"This volume celebrates the 25th [...] pastoral letter of the U.S. bishop [...] tion because Mark Allman has brough[...] retrieve insights of the letter and develop excellent ethical reflections app[...] [...]e to our present economic situation."

—Kenneth R. Himes, OFM, associate professor of theology, Boston College

"Twenty-five years ago the U.S. Catholic bishops published a document on Catholic social teaching and the U.S. economy. A group of nine scholars look now at that document and its contents. They keep alive the concern the bishops had then for an economy that is centered on the development of the human person, and especially how it treats the least among us and permits them to participate. They note the current changes toward a global economy and the desire to extend the bishops' concerns to the poor of the world. They analyze, challenge, and clarify where we are today and bring new light and insights to the world scene without losing sight of those who are most adversely affected. The book is certainly worth the read and is highly recommended."

—Archbishop Rembert G. Weakland, OSB

"This is an important book about a very important Church document and multi-year event. It invites us to study and understand *Economic Justice for All* and its ramifications for a just society. It reflects the theologian's role in the critical application of faith to reality and in stretching that faith to emerging realities. The book emphasizes important principles of Catholic social thought, including solidarity, participation, the universal destination of all creation, right relationships, and the preferential love of the poor. It applies these principles to contemporary challenges of globalization, poverty, welfare reform, racism, white economic advantage, immigrant justice, the world ecosystem, food security, and, perhaps surprisingly, worship.

"The reader's challenges are many: to understand what the pastoral letter did and did not say; to grasp the revolutionary participative process of widespread engagement in developing the document; to appreciate the funding of a three-year implementation office to produce educational and pastoral resources; to discern strengths and weaknesses of the pastoral, and, in assessing the commentators, to discern what is historically valid, what is hindsight, and the actual advances being made in Catholic social thought. Discussion questions at the end of chapters assist with this analysis."

—Fred Kammer, SJ, executive director of the Jesuit Social Research Institute, Loyola University New Orleans

"*The Almighty and the Dollar* is a vibrant reexamination of the U.S. Catholic bishops' seminal teaching in their historic pastoral letter *Economic Justice for All*. This book is both steeped in the history of the pastoral letter and energized by its application to today's world. It will be a touchstone for all who strive to live their faith in the marketplace."

—Simone Campbell, SSS
Executive director, NETWORK

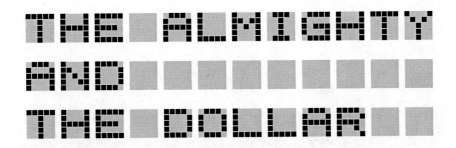

THE ALMIGHTY AND THE DOLLAR

Reflections on *Economic Justice for All*

Mark J. Allman, editor

ANSELM
A C A D E M I C

In memory of Monsignor John A. Ryan (1869–1945) and
Monsignor George G. Higgins (1916–2002),
staunch advocates of economic justice for all.

AUTHOR ACKNOWLEDGMENTS

I thank all those who made this volume possible: the United States Conference of Catholic Bishops for permission to reproduce significant portions of *Economic Justice for All*; the authors for sharing their wisdom and for cooperating throughout the editing process; *The Catholic Theological Society of America* for supporting a three-year interest group and *The Society of Christian Ethics* for hosting a panel, both of which allowed early drafts of these chapters to be presented at their annual meetings; Archbishop Rembert Weakland, OSB, not only for chairing the committee that drafted the economic pastoral but also for offering comments on this volume's publication; Meghan J. Clark, PhD, for reading early drafts of this volume and sharing insights; Merrimack College for supporting my scholarship with summer research grants and especially for my colleagues in the Department of Religious and Theological Studies for their camaraderie; Annie Belt for her keen attention in copyediting; and Anselm Academic, in particular Jerry Ruff and Brad Harmon, for their support and enthusiasm of scholarship and teaching. Finally, I thank my wife, Emily, for her love and patience.

PUBLISHER ACKNOWLEDGMENTS

Thank you to William Collinge of Mount Saint Mary's University, Emmitsburg, MD, for reviewing this work in progress.

CONTENTS

PART I

ECONOMIC JUSTICE FOR ALL: *PASTORAL LETTER ON CATHOLIC SOCIAL TEACHING AND THE U.S. ECONOMY* (EXCERPT WITH CHAPTERS I, II, IV, AND V) *United States Catholic Bishops, 1986*

PART II
FOUNDATIONAL ISSUES OF ECONOMIC JUSTICE

PART III
CONTEMPORARY ISSUES OF ECONOMIC JUSTICE

To download articles by John R. Donahue and Archbishop Rembert
Weakland on *Economic Justice for All*, go to www.anselmacademic.org
and visit the Web page for *The Almighty and the Dollar*.

INTRODUCTION

Serving Two Masters?

Mark J. Allman

"No man can serve two masters. He will either hate one and love the other, or be devoted to one and despise the other. You cannot serve God and mammon." (Mt 6:24)

The Catholic bishops of the United States in the 1980s produced two prophetic and challenging statements: *The Challenge of Peace* (1983), which focused on the ethics of war and peace, and *Economic Justice for All* (1986), which focused on economic ethics.[1] Both of these statements, called pastoral letters, are addressed to all Christians. They garnered significant attention in the church community[2] and in society at large because the bishops made ethical judgments about some of the most contentious political and economic issues of the day. These letters thrust the bishops into the center of political and economic life in the United States and injected Christian perspectives into the larger debate about domestic and foreign policy. On the tenth anniversaries of these pastoral letters, the bishops reissued each document along with additional statements intended to update their perspectives and apply Christian ethical principles to the contemporary context.[3]

On the twenty-fifth anniversary of *The Challenge of Peace* in 2008, however, with the United States embroiled in wars in Iraq and Afghanistan as well as fighting the so-called global war on terror, the United States Conference of Catholic Bishops (USCCB) made no official statements marking the peace pastoral's anniversary. Similarly, on the silver anniversary of *Economic Justice for All* (*EJA*), while the United States was experiencing the worst economic downturn

---

[1] National Conference of Catholic Bishops, *The Challenge of Peace: God's Promise and Our Response* (Washington, DC: United States Catholic Conference (USCC), 1984) and *Economic Justice for All: Pastoral Letter on Catholic Social Teaching and the U.S. Economy* (Washington, DC: USCC, 1986).

[2] When "church" is not capitalized in this text, as here, it refers to all Christian churches. When "Church" is capitalized it refers to a specific community, e.g., the Roman Catholic Church, the Lutheran Church, the Episcopal Church, etc.

[3] See *The Harvest of Justice Is Sown in Peace: A Reflection of the National Conference of Catholic Bishops on the Tenth Anniversary of* The Challenge of Peace (1993) and *A Decade after* "Economic Justice for All": *Continuing Principles, Changing Context, New Challenges* (1995), as well as a shorter statement, "A Catholic Framework for Economic Life" (1986).

since the Great Depression, with unemployment rates hovering around 10 percent, again the bishops chose not to mark the occasion. All of which begs the question, Why would the bishops ignore the anniversaries of arguably the two most influential statements they have ever issued, especially when the topic of each letter was immediately applicable to the current political and economic situation? Why would they choose not to exercise their role as moral teachers, especially in these times of crisis?

This book *The Almighty and the Dollar: Reflections on Economic Justice for All*, began when the peace pastoral's anniversary passed seemingly unnoticed by the bishops. Fearing the same would happen on the anniversary of *EJA*, and recognizing that the responsibility for teaching in the larger church community rests not only on the shoulders of bishops, but upon theologians as well, I invited prominent scholars to reflect on challenges and promises of the current economy in light of *EJA*. The original economic pastoral letter is both theoretical and practical. It draws on Scripture and Christian ethical norms to articulate the demands of social justice in the context of the contemporary economy (in 1986). While the application portions of the pastoral letter are now largely outdated, the portions of the letter that articulate Christian principles of economic justice are timeless.

The first part of this book reprints extensive excerpts from *EJA*. Following these, part II includes reflections by Christian ethicists on some of the ethical principles and norms expressed in *EJA* as well as the bishops' call for a "New American Experiment." Part III includes reflections by Christian ethicists on contemporary issues and challenges to economic justice. In essence, this book attempts to recreate the original focus of the letter by revisiting its ethical principles and norms and then applying them to the current context. A few key caveats need to be made:

1. The authors in this volume do not speak for the whole church, nor do they speak as a unified group. Each chapter contains the opinions of the individual author.

2. This is not an attempt to supplant or undermine the teaching authority of the bishops; it is an exercise of the vocation of theological ethicists.

3. This is not intended to be a comprehensive ethical analysis of the economy. That would be impossible. The chapters are intended to offer ethical analysis of *some* aspects of the economy, indeed a major lacuna in this collection is the absence of chapters focusing on women in the economy, ecology and the economy, and the role of global finance, although these concerns are raised in a number of the chapters.

Economic Justice for All sparked a nationwide conversation about Gospel demands and economic justice. This volume is intended to serve as an aid in reviving that conversation. Before one dives into that conversation, understanding the history and reaction to the original letter should prove helpful.

■ HISTORY AND REACTION

The Catholic bishops in the United States have nearly a century of speaking in one voice on matters of economic justice, dating back to 1919 and the National Catholic Welfare Conference, which ultimately became the USCCB.[4] Prior to the 1960s the bishops issued statements on industrial relations, defended organized labor (unions), advocated for decent wages for laborers, and warned against the dangers of communism. The 1960s proved to be a watershed period for the US church. In the early twentieth century, the Roman Catholic Church tended to be suspicious of modernism, even going so far as to require all clergy and seminary professors to swear an Oath Against Modernism.[5]

By the middle of the century, however, modern and secular ideas (in biblical studies, theology, philosophy, and ethics) began to influence Catholic intellectuals and members of the clergy. In the midst of the sociocultural revolutions of the age (the sexual revolution, civil rights movements, and political independence movements across the globe), Pope John XXIII (1958–1963) called for an ecumenical council (the Second Vatican Council or Vatican II), which was to be an *aggorniomento* (Italian for "an updating") of the Church. Vatican II (1962–1965) resulted in the Church taking a less defensive stance toward the modern world and calling for greater popular participation in the Church's life (in worship, service, and teaching). One of the signature documents of Vatican II, *The Pastoral Constitution on the Church in the Modern World* (*Gaudium et spes*), was written to "to explain to everyone how it [the Church] conceives of the presence and activity of the Church in the world of today."[6] The document opens with these words: "The joys and the hopes, the griefs and the anxieties of the men of this age, especially those who are poor or in any way afflicted, these are the joys and hopes, the griefs and anxieties of the followers of Christ."[7] With Vatican II, the Catholic Church renewed its interest in Scripture study and liturgy (worship), changed its approach to how the Church relates to the modern and increasingly secular world, and granted greater authority and autonomy to national conferences of bishops, who were encouraged to carry on the Church's "duty of scrutinizing the signs of the times and of interpreting them in the light of the

---

[4] This history of the document's formation is drawn principally from Charles Curran, "The Reception of Catholic Social and Economic Teaching in the United States," in *Modern Catholic Social Teaching: Commentaries and Interpretations*, ed. Kenneth R. Himes and others (Washington, DC: Georgetown University Press, 2004), and Rembert Weakland's accounts of the process where noted below.

[5] Modernism was a movement in the late nineteenth and early twentieth centuries that challenged traditional theology by applying critical literary and historical studies to Scripture and doctrine. It emphasized the human element in Scripture and the influence of historical and cultural contexts on Church teaching, thereby challenging notions that Church teachings were timeless, universal, and unchanging.

[6] *Pastoral Constitution on the Church in the Modern World*, no. 2, *http://www.vatican.va/archive/hist_councils/ii_vatican_council/documents/vat-ii_cons_19651207_gaudium-et-spes_en.html*.

[7] Ibid., no. 1.

Gospel."[8] The US bishops in the 1980s, with their prophetic and challenging pastoral letters, were responding directly to the Vatican II call for renewal and Pope Paul VI's (1963–1978) demand that "it is up to the Christian communities to analyze with objectivity the situation which is proper to their own country"[9] in light of Gospel values and the social teachings of the Church.

The US bishops were also inspired by the process at Vatican II. Drafts (called *schemata*) of the council documents were circulated in advance and commentaries from experts were solicited, including laypeople, and members of other Christian denominations and other religions. The final documents were then revised based on these consultations. In November 1980, during a debate about a pastoral letter on Christianity and Marxism, the US bishops decided they should also write a letter on Christianity and capitalism. Archbishop Rembert Weakland, OSB, of Milwaukee was appointed chair of a five-bishop committee that also included a staff and consultants.[10] Three drafts of the pastoral letter on economics were published, with the committee soliciting responses from theologians, economists, sociologists, business leaders, union leaders, community organizers, and congressional staff. Special sessions with the World Council of Churches and Jewish scholars and rabbis were held and listening sessions across the country were hosted, from which ten thousand written commentaries were received. On November 13, 1986, the final draft was adopted by the bishops' conference by a vote of 225 in favor and 9 opposed.[11]

The drafting committee decided early on that the economic pastoral should not be a theoretical analysis of capitalism because capitalism has no single philosophy or approach. Instead the economic pastoral explores Scripture and ethical norms drawn from the Church's social justice tradition (see Principles

---

[8] Ibid., no. 4.

[9] "A Call to Action on the Eightieth Anniversary of *Rerum novarum*," no. 4, *http://www.vatican. va/holy_father/paul_vi/apost_letters/documents/hf_p-vi_apl_19710514_octogesima-adveniens_en.html.*

[10] The committee included Archbishop Thomas Donnellan (Atlanta, GA, who replaced Bishop Joseph Daley of Harrisburg, PA, due to illness), Bishop George Speltz (St. Cloud, MN), Bishop William Weigand (Salt Lake City, UT), and Auxiliary Bishop Peter Rosazza (Hartford, CT). The committee was also aided by Rev. Michael Lavelle, SJ, and Sister Ann Margaret Cahill, OP, who represented men and women religious; members of the US Catholic Conference (Thomas Quigley, Rev. Bryan Hehir, Ronald Krietemeyer, Rev. William Lewers, CSC, and Msgr. George Higgins); and a host of other invited consultants including Dr. Donald Warwick (Harvard University Institute for International Development), Dr. Charles Wilber (Dept. of Economics, University of Notre Dame), Rev. David Hollenbach, SJ (Weston School of Theology), Rev. John Donahue, SJ (Jesuit School of Theology at Berkeley), and two Nobel laureates in Economics: James Tobin and Lawrence Kline. See Rembert Weakland, "Report by Archbishop Rembert Weakland, OSB . . ." *Origins* 13, no. 26 (December 1, 1983), Rembert Weakland, *A Pilgrim in a Pilgrim Church: Memoirs of a Catholic Archbishop* (Grand Rapids: Eerdmans, 2009), 273–93, and Bishop Ricardo Ramirez, CSB, "The U.S. Bishops Pastoral Letter 'Economic Justice for All' Twenty Years After." University of St. Thomas Social Justice Summer Institute, June 2, 2006, *http://www.dioceseoflascruces.org/includes/tinymce/ jscripts/tiny_mce/plugins/filemanager/files/spch/bp_sp_16.pdf.*

[11] Ramirez, "The U.S. Bishops Pastoral Letter 'Economic Justice for All' Twenty Years After."

of Catholic Social Teaching at the end of this introduction) and applies them to four areas: employment, poverty, food and agriculture, and global poverty. In their ethical analysis of economic justice in the United States, the bishops stressed the preferential option for the poor, participation, the common good, solidarity, and subsidiarity.

Because the drafts were widely distributed, the final letter garnered significant attention. Business media, such as the *Wall Street Journal, Forbes*, and *Business Week*, criticized the letter for being antibusiness, anticapitalist, and advocating for a planned economy (in which a central authority, typically government, makes decisions regarding production, pricing, and investment). A *Wall Street Journal* editorial asked, "What does any of this have to do with 'Catholic matters?'"[12] For those who believe that churches should concern themselves only with "spiritual matters," this foray into the public square seemed out of place and possibly a violation of the long-cherished American belief in the separation of church and state. In the eyes of many bishops, however, such comments revealed a lack of understanding of the role of the church. Against this criticism, Weakland said, "The church . . . does not accept that political and social issues are without ethical or moral consequences. Moreover, the church distinguishes between state and society and does not see the church as separate from society."[13] Other popular media (the *New York Times* and many local newspapers) reacted favorably and were enamored of the bishops' transparent and dialogical process for writing the letter.

Critics of the consultative process worried that seeking input from a wide variety of people would weaken the teaching authority of the bishops because it might imply that the bishops were unable to teach on their own. Weakland responded, "The [teaching] model adopted by the U.S. conference believes that the Holy Spirit resides in all members of the church and that the hierarchy must listen to what the Spirit is saying to the whole church."[14] Questions on the authority of the statement were also raised. Weakland explained the different levels of authority in his letter:

> Distinctions must also be made concerning the nature of the material taught. If a bishops' conference is reiterating truth held by the universal church and proposed as such, it carries more weight. . . . General principles carry with them more certitude when taught by bishops than practical applications of these same principles.[15]

---

[12] "On Disagreeing with Bishops," *Wall Street Journal*, November 17, 1986, 1.

[13] Weakland, "Developing a Pastoral Letter on the Economy: Action and Reflection," *Origins* 13, no. 46 (April 26, 1984). Archbishop John J. O'Connor of New York made similar comments in his 1984 Labor Day statement, in which he said the Church "is seeking to make clear the human and moral consequences of the technical choices we make as a nation" (quoted in Hugh J. Nolan, ed., *Pastoral Letters of the United States Catholic Bishops, 1983–1988*, vol. 5 [USCC, 1989], 274).

[14] Weakland, "Developing a Pastoral Letter."

[15] Ibid.

Thus statements about general ethical and biblical principles are considered to be more authoritative than statements applying those principles to particular situations (e.g., employment, wages, agriculture, legislation, public assistance programs, etc.).

The most strident criticism of the economic pastoral came from Catholic neoconservatives such as Michael Novak, Richard John Neuhaus, and George Wiegal. Under Novak's leadership a lay group published *Toward the Future: Catholic Social Thought and the U.S. Economy* prior to the first draft of the pastoral letter being distributed.[16] The neoconservative critics of the bishops' approach claimed that the bishops (1) place too much emphasis on the distribution of resources and ignore the positive role and effect of wealth creation; (2) tend to view the poor as victims and fail to stress personal responsibility; (3) do not take human sinfulness seriously and naively assume that wealth and prosperity is natural and poverty is abnormal; and (4) endorse the notion of economic rights (e.g., the rights to work, to a living wage, to collective bargaining, social safety net programs, etc.), which runs contrary to the American ideal of a limited role for government. Novak, in particular, emphasizes the importance of "equal opportunity for all" as opposed to a host of economic rights that government is to provide.

Criticisms of the pastoral were not limited to those from the right. Progressive Catholics lamented that the pastoral letter did not offer a robust criticism of capitalism nor did the US bishops follow the lead of the Latin American and Canadian bishops' conferences, which had produced more radical statements about capitalism in light of the preferential option for the poor.[17] Rev. Charles Curran, for example, a prominent progressive American Catholic moral theologian, criticized the pastoral for (1) focusing on Catholic social *teaching* (which includes official teachings by members of the magisterium only) but ignoring the wider category of Catholic social *thought*, which includes scholars as well as the experience of grassroots efforts within the Church that work for economic justice (e.g., Catholic Campaign for Human Development, Catholic Relief Services, Catholic Worker movement); (2) ignoring fundamental issues in the US economy, such as the profit motive, the role of markets, and the dehumanizing aspects of technology; (3) strongly focusing on the need for structural change, but failing to adequately address personal and spiritual matters (e.g., the need for a change of heart and the responsibilities of the baptized in matters of social justice); and (4) not acknowledging the role of power. For Curran, the letter appeals to the "reason and good will . . . of the elite and leaders to put into practice the principles proposed,"[18] but does not consider that change can also come from the

---

[16] Michael Novak and Michael Joyce, *Toward the Future: Catholic Social Thought and the U.S. Economy* (Lanham, MD: University Press of America, 1985).

[17] Gregory Baum, "A Canadian Perspective of on the U.S. Pastoral," *Christianity and Crisis* 44, no. 22 (January 21, 1985): 516–8.

[18] Curran, "The Reception of Catholic Social and Economic Teaching," 483.

bottom up. In Curran's estimation, "The pastoral letters of the U.S. bishops in the 1980s on nuclear war and deterrence and the economy had a greater effect on the American public in general and the Catholic Church in the United States than any other documents coming from the U.S. bishops,"[19] which returns us to the question asked earlier: why were the bishops such public participants in debates on war and economics in the 1980s—willing to take controversial positions based on the Gospel—but today, as a collective group, remain silent on these issues?

For Curran the effect and influence of these letters were due to the process used to write them, their quality, and the timing. As to why "nothing the bishops have done since 1986 has come close to the impact made by their pastoral letters on peace and the economy,"[20] Curran cites three reasons: (1) an attempt to write a pastoral letter on the role of women in the Church using the same transparent consultative process ended disastrously in the early 1990s; (2) a shift in the global Roman Catholic Church that downplays the role of national bishops' conferences, placing greater emphasis on the Vatican, coupled with cardinals exercising more influence on the local/national level; and (3) the appointment of more conservative bishops during the pontificate of John Paul II, a group that tends to believe open consultative approaches to teaching weakens the authority of bishops.[21] To this list one must now add the national clergy sexual abuse scandals, beginning in the early 1990s, which weakened the bishops' teaching authority, especially on morality. None of this should suggest that the bishops have done nothing in terms of advocating for social justice since 1986. The USCCB continues to exert pressure in Washington, DC, and nationwide on a host of economic issues including welfare reform, health care, immigration, and the minimum (living) wage. But the bishops continue to be criticized for focusing most of their attention on two issues, abortion and same-sex marriage, while largely ignoring other questions of social justice.[22]

One of the greatest successes of *Economic Justice for All* was that it generated an intelligent national conversation about economic justice and the demands of the Christian faith. Even if one disagrees with the letter's views, one must wrestle with its perspectives and arguments. In the opening paragraphs of *Economic Justice or All*, the bishops explain why they wrote the pastoral.

> We are believers called to follow Our Lord Jesus Christ and proclaim his Gospel in the midst of a complex and powerful economy. . . . Our

---

[19] Ibid.

[20] Ibid., 484.

[21] Ibid., 484–5.

[22] See Francis X. Doyle, "For U.S. Bishops, Economic Justice Isn't on the Agenda," *Baltimore Sun*, November 14, 2011, *http://articles.baltimoresun.com/2011-11-14/news/bs-ed-bishops-20111111_1_catholic-bishops-catholic-leaders-catholic-lawmakers* and Patricia Zapor, "Debate Fresh 25 Years after 'Economic Justice for All,'" *NCRonline.org*, December 9, 2011, *http://ncronline.org/news/debate-still-fresh-25-years-after-economic-justice-all.*

faith calls us to measure this economy not only by what it produces, but also by how it touches human life and whether it protects or undermines the dignity of the human person. (no. 1)

. . . We write to share our teaching, to raise questions, to challenge one another to live our faith in the world. (no. 4)

Their words reflect why this volume was published as well.

▪▪ PRINCIPLES OF CATHOLIC SOCIAL TEACHING

In *EJA* and in the chapters in parts II and III of this volume, the authors frequently refer to Catholic social *teaching* and Catholic social *thought*. Catholic social teaching refers to a collection of writings by popes and bishops over the centuries on matters of social, political, and economic justice. Catholic social thought is a larger body of writings that includes all of Catholic social teaching and the reflections of theologians, philosophers, other scholars, and people involved in grassroots advocacy and acts of charity on the same issues.

While there is no official list of what constitute Catholic social teaching, most scholars focus on the papal social teachings since the Industrial Revolution (often found in statements called encyclicals) and the teachings of bishops' conferences. In these documents, certain themes, principles, or norms emerge. The following list of principles in Catholic social teaching is provided as an aid in reading the rest of this book, especially for those who are unfamiliar with this tradition.[23]

Dignity of the Human Person. All human beings are made in the image and likeness of God and are redeemed by Christ, which grants them an inherent and inviolable dignity. From this comes the defense of all human life, which is considered sacred. This principle informs the Church's opposition to abortion, capital punishment, euthanasia, as well as the Church's work to enhance the life and dignity of the poor.

The human person is the clearest reflection of God's presence in the world; all of the Church's work in pursuit of both justice and peace is designed to protect and promote the dignity of every person. For each person not only reflects God, but is the expression of God's creative

---

[23] There are many lists of key principles of Catholic social teaching, including those in Catholic Charities of St. Paul and Minneapolis, "Major Themes of Catholic Social Teaching" *http://www. ccspm.org/page.aspx?pid=436*; William J. Byron, "Ten Building Blocks of Catholic Social Teaching," *America*, October 31, 1998, *http://www.americamagazine.org/content/article.cfm?article_id=11297*; and USCCB, "Seven Themes of Catholic Social Teaching," *http://usccb.org/beliefs-and-teachings/what-we-believe/catholic-social-teaching/seven-themes-of-catholic-social-teaching.cfm*.

work and the meaning of Christ's redemptive ministry. . . . God is the Lord of life, and so each human life is sacred.[24]

Human Rights and Obligations. Basic rights (food, clothing, shelter, and health care) refer to the minimum needs of all human beings. In addition to basic rights, all people enjoy a host of social, political, and economic rights. Typically it is the responsibility of government to safeguard these rights (see subsidiarity). All rights come with concomitant duties, including the recognition that all others enjoy the same rights and the obligation to exercise one's rights in the name of the common good. Some of the rights that figure prominently in Catholic social teaching are the right to life, the right to private property, the right to work, the right to a living wage, and the right to religious liberty.

> Indeed, precisely because he is a person he has rights and obligations flowing directly and simultaneously from his very nature. And as these rights and obligations are universal and inviolable so they cannot in any way be surrendered.[25]

The Common Good. Because human beings are social animals, the wide array of human relationships (interpersonal, family, and communal) is necessary for safeguarding human dignity. Society must organize its various institutions (social, political, economic, judicial, educational, recreational, etc.) in ways that promote human sociality and the good of society as a whole.

> [The common good is] the sum total of social conditions which allow people, either as groups or as individuals, to reach their fulfillment more fully and more easily.[26]

Preferential Option for the Poor. The moral measure of any society is how it treats its weakest and most vulnerable members. This is not an option against the rich, rather it holds that all social, political, and economic decisions and programs ought to be evaluated first by the impact they have on the poor and vulnerable.

> The obligation to evaluate social and economic activity from the viewpoint of the poor and the powerless arises from the radical command to love one's neighbor as one's self. Those who are marginalized and whose rights are denied have privileged claims if society is to provide justice for *all* (*EJA*, no. 87, italics in the original).
>
> . . . The way society responds to the needs of the poor through its public policies is the litmus test of its justice or injustice (*EJA*, no. 123).

---

[24] National Conference of Catholic Bishops, *The Challenge of Peace*, no. 15.

[25] Pope John XXIII, *Peace on Earth* (1963), no. 9.

[26] Vatican II, *The Church in the Modern World*, no. 26.

Solidarity. Best described as a virtue, solidarity is the commitment to the good of all. It is an expression of neighborly love that extends beyond immediate relationships to encompass the entire world. Solidarity is a commitment to seeing every person as a brother or sister and then acting accordingly. As such it requires sacrifice.

> [Solidarity] is not a feeling of vague compassion or shallow distress at the misfortunes of so many people, both near and far. On the contrary, it is a firm and persevering determination to commit oneself to the common good; that is to say to the good of all and of each individual, because we are all really responsible for all.[27]

Participation. Because all human beings have an inherent dignity and because they are social animals, all human beings have a right and a duty to play an active role in the social, political, and economic life of society.

> [B]asic justice demands the establishment of minimum levels of participation in the life of the human community for all persons. The ultimate injustice is for a person or group to be treated actively or abandoned passively as if they were nonmembers of the human race. To treat people this way is effectively to say they simply do not count as human beings (*EJA*, no. 77, italics in the original).

Work. The modern Catholic social teaching tradition began during the Industrial Revolution. In that crisis, Pope Leo XIII defended the right of workers to collective bargaining, unionization, a living wage, and humane work conditions. Like all rights, labor rights come with obligations. Work is seen as essential to human dignity because it is how people provide for themselves and their families, a principal means of human sociality, how most people contribute to the common good, and a participation in the creative activity of God. Work is not reduced to simply employment it includes any activity.

> Awareness that man's work is a participation in God's activity ought to permeate . . . even *"the most ordinary everyday activities*. For, while providing the substance of life for themselves and their families, men and women are performing their activities in a way which appropriately benefits society. They can justly consider that by their labour they are unfolding the Creator's work, consulting the advantages of their brothers and sisters, and contributing by their personal industry to the realization in history of the divine plan."[28]

---

[27] John Paul II, *On Social Concern* (1987), no. 38.

[28] John Paul II, *On Human Work* (1981), no. 25. Internal quote from Vatican II, *The Church in the Modern World*, no. 34 (italics in the original).

Subsidiarity and Government. The purpose of government is to safeguard the common good, promote human dignity, and secure the rights of all. Government is also responsible for enabling citizens to participate in society. The principle of subsidiarity affirms that the tasks of governance should be carried out at the lowest (most local) level possible, so long as it can be carried out properly.

> Just as it is gravely wrong to take from individuals what they can accomplish by their own initiative and industry and give it to the community, so also it is an injustice and at the same time a grave evil and disturbance of right order to assign to a greater and higher association what lesser and subordinate organizations can do. For every social activity ought of its very nature to furnish help to the members of the body social, and never destroy and absorb them.[29]

Development. The purpose of economic activity is not merely the generation of wealth. The purpose of economic activity is to serve human beings. True development is not measured by the size of an economy but by whether the economic, political, and social structures enable people to live authentically human lives. While underdevelopment plagues poorer nations and prevents their peoples from living in a state worthy of a human being because of hunger, lack of clean water, and disease, wealthier nations are often plagued by super-development wherein people are seduced or distracted by materialism, consumerism, and technology, and confuse *having* with *being*.

> [T]he mere accumulation of goods and services, even for the benefit of the majority, is not enough for the realization of human happiness . . . side-by-side with the miseries of underdevelopment, themselves unacceptable, we find ourselves up against a form of superdevelopment . . . [both are] contrary to what is good and to true happiness.[30]

Peace. Peace is not simply the absence of war, it is the result of justice; or as Paul VI said, "If you want peace, work for justice."[31] When society is rightly ordered, when the individual liberties of all are guaranteed and all are working for the good of all, then peace will ensue.

> Peace is not merely the absence of war. Nor can it be reduced solely to the maintenance of a balance of power between enemies. Nor is it brought about by dictatorship. Instead, it is rightly and appropriately called "an enterprise of justice" (Is. 32:7). Peace results from that

---

[29] Pius XI, *On the Fortieth Year* (1931), no. 79.

[30] John Paul II, *On Social Concern* (1987), no. 28.

[31] Paul VI, *If You Want Peace, Work for Justice*, Day of Peace message (January 1, 1972).

harmony built into human society by its divine founder, and actualized by men as they thirst after ever greater justice.[32]

Stewardship. Ecological stewardship concerns the proper use of and care for the environment. Creation is understood as a gift from God for the benefit of all. While stewardship of creation is a recent focus of Catholic social teaching, the idea that the goods of the earth were intended by God to be used by all (traditionally called the "universal destination of goods") has enjoyed a long standing and is often addressed in conjunction with the right to private property.

> Stewardship—defined in this case as the ability to exercise moral responsibility to care for the environment—requires freedom to act. Significant aspects of this stewardship include the right to private initiative, the ownership of property, and the exercise of responsible freedom in the economic sector. Stewardship requires a careful protection of the environment and calls us to use our intelligence "to discover the earth's productive potential and the many different ways in which human needs can be satisfied."[33]

A final note about Catholic social teaching: Many people first struggle with Catholic social teaching because they try to categorize it as either liberal or conservative. But Catholic social teaching is neither. Sometimes described as a "third way" or "middle way" theory, it espouses and condemns positions that are commonly considered liberal or conservative. For example, Catholic social teaching condemns abortion and the death penalty; it supports the right of workers to form unions and defends the right to private property; it warns against the evils and excesses of both Marxism and capitalism; it defends pacifism and notions of justified war. What unifies Catholic social teaching is its commitment to the inherent dignity of every human being and its affirmation of the social nature of the human person. All of the principles of Catholic social teaching rest on this foundation.

---

[32] Vatican II, *The Church in the Modern World*, no. 78.

[33] USCCB, "Global Climate Change: A Plea for Dialogue, Prudence, and the Common Good" (2001), no. 16. Internal quote from John Paul II *Centesimus annus*, (On the Hundredth Anniversary of *Rerum novarum*) (1991), no. 32.

PART I

ECONOMIC JUSTICE FOR ALL

*Pastoral Letter on Catholic Social Teaching
and the U.S. Economy*

Excerpt with Chapters I, II, IV, and V

United States Catholic Bishops, 1986

A Pastoral Message: Economic Justice for All

Brothers and Sisters in Christ:

1. We are believers called to follow Our Lord Jesus Christ and proclaim his Gospel in the midst of a complex and powerful economy. This reality poses both opportunities and responsibilities for Catholics in the United States. Our faith calls us to measure this economy, not by what it produces but also by how it touches human life and whether it protects or undermines the dignity of the human person. Economic decisions have human consequences and moral content; they help or hurt people, strengthen or weaken family life, advance or diminish the quality of justice in our land.

2. This is why we have written *Economic Justice for All: A Pastoral Letter on Catholic Social Teaching and the U.S. Economy*. This letter is a personal invitation to Catholics to use the resources of our faith, the strength of our economy, and the opportunities of our democracy to shape a society that better protects the dignity and basic rights of our sisters and brothers, both in this land and around the world.

3. This pastoral letter has been a work of careful inquiry, wide consultation, and prayerful discernment. The letter has been greatly enriched by this process of listening and refinement. We offer this introductory pastoral message to Catholics in the United States seeking to live their faith in the marketplace—in homes, offices, factories, and schools; on farms and ranches; in boardrooms and union halls; in service agencies and legislative chambers. We seek to explain why we wrote the pastoral letter, to introduce its major themes, and to share our hopes for the dialogue and action it might generate.

▓ WHY WE WRITE

4. We write to share our teaching, to raise questions, to challenge one another to live our faith in the world. We write as heirs of the biblical

prophets who summon us "to do right, and to love goodness, and to walk humbly with your God" (Mi. 6:8). We write as followers of Jesus who told us in the Sermon on the Mount: "Blessed are the poor in spirit. . . . Blessed are the meek. . . . Blessed are they who hunger and thirst for righteousness. . . . You are the salt of the earth. . . . You are the light of the world" (Mt 5:1–6, 13–14). These words challenge us not only as believers but also as consumers, citizens, workers, and owners. In the parable of the Last Judgment, Jesus said, "For I was hungry and you gave me food, I was thirsty and you gave me drink. . . . As often as you did it for one of my least brothers, you did it for me" (Mt. 25:35–40). The challenge for us is to discover in our own place and time what it means to be "poor in spirit" and "the salt of the earth" and what it means to serve "the least among us" and to "hunger and thirst for righteousness."

5. Followers of Christ must avoid a tragic separation between faith and everyday life. They can neither shirk their earthly duties nor, as the Second Vatican Council declared, "immerse [them]selves in earthly activities as if these latter were utterly foreign to religion, and religion were nothing more than the fulfillment of acts of worship and the observance of a few moral obligations" (*Pastoral Constitution on the Church in the Modern World*, no. 43).

6. Economic life raises important social and moral questions for each of us and for the society as a whole. Like family life, economic life is one of the chief areas where we live out our faith, love our neighbor, confront temptation, fulfill God's creative design, and achieve holiness. Our economic activity in factory, field, office, or shop feeds our families—or feeds our anxieties. It exercises our talents—or wastes them. It raises our hopes—or crushes them. IT brings us into cooperation with others—or sets us at odds. The Second Vatican Council instructs us "to preach the message of Christ in such a way that the light of the Gospel will shine on all activities of the faithful" (Pastoral Constitution, no. 43). In this case, we are trying to look at economic life through the eyes of faith, applying traditional church teaching to the U.S. economy.

7. In our letter, we write as pastors, not public officials. We speak as moral teachers, not economic technicians. We seek not to make some political or ideological point but to lift up the human and ethical dimensions of economic life, aspects too often neglected in public discussion. We bring to this task a dual heritage of Catholic social teaching and traditional American values.

8. As Catholics, we are heirs of a long tradition of thought and action on the moral dimensions of economic activity. The life and words of Jesus and the teaching of his Church call us to serve those in need and to work actively for social and economic justice. As a community of believers, we know that our faith is tested by the quality of justice among us, that we can best measure our life together by how the poor and the vulnerable are treated. This is not

a new concern for us. It is as old as the Hebrew prophets, as compelling as the Sermon on the Mount, and as current as the powerful voice of Pope John Paul II defending the dignity of the human person.

9. As Americans, we are grateful for the gift of freedom and committed to the dream of "liberty and justice for all." This nation, blessed with extraordinary resources, has provided an unprecedented standard of living for millions of people. We are proud of the strength, productivity, and creativity of our economy, but we also remember those who have been left behind in our progress. We believe that we honor our history best by working for the day when all our sisters and brothers share adequately in the American dream.

10. As bishops, in proclaiming the Gospel for these times we also manage institutions, balance budgets, meet payrolls. In this we see the human face of our economy. We feel the hurts and hopes of our people. We feel the pain of our sisters and brothers who are poor, unemployed, homeless, living on the edge. The poor and vulnerable are on our doorsteps, in our parishes, in our service agencies, and in our shelters. We see too much hunger and injustice, too much suffering and despair, both in our country and around the world.

11. As pastors, we also see the decency, generosity, and vulnerability of our people. We see the struggles of ordinary families to make ends meet and to provide a better future for their children. We know the desire of managers, professionals, and business people to shape what they do by what they believe. It is the faith, good will, and generosity of our people that gives us hope as we write this letter.

▪▪ PRINCIPAL THEMES OF THE PASTORAL LETTER

12. The pastoral letter is not a blueprint for the American economy. It does not embrace any particular theory of how the economy works, nor does it attempt to resolve disputes between different schools of economic thought. Instead, our letter turns to Scripture and to the social teaching of the Church. There, we discover what our economic life must serve, what standards it must meet. Let us examine some of these basic moral principles.

13. Every economic decision and institution must be judged in light of whether it protects or undermines the dignity of the human person. The pastoral letter begins with the human person. We believe the person is sacred—the clearest reflection of God among us. Human dignity comes from God, not from nationality, race, sex, economic status, or any human accomplishment. We judge any economic system by what it does *for* and *to* people and by how it permits all to *participate* in it. The economy should serve people, not the other way around.

14. Human dignity can be realized and protected only in community. In our teaching, the human person is not only sacred but social. How we organize our society—in economics and politics, in law and policy—directly affects human dignity and the capacity of individuals to grow in community. The obligation to "love our neighbor" has an individual dimension, but it also requires a broader social commitment to the common good. We have many partial ways to measure and debate the health of our economy: Gross National Product, per capita income, stock market prices, and so forth. The Christian vision of economic life looks beyond them all and asks, Does economic life enhance or threaten our life together as a community?

15. All people have a right to participate in the economic life of society. Basic justice demands that people be assured a minimum level of participation in the economy. It is wrong for a person or a group to be excluded unfairly or to be unable to participate or contribute to the economy. For example, people who are both able and willing, but cannot get a job are deprived of the participation that is so vital to human development. For, it is through employment that most individuals and families meet their material needs, exercise their talents, and have an opportunity to contribute to the larger community. Such participation has a special significance in our tradition because we believe that it is a means by which we join in carrying forward God's creative activity.

16. All members of society have a special obligation to the poor and vulnerable. From the Scriptures and church teaching, we learn that the justice of a society is tested by the treatment of the poor. The justice that was the sign of God's covenant with Israel was measured by how the poor and unprotected—the widow, the orphan, and the stranger—were treated. The kingdom that Jesus proclaimed in his word and ministry excludes no one. Throughout Israel's history and in early Christianity, the poor are agents of God's transforming power. "The Spirit of the Lord is upon me, therefore he has anointed me. He has sent me to bring glad tidings to the poor" (Lk. 4:18). This was Jesus' first public utterance. Jesus takes the side of those most in need. In the Last Judgment, so dramatically described in St. Matthew's Gospel, we are told that we will be judged according to how we respond to the hungry, the thirsty, the naked, the stranger. As followers of Christ, we are challenged to make a fundamental "option for the poor"—to speak for the voiceless, to defend the defenseless, to assess life styles, policies, and social institutions in terms of their impact on the poor. This "option for the poor" does not mean pitting one group against another, but rather, strengthening the whole community by assisting those who are the most vulnerable. As Christians, we are called to respond to the needs of *all* our brothers and sisters, but those with the greatest needs require the greatest response.

17. Human rights are the minimum conditions for life in community. In Catholic teaching, human rights include not only civil and political rights but also

economic rights. As Pope John XXIII declared, "all people have a right to life, food, clothing, shelter, rest, medical care, education, and employment." This means that when people are without a chance to earn a living, and must go hungry and homeless, they are being denied basic rights. Society must ensure that these rights are protected. In this way, we will ensure that the minimum conditions of economic justice are met for all our sisters and brothers.

18. Society as a whole, acting through public and private institutions, has the moral responsibility to enhance human dignity and protect human rights. In addition to the clear responsibility of private institutions, government has an essential responsibility in this area. This does not mean that government has the primary or exclusive role, but it does have a positive moral responsibility in safeguarding human rights and ensuring that the minimum conditions of human dignity are met for all. In a democracy, government is a means by which we can act together to protect what is important to us and to promote our common values.

19. These six moral principles are not the only ones presented in the pastoral letter, but they give an overview of the moral vision that we are trying to share. This vision of economic life cannot exist in a vacuum; it must be translated into concrete measures. Our pastoral letter spells out some specific applications of Catholic moral principles. We call for a new national commitment to full employment. We say it is a social and moral scandal that one of every seven Americans is poor, and we call for concerted efforts to eradicate poverty. The fulfillment of the basic needs of the poor is of the highest priority. We urge that all economic policies be evaluated in light of their impact on the life and stability of the family. We support measures to halt the loss of family farms and to resist the growing concentration in the ownership of agricultural resources. We specify ways in which the United States can do far more to relieve the plight of poor nations and assist in their development. We also reaffirm church teaching on the rights of workers, collective bargaining, private property, subsidiarity, and equal opportunity.

20. We believe that the recommendations in our letter are reasonable and balanced. In analyzing the economy, we reject ideological extremes and start from the fact that ours is a "mixed" economy, the product of a long history of reform and adjustment. We know that some of our specific recommendations are controversial. As bishops, we do not claim to make these prudential judgments with the same kind of authority that marks our declarations of principle. But, we feel obliged to teach by example how Christians can undertake concrete analysis and make specific judgments on economic issues. The Church's teachings cannot be left at the level of appealing generalities.

21. In the pastoral letter, we suggest that the time has come for a "New American Experiment"—to implement economic rights, to broaden the sharing of economic power, and to make economic decisions more accountable to

the common good. This experiment can create new structures of economic partnership and participation within firms at the regional level, for the whole nation, and across borders.

22. Of course, there are many aspects of the economy the letter does not touch, and there are basic questions it leaves to further exploration. There are also many specific points on which men and women of good will may disagree. We look for a fruitful exchange among differing viewpoints. We pray only that all will take to heart the urgency of our concerns; that together we will test our views by the Gospel and the Church's teaching; and that we will listen to other voices in a spirit of mutual respect and open dialogue.

▪ A CALL TO CONVERSION AND ACTION

23. We should not be surprised if we find Catholic social teaching to be demanding. The Gospel is demanding. We are always in need of conversion, of a change of heart. We are richly blessed, and as St. Paul assures us, we are destined for glory. yet, it is also true that we are sinners; that we are not always wise or loving or just; that, for all our amazing possibilities, we are incompletely born, wary of life, and hemmed in by fears and empty routines. We are unable to entrust ourselves fully to the living God, and so we seek substituted forms of security in material things, in power, in indifference, in popularity, in pleasure. The Scriptures warn us that these things can become forms of idolatry. We know that, at times, in order to remain truly a community of Jesus' disciples, we will have to say "no" to certain aspects of our culture, to certain trends and ways of acting that are opposed to a life of faith, love and justice. Changes in our hearts lead naturally to a desire to change how we act. With what care, human kindness, and justice do I conduct myself at work? How will my economic decisions to buy, sell, invest, divest, hire, or fire serve human dignity and the common good? In what career can I best exercise my talents so as to fill the world with the Spirit of Christ? How do my economic choices contribute to the strength of my family and community, to the values of my children, to a sensitivity to those in need? In this consumer society, how can I develop a healthy detachment from things and avoid the temptation to assess who I am by what I have? How do I strike a balance between labor and leisure that enlarges my capacity for friendships, for family life, for community? What government policies should I support to attain the wellbeing of all, especially the poor and vulnerable?

24. The answers to such questions are not always clear—or easy to live out. But, conversion is a lifelong process. And, it is not undertaken alone. It occurs with the support of the whole believing community, through baptism, common prayer, and our daily efforts, large and small, on behalf of justice. As a Church,

we must be people after God's own heart, bonded by the Spirit, sustaining one another in love, setting our hearts on God's kingdom, committing ourselves to solidarity with those who suffer, working for peace and justice, acting as a sign of Christ's love and justice in the world. The Church cannot redeem the world from the deadening effects of sin and injustice unless it is working to remove sin and injustice in its own life and institutions. All of us must help the Church to practice in its own life what it preaches to others about economic justice and cooperation.

25. The challenge of this pastoral letter is not merely to think differently, but also to act differently. A renewal of economic life depends on the conscious choices and commitments of individual believers who practice their faith in the world. The road to holiness for most of us lies in our secular vocations. We need a spirituality that calls forth and supports lay initiative and witness not just in our churches but also in business, in the labor movement, in the professions, in education, and in public life. Our faith is not just a weekend obligation, a mystery to be celebrated around the altar on Sunday. It is a pervasive reality to be practiced every day in homes, offices, factories, schools, and businesses across our land. We cannot separate what we believe from how we act in the marketplace and the broader community, for this is where we make our primary contribution to the pursuit of economic justice.

26. We ask each of you to read the pastoral letter, to study it, to pray about it, and match it with your own experience. We ask you to join with us in service to those in need. Let us reach out personally to the hungry and the homeless, to the poor and the powerless, and to the troubled and the vulnerable. In serving them, we serve Christ. Our service efforts cannot substitute for just and compassionate public policies, but they can help us practice what we preach about human life and human dignity.

27. The pursuit of economic justice takes believers into the public arena, testing the policies of government by the principles of our teaching. We ask you to become more informed and active citizens, using your voices and votes to speak for the voiceless, to defend the poor and the vulnerable and to advance the common good. We are called to shape a constituency of conscience, measuring every policy by how it touches the least, the lost, and the left-out among us. This letter calls us to conversion and common action, to new forms of stewardship, service, and citizenship.

28. The completion of a letter such as this is but the beginning of a long process of education, discussion and action. By faith and baptism, we are fashioned into new creatures, filled with the Holy Spirit and with a love that compels us to seek out a new profound relationship with God, with the human family, and with all created things. Jesus has entered our history as God's anointed son who announces the coming of God's kingdom, a kingdom of justice and peace and freedom. And, what Jesus proclaims, he embodies in his actions.

His ministry reveals that the reign of God is something more powerful than evil, injustice, and the hardness of hearts. Through his crucifixion and resurrection, he reveals that God's love is ultimately victorious over all suffering, all horror, all meaninglessness, and even over the mystery of death. Thus, we proclaim words of hope and assurance to all who suffer and are in need.

29. We believe that the Christian view of life, including economic life, can transform the lives of individuals, families, schools, and our whole culture. We believe that with your prayers, reflection, service and action, our economy can be shaped so that human dignity prospers and the human person is served. This is the unfinished work of our nation. This is the challenge of our faith.

CHAPTER I

The Church and the Future of the U.S. Economy (nos. 1–27)

1. Every perspective on economic life that is human, moral, and Christian must be shaped by three questions: What does the economy do *for* people? What does it do *to* people? And how do people *participate* in it? The economy is a human reality: men and women working together to develop and care for the whole of God's creation. All this work must serve the material and spiritual well-being of people. It influences what people hope for themselves and their loved ones. It affects the way they act together in society. It influences their very faith in God.[1]

2. The Second Vatican Council declared that "the joys and hopes, the griefs and anxieties of the people of this age, especially those who are poor or in any way afflicted, these too are the joys and hopes, the griefs and anxieties of the followers of Christ."[2] There are many signs of hope in U.S. economic life today:

   - Many fathers and mothers skillfully balance the arduous responsibilities of work and family life. There are parents who pursue a purposeful and modest way of life and by their example encourage their children to follow a similar path. A large number of women and men, drawing on their religious tradition, recognize the challenging vocation of family life and child rearing in a culture that emphasizes material display and self-gratification.

   - Conscientious business people seek new and more equitable ways to organize resources and the workplace. They face hard choices over expanding or retrenching, shifting investments, hiring or firing.

   - Young people choosing their life's work ask whether success and security are compatible with service to others.

   - Workers whose labor may be toilsome or repetitive try daily to ennoble their work with a spirit of solidarity and friendship.

   - New Immigrants brave dislocations while hoping for the opportunities realized by millions who came before them.

3. These signs of hope are not the whole story. There have been failures—some of them massive and ugly:

   - Poor and homeless people sleep in community shelters and in our church basements: the hungry line up in soup lines.
   - Unemployment gnaws at the self-respect of both middle-aged persons who have lost jobs and the young who cannot find them.
   - Hardworking men and women wonder if the system of enterprise that helped them yesterday might destroy their jobs and their communities tomorrow.
   - Families confront major challenges: dwindling social supports for family stability; economic pressures that force both parents of young children to work outside the home; a driven pace of life among the successful that can sap love and commitment; lack of hope among those who have less or nothing at all. Very different kinds of families bear different burdens of our economic system.
   - Farmers face the loss of their land and way of life; young people find it difficult to choose farming as a vocation; farming communities are threatened; migrant farm workers break their backs in serf-like conditions for disgracefully low wages.

4. And beyond our own shores, the reality of 800 million people living in absolute poverty and 450 million malnourished or facing starvation casts an ominous shadow over all these hopes and problems at home.

5. Anyone who sees all this will understand our concern as pastors and bishops. People shape the economy and in turn are shaped by it. Economic arrangements can be sources of fulfillment, of hope, of community—or of frustration, isolation, and even despair. They teach values—or vices—and day by day help mold our characters. They affect the quality of people's lives; at the extreme even determining whether people live or die. Serious economic choices go beyond purely technical issues to fundamental questions of value and human purpose.[3] We believe that in facing these questions the Christian religious and moral tradition can make an important contribution.

▪▪ A. THE U.S. ECONOMY TODAY: MEMORY AND HOPE

6. The United States is among the most economically powerful nations on earth. In its short history the U.S. economy has grown to provide an unprecedented standard of living for most of its people. The nation has created productive work for millions of immigrants and enabled them to broaden their

freedoms, improve their families' quality of life, and contribute to the building of a great nation. Those who came to this country from other lands often understood their new lives in the light of biblical faith. They thought of themselves as entering a promised land of political freedom and economic opportunity. The United States *is* a land of vast natural resources and fertile soil. It *has* encouraged citizens to undertake bold ventures. Through hard work, self-sacrifice, and cooperation, families have flourished; towns, cities and a powerful nation have been created.

7. But we should recall this history with sober humility. The American experiment in social, political, and economic life has involved serious conflict and suffering. Our nation was born in the face of injustice to native Americans, and its independence was paid for with the blood of revolution. Slavery stained the commercial life of the land through its first two hundred and fifty years and was ended only by a violent civil war. The establishment of women's suffrage, the protection of industrial workers, the elimination of child labor, the response to the Great Depression of the 1930s, and the civil rights movement of the 1960s all involved a sustained struggle to transform the political and economic institutions of the nation.

8. The U.S. value system emphasizes economic freedom. It also recognizes that the market is limited by fundamental human rights. Some things are never to be bought or sold.[4] This conviction has prompted positive steps to modify the operation of the market when it harms vulnerable members of society. Labor unions help workers resist exploitation. Through their government, the people of the United States have provided support for education, access to food, unemployment compensation, security in old age, and protection of the environment. The market system contributes to the success of the U.S. economy, but so do many efforts to forge economic institutions and public policies that enable *all* to share in the riches of the nation. The country's economy has been built through a creative struggle; entrepreneurs, business people, workers, unions, consumers, and government have all played essential roles.

9. The task of the United States today is as demanding as that faced by our forebears. Abraham Lincoln's words at Gettysburg are a reminder that complacency today would be a betrayal of our nation's history: "It is for us, the living, rather to be dedicated here to the unfinished work . . . they have thus far nobly advanced."[5] There is unfinished business in the American experiment in freedom and justice for all.

■ B. URGENT PROBLEMS OF TODAY

10. The preeminent role of the United States in an increasingly interdependent global economy is a central sign of our times.[6] The United States is still the

world's economic giant. Decisions made here have immediate effects in other countries; decisions made abroad have immediate consequences for steelworkers in Pittsburgh, oil company employees in Houston, and farmers in Iowa. U.S. economic growth is vitally dependent on resources from other countries and on their purchases of our goods and services. Many jobs in U.S. industry and agriculture depend on our ability to export manufactured goods and food.

11. In some industries the mobility of capital and technology makes wages the main variable in the cost of production. Overseas competitors with the same technology but with wage rates as low as one-tenth of ours put enormous pressure on U.S. firms to cut wages, relocate abroad, or close. U.S. workers and their communities should not be expected to bear these burdens alone.

12. All people on this globe share a common ecological environment that is under increasing pressure. Depletion of soil, water and other natural resources endangers the future. Pollution of air and water threatens the delicate balance of the biosphere on which future generations will depend.[7] The resources of the earth have been created by God for the benefit of all, and we who are alive today hold them in trust. This is a challenge to develop a new ecological ethic, that will help shape a future that is both just and sustainable.

13. In short, nations separated by geography, culture, and ideology are linked in a complex commercial, financial, technological, and environmental network. These links have two direct consequences. First, they create hope for a new form of community among peoples, one built on dignity, solidarity and justice. Second, this rising global awareness calls for greater attention to the stark inequities across countries in the standards of living and control of resources. We must not look at the welfare of U.S. citizens as the only good to be sought. Nor may we overlook the disparities of power in the relationships between this nation and the developing countries. The United States is the major supplier of food to other countries, a major source of arms sales to developing nations, and a powerful influence in multilateral institutions such as the International Monetary Fund, the World Bank, and the United Nations. What Americans see as a growing interdependence is regarded by many in the less developed countries as a pattern of domination and dependence.

14. Within this larger international setting, there are also a number of challenges to the domestic economy that call for creativity and courage. The promise of the "American dream"—freedom for all persons to develop their God-given talents to the full—remains unfulfilled for millions in the United States today.

15. Several areas of U.S. economic life demand special attention. Unemployment is the most basic. Despite the large number of new jobs the U.S. economy has generated in the past decade, approximately 8 million people seeking work in this country are unable to find it, and many more are so discouraged they have stopped looking.[8] Over the past two decades the nation has

come to tolerate an increasing level of unemployment. The 6 to 7 percent rate deemed acceptable today would have been intolerable twenty years ago. Among the unemployed are a disproportionate number of blacks, Hispanics, young people, or women who are the sole support of their families.[9] Some cities and states have many more unemployed persons than others as a result of economic forces that have little to do with people's desire to work. Unemployment is a tragedy no matter whom it strikes, but the tragedy is compounded by the unequal and unfair way it is distributed in our society.

16. Harsh poverty plagues our country despite its great wealth. More than 33 million Americans are poor; by any reasonable standard another 20–30 million are needy. Poverty is increasing in the United States, not decreasing.[10] For a people who believe in "progress," this should be cause for alarm. These burdens fall most heavily on blacks, Hispanics, and Native Americans. Even more disturbing is the large increase in the number of women and children living in poverty. Today children are the largest single group among the nation's poor. This tragic fact seriously threatens the nation's future. That so many people are poor in a nation as rich as ours is a social and moral scandal that we cannot ignore.

17. Many working people and middle-class Americans live dangerously close to poverty. A rising number of families must rely on the wages of two or even three members just to get by. From 1968 to 1978 nearly a quarter of the U.S. population was in poverty part of the time and received welfare benefits in at least one year.[11] The loss of a job, illness, or the breakup of a marriage may be all it takes to push people into poverty.

18. The lack of a mutually supportive relation between family life and economic life is one of the most serious problems facing the United States today.[12] The economic and cultural strength of the nation is directly linked to the stability and health of its families.[13] When families thrive, spouses contribute to the common good through their work at home, in the community, and in their jobs; and children develop a sense of their own worth and of their responsibility to serve others. When families are weak or break down entirely, the dignity of parents and children is threatened. High cultural and economic costs are inflicted on society at large.

19. The precarious economic situation of so many people and so many families calls for examination of U.S. economic arrangements. Christian conviction and the American promise of liberty and justice for all give the poor and the vulnerable a special claim on the nation's concern. They also challenge all members of the Church to help build a more just society.

20. The investment of human creativity and material resources in the production of the weapons of war makes these economic problems even more difficult to solve. Defense Department expenditures in the United States are almost $300 billion per year. The rivalry and mutual fear between superpowers

divert into projects that threaten death, minds, and money that could better human life. Developing countries engage in arms races that they can ill afford, often with the encouragement of the superpowers. Some of the poorest countries of the world use scarce resources to buy planes, guns and other weapons when they lack the food, education and healthcare their people need. Defense policies must be evaluated and assessed, in light of their real contribution to freedom, justice and peace for the citizens of our own and other nations. We have developed a perspective on these multiple moral concerns in our 1983 pastoral letter, *The Challenge of Peace: God's Promise and Our Response.*[14] When weapons or strategies make questionable contributions to security, peace, and justice and will also be very expensive, spending priorities should be redirected to more pressing social needs.[15]

21. Many other social and economic challenges require careful analysis: the movement of many industries from the Snowbelt to the Sunbelt, the federal deficit and interest rates, corporate mergers and takeovers, the effects of new technologies such as robotics and information systems in U.S. industry, immigration policy, growing international traffic in drugs, and the trade imbalance. All of these issues do not provide a complete portrait of the economy. Rather they are symptoms of more fundamental currents shaping U.S. economic life today: the struggle to find meaning and value in human work, efforts to support individual freedom in the context of renewed social cooperation, the urgent need to create equitable forms of global interdependence in a world now marked by extreme inequality. These deeper currents are cultural and moral in content. They show that the long-range challenges facing the nation call for sustained reflection on the values that guide economic choices and are embodied in economic institutions. Such explicit reflection on the ethical content of economic choices and policies most become an integral part of the way Christians relate religious belief to the realities of everyday life. In this way, the "split between the faith which many profess and their daily lives,"[16] which Vatican II counted among the more serious errors of the modern age, will begin to be bridged.

▪▪ C. THE NEED FOR MORAL VISION

22. Sustaining a common culture and a common commitment to moral values is not easy in our world. Modern economic life is based on a division of labor into specialized jobs and professions. Since the industrial revolution, people have had to define themselves and their work ever more narrowly to find a niche in the economy. The benefits of this are evident in the satisfaction many people derive from contributing their specialized skills to society. But the costs are social fragmentation, a decline in seeing how one's work serves the whole community, and an increased emphasis on personal goals and

private interests.[17] This is vividly clear in discussions of economic justice. Here it is often difficult to find a common ground among people with different backgrounds and concerns. One of our chief hopes in writing this letter is to encourage and contribute to the development of this common ground.[18]

23. Strengthening common moral vision is essential if the economy is to serve all people more fairly. Many middle-class Americans feel themselves in the grip of economic demands and cultural pressures that go far beyond the individual family's capacity to cope. Without constructive guidance in making decisions with serious moral implications, men and women who hold positions of responsibility in corporations or government find their duties exacting a heavy price. We want these reflections to help them contribute to a more just economy.

24. The quality of the national discussion about our economic future will affect the poor most of all, in this country and throughout the world. The life and dignity of millions of men, women and children hang in the balance. Decisions must be judged in light of what they do *for* the poor, what they do *to* the poor, and what they enable the poor to do *for themselves*. The fundamental moral criterion for all economic decisions, policies, and institutions is this: They must be at the service of *all people, especially the poor*.

25. This letter is based on a long tradition of Catholic social thought, rooted in the Bible and developed over the past century by the popes and the Second Vatican Council in response to modern economic conditions. This tradition insists that human dignity, realized in community with others and with the whole of God's creation is the norm against which every social institution must be measured.[19]

26. This teaching has a rich history. It is also dynamic and growing.[20] Pope Paul VI insisted that all Christian communities have the responsibility "to analyze with objectivity the situation which is proper to their own country, to shed on it the light of the Gospel's unalterable words and to draw principles of reflection, norms of judgment, and directives for action from the social teaching of the Church."[21] Therefore, we build on the past work of our own bishops' conference, including the 1919 Program of Social Reconstruction and other pastoral letters.[22] In addition many people from Catholic, Protestant, and Jewish communities, in academic, business or political life and from many different economic backgrounds have also provided guidance. We want to make the legacy of Christian social thought a living, gorging resource that can inspire hope and help shape the future.

27. We write then, first of all to provide guidance for members of our own Church as they seek to form their consciences about economic matters. No one may claim the name of Christian and be comfortable in the face of hunger, homelessness, insecurity, and injustice found in this country and the world. At the same time, we want to add our voice to the public debate about the directions in which the U.S. economy should be moving. We seek the cooperation

and support of those who do not share our faith or tradition. The common bond of humanity that links all persons is the source of our belief that the country can attain a renewed moral vision. The questions are basic and the answers are often elusive; they challenge us to serious and sustained attention to economic justice.

Endnotes

1. Vatican Council II, *The Pastoral Constitution on the Church in the Modern World*, 33. [Note: This pastoral letter frequently refers to documents of the Second Vatican Council, papal encyclicals, and other official teachings of the Catholic Church. Most of these texts have been published by the United States Catholic Conference; many are available in collections, though no single collection is comprehensive. See selected bibliography.]

2. *Pastoral Constitution*, 1.

3. See ibid., 10, 42, 43; Congregation for the Doctrine of the Faith, *Instruction on Christian Freedom and Liberation* (Washington, D.C.: United States Catholic Conference, 1986), 34–36.

4. See Pope John Paul II, *On Human Work* (1981), 14; and Pope Paul VI, *Octogesima Adveniens* (1971), 35. See also Arthur Okun, *Equality and Efficiency: The Big Tradeoff* (Washington, D.C.: The Brookings Institution, 1975), ch. 1; Michael Walzer, *Spheres of Justice: A Defense of Pluralism and Equality* (New York: Basic Books, 1983), ch. 4; Jon P. Gunnemann, "Capitalism and Commutative Justice," paper presented at the 1985 meeting of the Society of Christian Ethics.

5. Abraham Lincoln, Address at Dedication of National Cemetery at Gettysburg, November 19, 1863.

6. Pope John XXIII, *Peace on Earth* (1963), 130–131.

7. Synod of Bishops, *Justice in the World* (1971), 8; Pope John Paul II, *Redeemer of Man* (1979), 15.

8. U.S. Department of Labor, Bureau of Labor Statistics, *The Employment Situation: August 1985* (September 1985); Table A-I.

9. Ibid.

10. U.S. Bureau of the Census, *Current Population Reports, Series P-60*, 145, *Money Income and Poverty Status of Families and Persons in the United States: 1983* (Washington, D.C.: Government Printing Office, 1984), 20.

11. Greg H. Duncan, *Years of Poverty, Years of Plenty: The Changing Economic Fortunes of American Workers and Their Families* (Ann Arbor, Mich.: Institute for Social Research, University of Michigan, 1984).

12. See John Paul II, *Familiaris Consortio* (1981), 46.

13. *Pastoral Constitution*, 47.

14. National Conference of Catholic Bishops, *The Challenge of Peace: God's Promise and Our Response* (Washington, D.C.: United States Catholic Conference, 1983).

15. Cardinal Joseph L. Bernardin and Cardinal John J. O'Connor, Testimony before the House Foreign Relations Committee, June 26, 1984, *Origins* 14:10 (August 10, 1984): 157.

16. *Pastoral Constitution*, 43.

17. See, for example, Peter Berger, Brigitte Berger, and Hansfried Kellner, *The Homeless Mind: Modernization and Consciousness* (New York: Vintage, 1974).

18. For a recent study of the importance and difficulty of achieving such a common language and vision see Robert N. Bellah, Richard Madsen, William M. Sullivan, Ann Swidler, and Stephen M. Tipton, *Habits of the Heart: Individualism and Commitment in American Life* (Berkeley, Calif.: University of California Press, 1985). See also Martin E. Marty, *The Public Church* (New York: Crossroads, 1981).

19. Pope John XXIII, *Mater et Magistra* (1961), 219; *Pastoral Constitution*, 40.

20. Congregation for the Doctrine of the Faith, *Instruction on Certain Aspects of the Theology of Liberation*, (Washington, D.C.: United States Catholic Conference, 1984); Pope Paul VI, *Octogesima Adveniens* (1971), 42.

21. *Octogesima Adveniens*, 4.

22. Administrative Committee of the National Catholic War Council, *Program of Social Reconstruction*, February 12, 1919. Other notable statements on the economy by our predecessors are *The Present Crisis*, April 25, 1933; *Statement on Church and Social Order*, February 4, 1940; The Economy: Human Dimensions, November 20, 1975. These and numerous other statements of the U.S. Catholic episcopate can be found in Hugh J. Nolan, ed., *Pastoral Letters of the U.S. Catholic Bishops*, 4 vols. (Washington, D.C.: United States Catholic Conference, 1984).

The Christian Vision of Economic Life

CHAPTER II

(nos. 28–126)

▪▪ THE CHRISTIAN VISION OF ECONOMIC LIFE

28. The basis for all that the Church believes about the moral dimensions of economic life is its vision of the transcendent worth—the sacredness—of human beings. *The dignity of the human person, realized in community with others, is the criterion against which all aspects of economic life must be measured.*[1] All human beings, therefore, are ends to be served by the institutions that make up the economy, not means to be exploited for more narrowly defined goals. Human personhood must be respected with a reverence that is religious. When we deal with each other, we should do so with the sense of awe that arises in the presence of something holy and sacred. For that is what human beings are: we are created in the image of God (Gn 1:27). Similarly, all economic institutions must support the bonds of community and solidarity that are essential to the dignity of persons. Wherever our economic arrangements fail to conform to the demands of human dignity lived in community, they must be questioned and transformed. These convictions have a biblical basis. They are also supported by a long tradition of theological and philosophical reflection and through the reasoned analysis of human experience by contemporary men and women.

29. In presenting the Christian moral vision, we turn first to the Scriptures for guidance. Though our comments are necessarily selective, we hope that pastors and other church members will become personally engaged with the biblical texts. The Scriptures contain many passages that speak directly of economic life. We must also attend to the Bible's deeper vision of God, of the purpose of creation, and of the dignity of human life in society. Along with other churches and ecclesial communities who are "strengthened by the grace of Baptism and the hearing of God's Word," we strive to become faithful hearers and doers of the word.[2] We also claim the Hebrew Scriptures as common heritage with our Jewish brothers and sisters, and we join with them in the quest for an economic life worthy of the divine revelation we share.

■■ A. BIBLICAL PERSPECTIVES

30. The fundamental conviction of our faith is that human life is fulfilled in the knowledge and love of the living God in communion with others. The Sacred Scriptures offer guidance so that men and women may enter into full communion with God and with each other, and witness to God's saving acts. We discover there is a God who is creator of heaven and earth, and of the human family. Though our first parents reject the God who created them, God does not abandon them, but from Abraham and Sarah forms a people of promise. When this people is enslaved in an alien land, God delivers them and makes a covenant with them in which they are summoned to be faithful to the torah or sacred teaching. The focal points of Israel's faith—creation, covenant, and community—provide a foundation for reflection on issues of economic and social justice.

1. Created in God's Image

31. After the exile, when Israel combined its traditions into a written *torah*, it prefaced its history as a people with the story of the creation of all peoples and of the whole world by the same God who created them as a nation (Gn 1–11). God is the creator of heaven and earth (Gn 14:19–22; Is 40:28; 45:18); creation proclaims God's glory (Ps 89:6–12) and is "very good" (Gn 1:31). Fruitful harvests, bountiful flocks, a loving family are God's blessings on those who heed God's word. Such is the joyful refrain that echoes throughout the Bible. One legacy of this theology of creation is the conviction that no dimension of human creation lies beyond God's care and concern. God is present to creation, and creative engagement with God's handiwork is itself reverence for God.

32. At the summit of creation stands the creation of man and woman, made in God's image (Gn 1:26–27). *As such every human being possesses an inalienable dignity that stamps human existence prior to any division into races or nations and prior to human labor and human achievement* (Gn 4–11). Men and women are also to share in the creative activity of God. They are to be fruitful, to care for the earth (Gn 2:15), and to have "dominion" over it (Gn 1:28), which means they are "to govern the world in holiness and justice and to render judgment in integrity of heart" (Wis 9:3). Creation is a gift; women and men are to be faithful stewards in caring for the earth. They can justly consider that by their labor they are unfolding the Creator's work.[3]

33. The narratives of Genesis 1–11 also portray the origin of the strife and suffering that mar the world. Though created to enjoy intimacy with God and the fruits of the earth, Adam and Eve disrupted God's design by trying to

live independently of God through a denial of their status as creatures. They turned away from God and gave to God's creation the obedience due to God alone. For this reason the prime sin in so much of the biblical tradition is idolatry: service of the creature rather than of the creator (Rom 1:25), and the attempt to overturn creation by making Do in human likeness. The Bible castigates not only the worship of idols, but also manifestations of idolatry, such as the quest for unrestrained power and the desire for great wealth (Is 40:12–20; 44:1–20; Wis 13:1–14:31; Col 3:5, "the greed that is idolatry"). The sin of our first parents had other consequences as well. Alienation from God pits brother against brother (Gn 4:8–16), in a cycle of war and vengeance (Gn 4:22–23). Sin and evil abound, and the primeval history culminates with another assault on the heavens, this time ending in a babble of tongues scattered over the face of the earth (Gn 11:1–0). Sin simultaneously alienates human beings from God and shatters the solidarity of the human community. Yet this reign of sin is not the final word. The primeval history is followed by the call of Abraham, a man of faith, who was to be the bearer of the promise to many nations (Gn 12:1–4). Throughout the Bible we find this struggle between sin and repentance. God's judgment on evil is followed by God's seeking out a sinful people.

34. The biblical vision of creation has provided one of the most enduring legacies of Church teaching. To stand before God as the creator is to respect God's creation, both the world of nature and of human history. *From the patristic period to the present, the church has affirmed that misuse of the world's resources or appropriation of them by a minority of the world's population betrays the gift of creation since "whatever belongs to god belongs to all."*[4]

2. A People of Covenant

35. When the people of Israel, our forerunners in faith, gathered in thanksgiving to renew their covenant (Jos 24:1–15), they recalled the gracious deeds of God (Dt 6:20–25; 26:5–11). When they lived as aliens in a strange land and experienced oppression and slavery, they cried out. The Lord, the God of their ancestors, heard their cries, knew their afflictions, and came to deliver them (Ex 3:7–8). By leading them out of Egypt, God created a people that was to be the Lord's very own (Jer 24:7; Hos 2:25). They were to imitate God by treating the alien and the slave in their midst as God had treated them (Ex 22:20–22; Jer 34:8–14).

36. In the midst of this saving history stands the covenant at Sinai (Ex 19–24). It begins with an account of what God has done for the people (Ex 19:1–6; cf Jos 24:1–13) and includes from God's side a promise of steadfast love (hesed) and faithfulness ('emeth, Ex 34:5–7). The people are summoned to ratify this

covenant by faithfully worshiping God alone and by directing their lives according to God's will, which was made explicit in Israel's great legal codes such as the Decalogue (Ex 20:1–17) and the Book of the Covenant (Ex 20:22–23:33). Far from being an arbitrary restriction on the life of the people, these codes made life in community possible.[5] The specific laws of the covenant protect human life and property, demand respect for parents and the spouses and children of one's neighbor, and manifest a special concern for the vulnerable members of the community: widows, orphans, the poor, and strangers in the land. Laws such as that for the Sabbath year when the land was left fallow (Ex 23:11; Lv 25:1–7) and for the year of release of debts (Dt 15:1–11) summoned people to respect the land as God's gift and reminded Israel that as a people freed by God from bondage they were to be concerned for the poor and oppressed in their midst. Every fiftieth year a jubilee was proclaimed as a year of "liberty throughout the land" and property was to be restored to its original owners (LV 25:8–17, cf Is 61:1–2; Lk 4:18–19).[6] The codes of Israel reflect the norms of the covenant: reciprocal responsibility, mercy, and truthfulness. They embody a life in freedom from oppression: worship of the One God, rejection of idolatry, mutual respect among people, care and protection for every member of the social body. Being free and being a co-responsible community are God's intentions for us.

37. When the people turn away from the living God to serve idols and no longer heed the commands of the covenant, God sends prophets to recall his saving deeds and to summon them to return to the one who betrothed them "in right and in justice, in love and in mercy" (Hos 2:21). The substance of prophetic faith is proclaimed by Micah: "to do justice, and to love kindness, and to walk humbly with your God" (Mi 6:8, RSV). Biblical faith in general, and prophetic faith especially, insist that fidelity to the covenant joins obedience to God with reverence and concern for the neighbor. The biblical terms which best summarize this double dimension of Israel's faith are sedaqah, justice (also translated as righteousness), and mishpat (right judgment or justice embodied in a concrete act or deed). The biblical understanding of justice gives a fundamental perspective to our reflections on social and economic justice.[7]

38. God is described as a "God of justice" (Is 30:18) who loves justice (Is 61:8, cf. Ps 11:7; 33:5; 37:28: 99:4) and delights in it (Jer 9:23). God demands justice from the whole people (Dt 16:20) and executes justice for the needy (Ps 140:13). Central to the biblical presentation of justice is that the justice of a community is measured by its treatment of the powerless in society, most often described as the widow, the orphan, the poor, and the stranger (non-Israelite) in the land. The Law, the Prophets, and the Wisdom literature of the Old Testament all show deep concern for the proper treatment of such people.[8] What these groups of people have in common is their vulnerability

and lack of power. They are often alone and have no protector or advocate. Therefore, it is God who hears their cries (Ps 109:21; 113:7), and the king who is God's anointed is commanded to have special concern for them.

39. Justice has many nuances.[9] Fundamentally, it suggests a sense of what is right or of what should happen. For example, paths are just when they bring you to your destination (Gn 24:48; Ps 23:3), and laws are just when they create harmony within the community, as Isaiah says: "Justice will bring about peace; right will produce calm and security" (Is 32:17). God is "just" by acting as God should, coming to the people's aid and summoning them to conversion when they stray. People are summoned to be "just," that is, to be in a proper relation to God, by observing God's laws which form them into a faithful community. Biblical justice is more comprehensive than subsequent philosophical definitions. It is not concerned with a strict definition of rights and duties, but with the rightness of the human condition before God and within society. Nor is justice opposed to love; rather, it is both a manifestation of love and a condition for love to grow.[10] Because God loves Israel, he rescues them from oppression and summons them to be a people that "does justice" and loves kindness. The quest for justice arises from loving gratitude for the saving acts of God and manifests itself in wholehearted love of God and neighbor.

40. These perspectives provide the foundation for a biblical vision of economic justice. Every human person is created as an image of God, and the denial of dignity to a person is a blot on this image. Creation is a gift to all men and women, not to be appropriated for the benefit of a few; its beauty is an object of joy and reverence. The same God who came to the aid of an oppressed people and formed them into a covenant community continues to hear the cries of the oppressed and to create communities which are responsive to God's word. God's love and life are present when people can live in a community of faith and hope. These cardinal points of faith of Israel also furnish the religious context for understanding the saving action of God in the life and teachings of Jesus.

3. The Reign of God and Justice

41. Jesus enters human history as God's anointed son who announces the nearness of the reign of God (Mk 1:9–14). This proclamation summons us to acknowledge God as creator and covenant partner and challenges us to seek ways in which God's revelation of the dignity and destiny of all creation might become incarnate in history. It is not simply the promise of the future victory of God over sin and evil, but that this victory has already begun—in the life and teaching of Jesus.

42. What Jesus proclaims by word, he enacts in his ministry. He resists temptations of power and prestige, follows his Father's will, and teaches us to pray that it be accomplished on earth. He warns against attempts to "lay up treasures on earth" (Mt 6:19) and exhorts his followers not to be anxious about material goods but rather to seek first God's reign and God's justice (Mt 6:25–33). His mighty works symbolize that the reign of God is more powerful than evil, sickness, and the hardness of the human heart. He offers God's loving mercy to sinners (Mk 2:17), takes up the cause of those who suffered religious and social discrimination (Lk 7:36–50; 15:1–2), and attacks the use of religion to avoid the demands of charity and justice (Mk 7:9–13; Mt 23:23).

43. When asked what was the greatest commandment, Jesus quoted the age-old Jewish affirmation of faith that God alone is One and to be loved with the whole heart, mind, and soul (Dt 6:4–5) and immediately adds: "You shall love your neighbor as yourself" (Lv 19:18, Mk 12:28–34). This dual command of love that is at the basis of all Christian morality is illustrated in the Gospel of Luke by the parable of a Samaritan who interrupts his journey to come to the aid of a dying man (Lk 10:29–37). Unlike the other wayfarers who look on the man and pass by, the Samaritan "was moved with compassion at the sight"; he stops, tends the wounded man, and takes him to a place of safety. In this parable compassion is the bridge between mere seeing and action: love is made real through effective action.[11]

44. Near the end of his life, Jesus offers a vivid picture of the last judgment (Mt 25:31–46). All the nations of the world will be assembled and will be divided into those blessed who are welcomed into God's kingdom or those cursed who are sent to eternal punishment. The blessed are those who fed the hungry, gave drink to the thirsty, welcomed the stranger, clothed the naked, and visited the sick and imprisoned; the cursed are those who neglected these works of mercy and love. Neither the blessed nor the cursed are astounded that they are judged by the Son of Man, nor that the judgment is rendered according to the works of charity. The shock comes when they find that in neglecting the poor, the outcast, and the oppressed, they were rejecting Jesus himself. Jesus who came as "Emmanuel" (God with us, Mt 1:23) and who promises to be with his people until the end of the age (Mt 28:20) is hidden in those most in need; to reject them is to reject God made manifest in history.

4. Called to be Disciples in Community

45. Jesus summoned his first followers to a change of heart and to take on the yoke of God's reign (Mk 1:14–15; Mt 11:29). They are to be the nucleus of the community which will continue the work of proclaiming and building God's

kingdom through the centuries. As Jesus called the first disciples in the midst of their everyday occupations of fishing and tax collecting; so he again calls people in every age in the home, in the workplace, and in the marketplace.

46. The Church is, as Pope John Paul II reminded us, "a community of disciples" in which "we must see first and foremost Christ saying to each member of the community: follow me."[12] To be a Christian is to join with others in responding to this personal call and in learning the meaning of Christ's life. It is to be sustained by that loving intimacy with the Father that Jesus experienced in his work, in his prayer, and in his suffering.

47. Discipleship involves imitating the pattern of Jesus' life by openness to God's will in the service of others (Mk 10:42–45). Disciples are also called to follow him on the way of the cross, and to heed his call that those who lose their lives for the sake of the Gospel will save them (Mk 8:34–35). Jesus' death is an example of that greater love which lays down one's life for others (cf. Jn 15:12–18). It is a model for those who suffer persecution for the sake of justice (Mt 5:10). The death of Jesus was not the end of his power and presence, for he was raised up by the power of God. Nor did it mark the end of the disciples' union with him. After Jesus had appeared to them and when they received the gift of the Spirit (Acts 2:1–12), they became apostles of the good news to the ends of the earth. In the face of poverty and persecution they transformed human lives and formed communities which became signs of the power and presence of God. Sharing in this same resurrection faith, contemporary followers of Christ can face the struggles and challenges that await those who bring the gospel vision to bear on our complex economic and social world.

5. Poverty, Riches, and the Challenge of Discipleship

48. The pattern of Christian life as presented in the Gospel of Luke has special relevance today. In her Magnificat, Mary rejoices in a God who scatters the proud, brings down the mighty, and raises up the poor and lowly (Lk 1:51–53). The first public utterance of Jesus is "The Spirit of the Lord is upon me, because he has anointed me to preach good news to the poor" (Lk 4:18 cf. Is 61:1–2). Jesus adds to the blessing on the poor a warning, "Woe to you who are rich, for you have received your consolation" (Lk 6:24). He warns his followers against greed and reliance on abundant possessions and underscores this by the parable of the man whose life is snatched away at the very moment he tries to secure his wealth (Lk 12:13–21). In Luke along, Jesus tells the parable of the rich man who does not see the poor and suffering Lazarus at his gate (Lk 16:19–31). When the rich man finally "sees" Lazarus, it is from the place of torment and the opportunity for conversion has passed. Pope

John Paul II has often recalled this parable to warn the prosperous not to be blind to the great poverty that exists beside great wealth.[13]

49. Jesus, especially in Luke, lives as a poor man, like the prophets takes the side of the poor, and warns of the dangers of wealth.[14] The terms used for the poor, while primarily describing lack of material goods, also suggest dependence and powerlessness. The poor are also an exiled and oppressed people whom God will rescue (Is 51:21–23) as well as a faithful remnant who will take refuge in God (Zep 3:12–13). Throughout the Bible, material poverty is a misfortune and a cause of sadness. A constant biblical refrain is that the poor must be cared for and protected and that when they are exploited, God hears their cries (Prv 22:22–23). Conversely, even though the goods of the earth are to be enjoyed and people are to thank God for material blessings, wealth is a constant danger. The rich are wise in their own eyes (Prv 28:11), and are prone to apostasy and idolatry (Am 5:4–13; Is 2:6–8), as well as to violence and oppression (Jas 2:6–7).[15] Since they are neither blinded by wealth nor make it into an idol, the poor can be open to God's presence; throughout Israel's history and in early Christianity the poor are agents of God's transforming power.

50. The poor are often related to the lowly (Mt 5:3, 5) to whom God reveals what was hidden from the wise (Mt 11:25–30). When Jesus calls the poor "blessed," he is not praising their condition of poverty, but their openness to God. When he states that the reign of God is theirs, he voices God's special concern for them, and promises that they are to be the beneficiaries of God's mercy, and justice. When he summons disciples to leave all and follow him, he is calling them to share his own radical trust in the Father and his freedom from care and anxiety (cf. Mt 6:25–34). The practice of evangelical poverty in the Church has always been a living witness to the power of that trust and to the joy that comes with that freedom.

51. Early Christianity saw the poor as an object of God's special love, but it neither canonized material poverty nor accepted deprivation as an inevitable fact of life. Though few early Christians possessed wealth or power (1 Cor 1:26–28; Jas 2:5), their communities had well-off members (Acts 16:14; 18:8). Jesus' concern for the poor was continued in different forms in the early Church. The early community at Jerusalem distributed its possessions so that "there was no needy person among them," and held "all things in common"—a phrase that suggests not only shared material possessions, but more fundamentally, friendship and mutual concern among all its members (Acts 4:32–34; 2:44). While recognizing the dangers of wealth, the early Church proposed the proper use of possessions to alleviate need and suffering, rather than universal dispossession. Beginning in the first century, and throughout history, Christian communities have developed varied structures to support and

sustain the weak and powerless in societies that were often brutally unconcerned about human suffering.

52. Such perspectives provide a basis today for what is called the "preferential option for the poor."[16] Though the Gospels and in the New Testament as a whole the offer of salvation is extended to all peoples, Jesus takes the side of the most in need, physically and spiritually. The example of Jesus poses a number of challenges to the contemporary Church. It imposes a prophetic mandate to speak for those who have no one to speak for them, to be a defender of the defenseless, who in biblical terms are the poor. It also demands a compassionate vision that enables the Church to see things from the side of the poor and powerless and to assess lifestyle, policies, and social institutions in terms of their impact on the poor. It summons the Church also to be an instrument in assisting people to experience the liberating power of God in their own lives so that they may respond to the Gospel in freedom and in dignity. Finally, and most radially, it calls for an emptying of self, both individually and corporately, that allows the Church to experience the power of God in the midst of poverty and powerlessness.

6. A Community of Hope

53. The biblical vision of creation, covenant, and community, as well as the summons to discipleship, unfolds under the tension between promise and fulfillment. The whole Bible is spanned by narratives of the first creation (Gn 1–3) and the vision of a restored creation at the end of history (Rv 21:1–4). Just as creation tells us that God's desire was one of wholeness and unity between God and the human family and within this family itself, the images of a new creation give hope that enmity and hatred will cease and justice and peace will reign (Is 11:4–6; 25:1–8). Human life unfolds "between the times," the time of the first creation and that of a restored creation (Rom 8:18–25). Although the ultimate realization of God's plan lies in the future, Christians in union with all people of good will are summed to shape history in the image of God's creative design, and in response to the reign of God proclaimed and embodied by Jesus.

54. A Christian is a member of a new community, "God's own people" (1 Pt 2:9–10), who, like the people of Exodus, owes its existence to the gracious gift of God and is summoned to respond to God's will made manifest in the life and teaching of Jesus. A Christian walks in the newness of life (Rom 6:4), and is "a new creation; the old has passed away, the new has come" (2 Cor 5:17). This new creation in Christ proclaims that God's creative love is constantly at work, offers sinners forgiveness, and reconciles a broken world. Our action on behalf of justice in our world proceeds from the conviction that, despite the

power of injustice and violence, life has been fundamentally changed by the entry of the Word made flesh into human history.

55. Christian communities that commit themselves to solidarity with those suffering and to confrontation with those attitudes and ways of acting which institutionalize injustice, will themselves experience the power and presence of Christ. They will embody in their lives the values of the new creation while they labor under the old. The quest for economic and social justice will always combine hope and realism, and must be renewed by every generation. It involves diagnosing those situations that continue to alienate the world from God's creative love as well as presenting hopeful alternatives that arise from living in a renewed creation. This quest arises from faith and is sustained by hope as it seeks to speak to a broken world of God's justice and loving kindness.

7. A Living Tradition

56. Our reflection on U.S. economic life today must be rooted in this biblical vision of the kingdom and discipleship, but it must also be shaped by the rich and complex tradition of Catholic life and thought. Throughout its history, the Christian community has listened to the words of Scripture and sought to enact them in the midst of daily life in very different historical and cultural contexts.

57. In the first centuries, when Christians were a minority in a hostile society, they cared for one another through generous almsgiving. In the patristic era, the church fathers repeatedly stressed that the goods of the earth were created by God for the benefit of every person without exception, and that all have special duties toward those in need. The monasteries of the Middle Ages were centers of prayer, learning, and education. They contributed greatly to the cultural and economic life of the towns and cities that sprang up around them. In the twelfth century the new mendicant orders dedicated themselves to following Christ in poverty and to the proclamation of the good news to the poor.

58. These same religious communities also nurtured some of the greatest theologians of the Church's tradition, thinkers who synthesized the call of Christ with the philosophical learning Greek, Roman, Jewish, and Arab worlds. Thomas Aquinas and the other scholastics devoted rigorous intellectual energy to clarifying the meaning of both personal virtue and justice in society. In more recent centuries Christians began to build a large network of hospitals, orphanages, and schools, to serve the poor and society at large. And beginning with Leo XIII's *Rerum Novarum*, down to the writings and speeches of John Paul II, the popes have more systematically addressed the rapid change of modern society in a series of social

encyclicals. These teachings of the modern popes and of the Second Vatican Council are especially significant for efforts to respond to the problems facing society today.[17]

59. We also have much to learn from the strong emphasis in Protestant traditions on the vocation of lay people in the world and from ecumenical efforts to develop an economic ethic that addresses newly emergent problems. And in a special way our fellow Catholics in developing countries have much to teach us about the Christian response to an ever more interdependent world.

60. Christians today are called by God to carry on this tradition through active love of neighbor, a love that responds to the special challenges of this moment in human history. The world is wounded by sin and injustice, in need of conversion and of the transformation that comes when persons enter more deeply into the mystery of the death and Resurrection of Christ. The concerns of this pastoral letter are not at all peripheral to the central mystery at the heart of the Church.[18] They are integral to the proclamation of the Gospel and part of the vocation of every Christian today.[19]

▦ B. ETHICAL NORMS FOR ECONOMIC LIFE

61. These biblical and theological themes shape the overall Christian perspective on economic ethics. This perspective is also subscribed to by many who do not share Christian religious convictions. Human understanding and religious belief are complementary, not contradictory. For human beings are created in God's image, and their dignity is manifest in the ability to reason and understand, in their freedom to shape their own lives and the life of their communities, and in the capacity for love and friendship. In proposing ethical norms, therefore, we appeal both to Christians and to all in our pluralist society to show that respect and reverence owed to the the dignity of every person. Intelligent reflection on the social and economic realities of today is also indispensable in the effort to respond to economic circumstances never envisioned in biblical times. Therefore, we now want to propose an ethical framework that can guide economic life today in ways that are both faithful to the Gospel and shaped by human experience and reason.

62. First we outline the *duties* all people have to each other and to the whole community: love of neighbor, the basic requirements of justice, and the special obligation to those who are poor or vulnerable. Corresponding to these duties are the *human rights* of every person; the obligation to protect the dignity of all demands respect for these rights. Finally these duties and rights entail several *priorities* that should guide the economic choices of individuals, communities, and the nation as a whole.

1. The Responsibilities of Social Living

63. Human life is life in community. Catholic social teaching proposes several complementary perspectives that show how moral responsibilities and duties in the economic sphere are rooted in this call to community.

a. Love and Solidarity

64. *The commandments to love god with all one's heart and to love one's neighbor as oneself are the heart and soul of christian morality.* Jesus offers himself as the model of this all-inclusive love: . . . love one another as I have loved you" (Jn 15:12). These commands point out the path toward true human fulfillment and happiness. They are not arbitrary restrictions on human freedom. Only active love of God and neighbor makes the fullness of community happen. Christians look forward in hope to a true communion among all persons with each other and with God. The Spirit of Christ labors in history to build up the bonds of solidarity among all persons until that day on which their union is brought to perfection in the Kingdom of God.[20] Indeed Christian theological reflection on the very reality of God as a trinitarian unity of persons—Father, Son, and Holy Spirit—shows that being a person means being united to other persons in mutual love."[21]

65. What the Bible and Christian tradition teach, human wisdom confirms. Centuries before Christ, the Greeks and Romans spoke of the human person as a "social animal" made for friendship, community, and public life. These insights show that human beings achieve self-realization not in isolation, but in interaction with others.[22]

66. The virtues of citizenship are an expression of Christian love more crucial in today's interdependent world than ever before. These virtues grow out of a lively sense of one's dependence on the commonweal and obligations to it. This civic commitment must also guide the economic institutions of society. In the absence of a vital sense of citizenship among the businesses, corporations, labor unions, and other groups that shape economic life, society as a whole is endangered. Solidarity is another name for this social friendship and civic commitment that make human moral and economic life possible.

67. The Christian tradition recognizes, of course, that the fullness of love and community will be achieved only when God's work in Christ comes to completion in the kingdom of God. This kingdom has been inaugurated among us, but God's redeeming and transforming work is not yet complete. Within history, knowledge of how to achieve the goal of social unity is limited. Human sin continues to wound the lives of both individuals and larger social bodies and places obstacles in the path toward greater social solidarity. If efforts to protect human dignity are to be effective, they must take these

limits on knowledge and love into account. Nevertheless, sober realism should not be confused with resigned or cynical pessimism. It is a challenge to develop a courageous hope that can sustain efforts that will sometimes be arduous and protracted.

b. Justice and Participation

68. Biblical justice is the goal we strive for. This rich biblical understanding portrays a just society as one marked by the fullness of love, compassion, holiness, and peace. On their path through history, however, sinful human beings need more specific guidance on how to move toward the realization of this great vision of God's Kingdom. This guidance is contained in the norms of basic or minimal justice. These norms state the minimum levels of mutual care and respect that all persons owe to each other in an imperfect world.[23] Catholic social teaching, like must philosophical reflection, distinguishes three dimensions of basic justice: commutative justice, distributive justice, and social justice.[24]

69. *Commutative justice calls for fundamental fairness in all agreements and exchanges between individuals or private social groups.* It demands respect for the equal human dignity of all persons in economic transactions, contracts, or promises. For example, workers owe their employers diligent work in exchange for their wages. Employers are obligated to treat their employees as persons, paying them fair wages in exchange for the work done and establishing conditions and patterns of work that are truly human.[25]

70. *Distributive justice requires that the allocation of income, wealth, and power in society be evaluated in light of its effects on persons whose basic material needs are unmet.* The Second Vatican Council stated: "The right to have a share of earthly goods sufficient for oneself and one's family belongs to everyone. The fathers and doctors of the Church held this view, teaching that we are obliged to come to the relief of the poor and to do so not merely out of our superfluous goods."[26] Minimum material resources are an absolute necessity for human life. If persons are to be recognized as members of the human community, then the community has an obligation to help fulfill these basic needs unless an absolute scarcity of resources makes this strictly impossible. No such scarcity exists in the United States today.

71. Justice also has implications for the way the larger social, economic, and political institutions of society are organized. *Social justice implies that persons have an obligation to be active and productive participants in the life of society and that society has a duty to enable them to participate in this way.* This form of justice can also be called "contributive," for it stresses the duty of all who are able to help create the goods, services, and other nonmaterial or spiritual values necessary for the welfare of the whole community. In the words of Pius XI, "It is of the very essence of social justice to demand from

each individual all that is necessary for the common good."[27] Productivity is essential if the community is to have the resources to serve the well-being of all. Productivity, however, cannot be measured solely by its output in goods and services. Patterns of production must also be measured in light of their impact on the fulfillment of basic needs, employment levels, patterns of discrimination, environmental quality, and sense of community.

72. The meaning of social justice also includes a duty to organize economic and social institutions so that people can contribute to society in ways that respect their freedom and the dignity of their labor. Work should enable the working person to become "more a human being," more capable of acting intelligently, freely, and in ways that lead to self-realization.[28]

73. Economic conditions that leave large numbers of able people unemployed, underemployed, or employed in dehumanizing conditions fail to meet the converging demands of these three forms of basic justice. Work with adequate pay for all who seek it is the primary means of achieving basic justice in our society. Discrimination in job opportunities or income levels on the basis of race, sex, or other arbitrary standards can never be justified.[29] It is a scandal that such discrimination continues in the United States today. Where the effects of past discrimination persist, society has an obligation to take positive steps to overcome the legacy of injustice. Judiciously administered affirmative action programs in education and employment can be important expressions of the drive for solidarity and participation that is at the heart of true justice. Social harm calls for social relief.

74. Basic justice also calls for the establishment of a floor of material well-being on which all can stand. This is a duty of the whole of society and it creates particular obligations for those with greater resources. This duty calls into question extreme inequalities of income and consumption when so many lack basic necessities. Catholic social teaching does not maintain that a flat, arithmetical equality of income and wealth is a demand of justice, but it does challenge economic arrangements that leave large numbers of people impoverished. Further, it sees extreme inequality as a threat to the solidarity of the human community, for great disparities lead to deep social divisions and conflict.[30]

75. This means that all of us must examine our way of living in the light of the needs of the poor. Christian faith and the norms of justice impose distinct limits on what we consume and how we view material goods. The great wealth of the United States can easily blind us to the poverty that exists in this nation and the destitution of hundreds of millions of people in other parts of the world. Americans are challenged today as never before to develop the inner freedom to resist the temptation constantly to seek more. Only in this way will the nation avoid what Paul VI called "the most evident form of moral underdevelopment," namely greed.[31]

76. These duties call not only for individual charitable giving but also for a more systematic approach by businesses, labor unions, and the many other groups that shape economic life—as well as government. The concentration of privilege that exists today results far more from institutional relationships distribute power and wealth inequitably than from differences in talent or lack of desire to work. These institutional patterns must be examined and revised if we are to meet the demands of basic justice. For example, a system of taxation based on assessment according to ability to pay[32] is a prime necessity for the fulfillment of these social obligations.

c. Overcoming Marginalization and Powerlessness

77. These fundamental duties can be summarized this way: *basic justice demands the establishment of minimum levels of participation in the life of the human community for all persons.* The ultimate injustice is for a person or group to be treated actively or abandoned passively as if they were nonmembers of the human race. To treat people this way is effectively to say they simply do not count as human beings. This can take many forms, all of which can be described as varieties of marginalization, or exclusion from social life.[33] This exclusion can occur in the political sphere: restriction of free speech, concentration of power in the hands of a few, or outright repression by the state. It can also take economic forms that are equally harmful. Within the United States, individuals, families, and local communities fall victim to a downward cycle of poverty generated by economic forces they are powerless to influence. The poor, the disabled, and the unemployed too often are simply left behind. This pattern is even more severe beyond our borders in the least-developed countries. Whole nations are prevented from fully participating in the international economic order because they lack the power to change their disadvantaged position. Many people within the less developed countries are excluded from sharing in the meager resources available in their homelands by unjust elites and unjust governments. These patterns of exclusion are created by free human beings. In this sense they can be called forms of social sin.[34] Acquiescence in them or the failure to correct them when it is possible to do so is a sinful dereliction of Christian duty.

78. Recent Catholic social thought regards the task of overcoming these patterns of exclusion and powerlessness as a most basic demand of justice. Stated positively, justice demands that social institutions be ordered in a way that guarantees all persons the ability to participate actively in the economic, political, and cultural life of society.[35] The level of participation may be legitimately greater for some persons than for others, but there is a basic level of access that must be made available for all. Such participation is an essential expression of the social nature of human beings and of their communitarian vocation.

2. Human Rights: The Minimum Conditions for Life in Community

79. Catholic social teaching spells out the basic demands of justice in greater detail in the human rights of every person. These fundamental rights are prerequisites for a dignified life in community. The Bible vigorously affirms the sacredness of every person as a creature formed in the image and likeness of God. The biblical emphasis on covenant and community also shows that human dignity can only be realized and protected in solidarity with others. In Catholic social thought, therefore, respect for human rights and a strong sense of both personal and community responsibility are linked, not opposed. Vatican II described the common good as "the sum of those conditions of social life which allow social groups and their individual members relatively thorough and ready access to their own fulfillment."[36] These conditions include the right to fulfillment of material needs, a guarantee of fundamental freedoms, and the protection of relationships that are essential to participation in the life of society.[37] These rights are bestowed on human beings by God and grounded in the nature and dignity of human persons. They are not created by society. Indeed society has a duty to secure and protect them.[38]

80. The full range of human rights has been systematically outlined by John XXIII in his encyclical *Peace on Earth* (*Pacem in Terris*). His discussion echoes the United Nations Universal Declaration of Human Rights and implies that internationally accepted human rights standards are strongly supported by Catholic teaching. These rights include the civil and political rights to freedom of speech, worship, and assembly. A number of human rights also concern human welfare and are of a specifically economic nature. First among these are the rights to life, food, clothing, shelter, rest, medical care, and basic education. These are indispensable to the protection of human dignity. In order to ensure these necessities, all persons have a right to earn a living, which for most people in our economy is through remunerative employment. All persons also have a right to security in the event of sickness, unemployment, and old age. Participation in the life of the community calls for the protection of this same right to employment, as well as the right to healthful working conditions, to wages, and other benefits sufficient to provide individuals and their families with a standard of living in keeping with human dignity, and to the possibility of property ownership.[39] These fundamental personal rights—civil and political as well as social and economic—state the minimum conditions for social institutions that respect human dignity, social solidarity, and justice. They are all essential to human dignity and to the integral development of both individuals and society, and are thus moral issues.[40] Any denial of these rights harms persons and wounds the human community. Their

serious and sustained denial violates individuals and destroys solidarity among persons.

81. Social and economic rights call for a mode of implementation different from that required to secure civil and political rights. Freedom of worship and of speech imply immunity from interference on the part of both other persons and the government. The rights to education, employment, and social security, for example, are empowerments that call for positive action by individuals and society at large.

82. However, both kinds of rights call for positive action to create social and political institutions that enable all persons to become active members of society. Civil and political rights allow persons to participate freely in the public life of the community, for example, through free speech, assembly, and the vote. In democratic countries these rights have been secured through a long and vigorous history of creating the institutions of constitutional government. In seeking to secure the full range of social and economic rights today, a similar effort to shape new economic arrangements will be necessary.

83. The first step in such an effort is the development of a new cultural consensus that the basic economic conditions of human welfare are essential to human dignity and are due persons by right. Second, the securing of these rights will make demands on all members of society, on all private sector institutions, and on government. A concerted effort on all levels in our society is needed to meet these basic demands of justice and solidarity. Indeed political democracy and a commitment to secure economic rights are mutually reinforcing.

84. Securing economic rights for all will be an arduous task. There are a number of precedents in the U.S. history, however, which show that the work has already begun.[41] The country needs a serious dialogue about the appropriate levels of private and public sector involvement that are needed to move forward. There is certainly room for diversity of opinion in the Church and in U.S. society on "how" to protect the human dignity and economic rights of all our brothers and sisters.[42] In our view, however, there can be no legitimate disagreement on the basic moral objectives.

3. Moral Priorities for the Nation

85. *The common good demands justice for all, the protection of the human rights for all.*[43] Making cultural and economic institutions more supportive of the freedom, power, and security of individuals and families must be a central, long-range objective for the nation. Every person has a duty to contribute to building up the commonweal. All have a responsibility to develop their talents through education. Adults must contribute to society through their individual vocations and talents. Parents are called to guide their children

to the maturity of Christian adulthood and responsible citizenship. Everyone has special duties toward the poor and marginalized. Living up to these responsibilities, however, is often made difficult by the social and economic patterns of society. Schools and educational policies both public and private often serve the privileged exceedingly well, while the children of the poor are effectively abandoned as second-class citizens. Great stresses are created in family life by the way wok is organized and scheduled, and by the social and cultural values communicated on TV. Many in the lower middle class are barely getting by and fear becoming victims of economic forces over which they have no control.

86. *The obligation to provide justice for all means that the poor have the single most urgent economic claim on the conscience of the nation.* Poverty can take many forms, spiritual as well as material. All people face struggles of the spirit as they ask deep questions about their purpose in life. Many have serious problems in marriage and family life at some time in their lives, and all of us face the certain reality of sickness and death. The Gospel of Christ proclaims that God's love is stronger than all these forms of diminishment. Material deprivation, however, seriously compounds such sufferings of the spirit and heart. To see a loved one sick is bad enough, but to have no possibility of obtaining health care is worse. To face family problems, such as death of a spouse or a divorce, can be devastating, but to have these lead to the loss of one's home and end with living on the streets is something no one should have to endure in a country as rich as ours. In developing countries these human problems are even more greatly intensified by extreme material deprivation. This form of human suffering can be reduced if our own country, so rich in resources, chooses to increase its assistance.

87. As individuals and as a nation, therefore, we are called to make a fundamental "option for the poor."[44] The obligation to evaluate social and economic activity from the viewpoint of the poor and the powerless arises from the radical command to love one's neighbor as one's self. Those who are marginalized and whose rights are denied have privileged claims if society is to provide justice for *all*. This obligation is deeply rooted in Christian belief. As Paul VI stated:

> "In teaching us charity, the Gospel instructs us in the preferential respect due to the poor and the special situation they have in society: the more fortunate should renounce some of their rights so as to place their goods more generously at the service of others."[45]

> John Paul II has described this special obligation to the poor as "a call to have a special openness with the small and the weak, those that suffer and weep, those that are humiliated and left

on the margin of society, so as to help them win their dignity as human persons and children of God."[46]

88. The primary purpose of this special commitment to the poor is to enable them to become active participants in the life of society. It is to enable all persons to share in and contribute to the common good.[47] The "option for the poor," therefore, is not an adversarial slogan that pits one group or class against another. Rather it states that the deprivation and powerlessness of the poor wounds the whole community. The extent of their suffering is a measure of how far we are from being a true community of persons. These wounds will be healed only by greater solidarity with the poor and among the poor themselves.

89. In summary, the norms of love, basic justice, and human rights imply that personal decisions, social policies, and economic institutions should be governed by several key priorities. These priorities do not specify everything that must be considered in economic decision making. They do indicate the most fundamental and urgent objectives.

90. a. The fulfillment of the basic needs of the poor is of the highest priority. Personal decisions, policies of private and public bodies, and power relationships must be all evaluated by their effects on those who lack the minimum necessities of nutrition, housing, education, and health care. In particular, this principle recognizes that meeting fundamental human needs must come before the fulfillment of desires for luxury consumer goods, for profits not conducive to the common good, and for unnecessary military hardware.

91. b. Increasing active participation in economic life by those who are presently excluded or vulnerable is a high social priority. The human dignity of all is realized when people gain the power to work together to improve their lives, strengthen their families, and contribute to society. Basic justice calls for more than providing help to the poor and other vulnerable members of society. It recognizes the priority of policies and programs that support family life and enhance economic participation through employment and widespread ownership of property. It challenges privileged economic power in favor of the well-being of all. It points to the need to improve the present situation of those unjustly discriminated against in the past. And it has very important implications for both the domestic and the international distribution of power.

92. c. The investment of wealth, talent, and human energy should be specially directed to benefit those who are poor or economically insecure. Achieving a more just economy in the United States and the world depends in part on increasing economic resources and productivity. In addition, the ways these resources are invested and managed must be scrutinized in light of their effects on non-monetary values. Investment and management decisions have

crucial moral dimensions: they create jobs or eliminate them; they can push vulnerable families over the edge into poverty or give them new hope for the future; they help or hinder the building of a more equitable society. They can have either positive or negative influence on the fairness of the global economy. Therefore, this priority presents a strong moral challenge to policies that put large amounts of talent and capital into the production of luxury consumer goods and military technology while failing to invest sufficiently in education, health, the basic infrastructure of our society and economic sectors that produce urgently needed jobs, goods and services.

93. d. Economic and social policies as well as organization of the work world should be continually evaluated in light of their impact on the strength and stability of family life. The long-range future of this nation is intimately linked with the well-being of families, for the family is the most basic form of human community.[48] Efficiency and competition in the marketplace must be moderated by greater concern for the way work schedules and compensation support or threaten the bonds between spouses and between parents and children. Health, education and social service programs should be scrutinized in light of how well they ensure both individual dignity and family integrity.

94. These priorities are not policies. They are norms that should guide the economic choices of all and shape economic institutions. They can help the United States move forward to fulfill the duties of justice and protect economic rights. They were strongly affirmed as implications of Catholic social teaching by Pope John Paul II during his visit to Canada in 1984: "The needs of the poor take priority over the desires of the rich; the rights of workers over the maximization of profits; the preservation of the environment over uncontrolled industrial expansion; the production to meet social needs over production for military purposes."[49] There will undoubtedly be disputes about the concrete applications of these priorities in our complex world. We do not seek to foreclose discussion about them. However, we believe that an effort to move in the direction they indicate is urgently needed.

95. The economic challenge of today has many parallels with the political challenge that confronted the founders of our nation. In order to create a new form of political democracy they were compelled to develop ways of thinking and political institutions that had never existed before. Their efforts were arduous and their goals imperfectly realized, but they launched an experiment in the protection of civil and political rights that has prospered through the efforts of those who came after them. *We believe the time has come for a similar experiment in securing economic rights: the creation of an order that guarantees the minimum conditions of human dignity in the economic sphere for every person.* By drawing on the resources of the Catholic moral-religious tradition, we hope to make a contribution through this letter to such a new "American Experiment": a new venture to secure economic justice for all.

▦ C. WORKING FOR GREATER JUSTICE: PERSONS AND INSTITUTIONS

96. The economy of this nation has been built by the labor of human hands and minds. Its future will be forged by the ways persons direct all this work toward greater justice. The economy is not a machine that operates according to its own inexorable laws, and persons are not mere objects tossed about by economic forces. Pope John Paul II has stated that "human work is a key, probably the essential key, to the whole social question."[50] The Pope's understanding of work includes virtually all forms of productive human activity: agriculture, entrepreneurship, industry, the care of children, the sustaining of family life, politics, medical care, and scientific research. Leisure, prayer, celebration, and the arts are also central to the realization of human dignity and to the development of a rich cultural life. It is in their daily work, however, that persons become the subjects and creators of the economic life of the nation.[51] Thus, it is primarily through their daily labor that people make their most important contributions to economic justice.

97. All work has a threefold moral significance. First, it is a principal way that people exercise the distinctive human capacity for self-expression and self-realization. Second, it is the ordinary way for human beings to fulfill their material needs. Finally, work enables people to contribute to the well-being of the larger community. Work is not only for one's self. It is for one's family, for the nation, and indeed for the benefit of the entire human family.[52]

98. These three moral concerns should be visible in the work of all, no matter what their role in the economy: blue collar workers, managers, homemakers, politicians, and others. They should also govern the activities of the many different, overlapping communities and institutions that make up society: families, neighborhoods, small businesses, giant corporations, trade unions, the various levels of government, international organizations, and a host of other human associations including communities of faith.

99. Catholic social teaching calls for respect for the full richness of social life. The need for vital contributions from different human associations—ranging in size from the family to government—has been classically expressed in Catholic social teaching in the "principle of subsidiarity":

> "Just as it is gravely wrong to take from individuals what they can accomplish by their own initiative and industry and give it to the community, so also it is an injustice and at the same time a grave evil and disturbance of right order to assign a greater and higher association what lesser and subordinate organizations can do. For every social activity ought of its very nature to furnish help (*subsidium*) to the members of the body social, and never destroy and absorb them."[53]

100. This principle guarantees institutional pluralism. It provides space for freedom, initiative, and creativity on the part of many social agents. At the same time, it insists that all these agents should work in ways that help build up the social body. Therefore, in all their activities these groups should be working in ways that express their distinctive capacities for action, that help meet human needs, and that make true contributions to the common good of the human community. The task of creating a more just U.S. economy is a vocation of all and depends on strengthening the virtues of public service and responsible citizenship in personal life and on all levels of institutional life.[54]

101. Without attempting to describe the tasks of all the different groups that make up society, we want to point to the specific rights and duties of some of the persons and institutions whose work for justice will be particularly important to the future of the United States economy. These rights and duties are among the concrete implications of the principle of subsidiarity. Further implications will be discussed in Chapter IV of this letter.

1. Working People and Labor Unions

102. Though John Paul II's understanding of work is a very inclusive one, it fully applies to those customarily called "workers" or "labor" in the United States. Labor has a great dignity, so great that all who are able to work are obligated to do so. The duty to work derives both from God's command and from a responsibility to one's own humanity and to the common good.[55] The virtue of industriousness is also an expression of a person's dignity and solidarity with others. All working people are called to contribute to the common good by seeking excellence in production and service.

103. Because work is this important, people have a right to employment. In return for their labor, workers have a right to wages and other benefits sufficient to sustain life in dignity. As Pope Leo XIII stated, every working person has "the right of securing things to sustain life."[56] The way power is distributed in a free market economy frequently gives employers greater bargaining power than employees in the negotiation of labor contracts. Such unequal power may press workers into a choice between an inadequate wage or no wage at all. But justice, not charity, demands certain minimum wage guarantees. The provision of wages and other benefits sufficient to support a family in dignity is a basic necessity to prevent this exploitation of workers. The dignity of workers also requires adequate health care, security for old age or disability, unemployment compensation, healthful working conditions, weekly rest, periodic holidays for recreation and leisure, and reasonable security against arbitrary dismissal.[57] These provisions are all essential if workers are to be treated as persons rather than simply a "factor of production."

104. The Church fully supports the right of workers to form unions or other associations to secure their rights to fair wages and working conditions. This is a specific application of the more general right to associate. In the words of Pope John Paul II, "The experience of history teaches that organizations of this type are an indispensable element of social life, especially in modern industrial societies."[58] Unions may also legitimately resort to strikes where this is the only available means to the justice owed to workers.[59] No one may deny the right to organize without attacking human dignity itself. Therefore, we firmly oppose organized efforts, such as those regrettably now seen in this country, to break existing unions and prevent workers from organizing. Migrant agricultural workers today are particularly in need of the protection, including the right to organize and bargain collectively. U.S. labor law reform is needed to meet these problems as well as to provide more timely and effective remedies for unfair labor practices.

105. Denial of the right to organize has been pursued ruthlessly in many countries beyond our borders. We vehemently oppose violations of the freedom to associate, wherever they occur, for they are an intolerable attack on social solidarity.

106. Along with the rights of workers and unions go a number of important responsibilities. Individual workers have obligations to their employers, and trade unions also have duties to society as a whole. Union management in particular carries a strong responsibility for the good name of the entire union movement. Workers must use their collective power to contribute to the well-being of the whole community and should avoid pressing demands whose fulfillment would damage the common good and the rights of more vulnerable members of society.[60] It should be noted, however, that wages paid to workers are but one of the factors affecting the competitiveness of industries. Thus, it is unfair to expect unions to make concessions if managers and shareholders do not make at least equal sacrifices.

107. Many U.S. unions have exercised leadership in the struggle for justice for minorities and women. Racial and sexual discrimination, however, have blotted the record of some unions. Organized labor has a responsibility to work positively toward eliminating the injustice this discrimination has caused.

108. Perhaps the greatest challenge facing United States workers and unions today is that of developing a new vision of their role in the United States economy of the future. The labor movement in the United States stands at a crucial moment. The dynamism of the unions that led to their rapid growth in the middle decades of this century has been replaced by a decrease in the percentage of U.S. workers who are organized. American workers are under heavy pressures today that threaten their jobs. The restrictions on the right to organize in many countries abroad make labor costs lower there, threaten American workers and their jobs, and lead to the exploitation of workers in these countries. In these difficult circumstances, guaranteeing the rights of

U.S. workers calls for imaginative vision and creative new steps, not reactive or simply defensive strategies. For example, organized labor can play a very important role in helping provide the education and training needed to help keep workers employable. Unions can also help both their own members and workers in developing countries by increasing their international efforts. A vital labor movement will be one that looks to the future with a deepened sense of global interdependence.

109. There are many signs that these challenges are being discussed by creative labor leaders today. Deeper and broader discussions of this sort are needed. This does not mean that only organized labor faces these new problems. All other sectors and institutions in the U.S. economy need similar vision and imagination. Indeed new forms of cooperation among labor, management, government, and other social groups are essential, and will be discussed in Chapter VI of this letter.

2. Owners and Managers

110. The economy's success in fulfilling the demands of justice will depend on how its vast resources and wealth are managed. Property owners, managers, and investors of financial capital must all contribute to creating a more just society. Securing economic justice depends heavily on the leadership of men and women in business and on the wise investment by private enterprises. Pope John Paul II has pointed out, "The degree of well-being which society today enjoys would be unthinkable without the dynamic figure of the business person, whose function consists of organizing human labor and the means of production so as to give rise to the goods and services necessary for the prosperity and progress of the community."[61] The freedom of entrepreneurship, business, and finance should be protected, but the accountability of this freedom to the common good and the norms of justice must be assured.

111. Persons in management face many hard choices each day, choices on which the well-being of many others depends. Commitment to the public good and not simply the private good of their firms is at the heart of what it means to call their work a vocation and simply a career or a job. We believe that the norms and priorities discussed in this letter can be of help as they pursue their important tasks. The duties of individuals in the business world, however, do not exhaust the ethical dimensions of business and finance. The size of a firm or bank is in many cases an indicator of relative power. Large corporations and large financial institutions have considerable power to help shape economic institutions within the United States and throughout the world. With this power goes responsibility and the need for those who manage it to be held to moral and institutional accountability.

112. Business and finance have the duty to be faithful trustees of the resources at their disposal. No one can ever own capital resources absolutely or control their use without regard for others and society as a whole.[62] This applies first of all to land and natural resources. Short-term profits reaped at the cost of depletion of natural resources or the pollution of the environment violate this trust.

113. Resources created by human industry are also held in trust. Owners and managers have not created this capital on their own. They have benefited from the work of many others and from the local communities that support their endeavors.[63] They are accountable to these workers and communities when making decisions. For example, reinvestment in technological innovation is often considered crucial for the long-term viability of a firm. The use of financial resources solely in pursuit of short-term profits can stunt the production of needed goods and services; a broader vision of managerial responsibility is needed.

114. The Catholic tradition has long defended the right to private ownership of productive property.[64] This right is an important element in a just economic policy. It enlarges our capacity for creativity and initiative.[65] Small and medium-sized farms, businesses, and entrepreneurial enterprises are among the most creative and efficient sectors of our economy. They should be highly valued by the people of the United States, as are land ownership and home ownership. Widespread distribution of property can help avoid excessive concentration of economic and political power. For these reasons ownership should be made possible for a broad sector of our population.[66]

115. The common good may sometimes demand that the right to own be limited by public involvement in the planning or ownership of certain sectors of the economy. Support of private ownership does not mean that anyone has the right to unlimited accumulation of wealth. "Private property does not constitute for anyone an absolute or unconditional right. No one is justified in keeping for his exclusive use what he does not need, when others lack necessities."[67] Pope John Paul II has referred to limits placed on ownership by the duty to serve the common good as a "social mortgage" on private property.[68] For example, these limits are the basis of society's exercise of eminent domain over privately owned land needed for roads or other essential public goods. The Church's teaching opposes collectivist and statist economic approaches. But it also rejects the notion that a free market automatically produces justice. Therefore, as Pope John Paul II has argued, "One cannot exclude the socialization, in suitable conditions, of certain means of production."[69] The determination of when such conditions exist must be made on a case by case basis in light of the demands of the common good.

116. United States business and financial enterprises can also help determine the justice or injustice of the world economy. They are not all-powerful, but their real power is unquestionable. Transnational corporations and financial institutions can make positive contributions to development and global solidarity. Pope John Paul II has pointed out, however, that the desire to maximize profits and reduce cost of natural resources and labor has often tempted these transnational enterprises to behavior that increases inequality and decreases the stability of the international order.[70] By collaborating with those national governments that serve their citizens justly and with intergovernmental agencies, these corporations can contribute to overcoming the desperate plight of many persons throughout the world.

117. Business people, managers, investors, and financiers follow a vital Christian vocation when they act responsibly and seek the common good. We encourage and support a renewed sense of vocation in the business community. We also recognize that the way business people serve society is governed and limited by the incentives which flow from tax policies, and availability of credit, and other public policies.

118. Businesses have a right to an institutional framework that does not penalize enterprises that act responsibly. Governments must provide regulations and a system of taxation which encourage firms to preserve the environment, employ disadvantaged workers, and create jobs in depressed areas. Managers and stockholders should not be torn between their responsibilities to their organizations and their responsibilities toward society as a whole.

3. Citizens and Government

119. In addition to rights and duties related to specific roles in the economy, everyone has obligations based simply on membership in the social community. By fulfilling these duties, we create a true commonwealth. Volunteering time, talent, and money to work for greater justice is a fundamental expression of Christian love and social solidarity. All who have more than they need must come to the aid of the poor. People with professional or technical skills needed to enhance the lives of others have a duty to share them. And the poor have similar obligations: to work together as individuals and families to build up their communities by acts of social solidarity and justice. These voluntary efforts to overcome injustice are part of the Christian vocation.

120. Every citizen also has the responsibility to work to secure justice and human rights through an organized social response. In the words of Pius XI, "Charity will never be true charity unless it takes justice into account. . . . Let no one attempt with small gifts of charity to exempt himself from the great duties imposed by justice."[71] The guaranteeing of

basic justice for all is not an optional expression of largesse but an inescapable duty for the whole of society.

121. The traditional distinction between society and the state in Catholic social teaching provides the basic framework for such organized public efforts. The Church opposes all statist and totalitarian approaches to socioeconomic questions. Social life is richer than governmental power can encompass. All groups that compose society have responsibilities to respond to the demands of justice. We have just outlined some of the duties of labor unions and business and financial enterprises. These must be supplemented by initiatives by local community groups, professional associations, educational institutions, churches, and synagogues. All the groups that give life to this society have important roles to play in pursuit of economic justice.

122. For this reason, it is all the more significant that the teachings of the Church insist that *government has a moral function: protecting human rights and securing basic justice for all members of the commonwealth.*[72] Society as a whole and in all its diversity is responsible for building up the common good. But it is the government's role to guarantee the minimum conditions that make this rich social activity possible, namely, human rights and justice.[73] This obligation also falls on individual citizens as they choose their representatives and participate in shaping public opinion.

123. More specifically, it is the responsibility of all citizens, acting through their government, to assist and empower the poor, the disadvantaged, the handicapped, and the unemployed. Government should assume a positive role in generating employment and establishing fair labor practices, in guaranteeing the provision and maintenance of the economy's infrastructure, such as roads, bridges, harbors, public means of communication, and transport. It should regulate trade and commerce in the interest of fairness.[74] Government may levy the taxes necessary to meet these responsibilities, and citizens have a moral obligation to pay those taxes. The way society responds to the needs of the poor through its public policies is the litmus test of its justice or injustice. The political debate about these policies is the indispensable forum for dealing with the conflicts and tradeoffs that will always be present in the pursuit of a more just economy.

124. The primary norm for determining the scope and limits of governmental intervention is the "principle of subsidiarity" cited above. This principle states that, in order to protect basic justice, government should undertake only those initiatives which exceed the capacities of individuals or private groups acting independently. Government should not replace or destroy smaller communities and individual initiative. Rather it should help them contribute more effectively to social well-being and supplement their activity when the demands of justice exceed their capacities. These does not mean, however, that the government that governs least, governs best. Rather it defines good

government intervention as that which truly "helps" other social groups contribute to the common good by directing, urging, restraining, and regulating economic activity as "the occasion requires and necessity demands."[75] This calls for cooperation and consensus building among the diverse agents in our economic life, including government. The precise form of government involvement in this process cannot be determined in the abstract. It will depend on an assessment of specific needs and the most effective ways to address them.

▪▪ D. CHRISTIAN HOPE
AND THE COURAGE TO ACT

125. The Christian vision is based on the conviction that God has destined the human race and all creation for "a kingdom of truth and life, of holiness and grace, of justice, love and peace."[76] This conviction gives Christians strong hope as they face the economic struggles of the world today. This hope is not a naive optimism that imagines that simple formulas for creating a fully just society are ready at hand. The Church's experience through history and in nations throughout the world today has made it wary of all ideologies that claim to have the final answer to humanity's problems.[77] Christian hope has a much stronger foundation than such ideologies, for it rests on the knowledge that God is at work in the world, "preparing a new dwelling place and a new earth where justice will abide."[78]

126. This hope stimulates and strengthens Christian efforts to create a more just economic order in spite of difficulties and setbacks.[79] Christian hope is strong and resilient, for it is rooted in a faith that knows that the fullness of life comes to those who follow Christ in the way of the Cross. In pursuit of concrete solutions, all members of the Christian community are called to an ever finer discernment of the hurts and opportunities in the world around them, in order to respond to the most pressing needs and thus build up a more just society.[80] This is a communal task calling for dialogue, experimentation, and imagination. It also calls for deep faith and a courageous love.

Endnotes

1. *Mater et Magistra*, 219–220. See *Pastoral Constitution*, 63.

2. Vatican Council II, *Decree on Ecumenism*, 22–23.

3. C. Westermann, *Creation* (Philadelphia: Fortress Press, 1974); and B. Vawter, *On Genesis: A New Reading* (Garden City, N.Y.: Doubleday, 1977). See also *Pastoral Constitution*, 34.

4. St. Cyprian, *On Works and Almsgiving*, 25, trans. R. J. Deferrari, *St. Cyprian: Treatises*, 36 (New York: Fathers of the Church, 1958), 251. Original text in Migne, Patrologia Latina,

vol. 4, 620. *On the Patristic teaching*, see C. Avila, *Ownership: Early Christian Teaching* (Maryknoll, N.Y.: Orbis Books, 1983). Collection of original texts and translations.

5. T. T. Ogletree, *The Use of the Bible in Christian Ethics* (Philadelphia: Fortress Press, 1983), 47–85.

6. Though scholars debate whether the Jubilee was a historical institution or an ideal, its images were continually evoked to stress God's sovereignty over the land and God's concern for the poor and the oppressed (e.g., Is. 61:1–2; Lk 4:16–19). See R. North, *Sociology of the Biblical Jubilee* (Rome: Biblical Institute, 1954); S. Ringe, *Jesus, Liberation and the Biblical Jubilee: Images for Ethics and Christology* (Philadelphia: Fortress Press, 1985).

7. On justice, see J. R. Donahue, "Biblical Perspectives on Justice," in Haughey, ed., *The Faith That Does Justice* (New York: Paulist Press, 1977), 68–112; and S. C. Mott, *Biblical Ethics and Social Change* (New York: Oxford University Press, 1982).

8. See Ex 22:20–26; Dt 15:1–11; Jb 29:12–17; Pss 69:34; 72:2, 4,12–24; 82:3–4; Prv 14:21, 31; Is 3:14–15, 10:2; Jer 22:16; Zec 7:9–10.

9. J. Pedersen, *Israel: Its Life and Culture*, vols. I–II (London: Oxford University Press, 1926), 337–340.

10. J. Alfaro, *Theology of Justice in the World* (Rome: Pontifical Commission on Justice and Peace, 1973), 40–41; E. McDonagh, *The Making of Disciples* (Wilmington, Del.: Michael Glazier, 1982), 119.

11. Pope John Paul II has drawn on this parable to exhort us to have a "compassionate heart" to those in need in his Apostolic Letter "On the Christian Meaning of Human Suffering" (*Salvifici Doloris*) (Washington, D.C.: United States Catholic Conference, 1984), 34–39.

12. *Redeemer of Man*, 21.

13. Address to Workers at Sao Paulo, 8, *Origins* 10:9 (July 31, 1980), 139; and Address at Yankee Stadium, *Origins* 9:19 (October 25, 1979), 311–312.

14. J. Dupont and A. George, eds., *La pauvreté évangelique* (Paris: Cerf, 1971); M. Hengel, *Property and Riches in the Early Church* (Philadelphia: Fortress Press, 1974); L. Johnson, *Sharing Possessions: Mandate and Symbol of Faith* (Philadelphia: Fortress Press, 1981); D. L. Mealand, *Poverty and Expectation in the Gospels* (London: SPCK, 1980); W. Pilgrim, *Good News to the Poor: Wealth and Poverty in Luke-Acts* (Minneapolis: Augsburg, 1981); and W. Stegemann, *The Gospel and the Poor* (Philadelphia: Fortress Press, 1984).

15. See Am 4:1–3; Jb 20:19; Sir 13:4–7; Jas 2:6; 5:1–6; Rv 18:11–19.

16. See paras. 85–91.

17. See Selected Bibliography.

18. Extraordinary Synod of Bishops (1985), *The Final Report, II, A* (Washington, D.C.: United States Catholic Conference, 1986).

19. Pope Paul VI, *On Evangelization in the Modern World*, 31.

20. Ibid., 24.

21. *Pastoral Constitution*, 32.

22. Ibid., 25.

23. See para. 39.

24. Josef Pieper, *The Four Cardinal Virtues* (Notre Dame, Ind.: University of Notre Dame Press, 1966), 43–116; David Hollenbach, "Modern Catholic Teachings Concerning Justice," in John C. Haughey, ed., *The Faith That Does Justice* (New York: Paulist Press, 1977), 207–231.

25. Jon P. Gunnemann, "Capitalism and Commutative Justice," presented at the 1985 meeting of the Society of Christian Ethics, published in *The Annual of the Society of Christian Ethics*.

26. *Pastoral Constitution*, 69.

27. Pope Pius XI, *Divini Redemptoris*, 51. See John A. Ryan, *Distributive Justice, third edition* (New York: Macmillan, 1942), 188. The term "social justice" has been used in several different but related ways in the Catholic ethical tradition. See William Ferree, "The Act of Social Justice," *Philosophical Studies*, vol. 72 (Washington, D.C.: The Catholic University of America Press, 1943).

28. *On Human Work*, 6, 9.

29. *Pastoral Constitution*, 29.

30. Ibid. See below, paras. 180–182.

31. Pope Paul VI, *On the Development of Peoples* (1967), 19.

32. *Mater et Magistra*, 132.

33. *Justice in the World*, 10, 16; and *Octogesima Adveniens*, 15.

34. *Pastoral Constitution*, 25; *Justice in the World*, 51; Pope John Paul II, *The Gift of the Redemption, Apostolic Exhortation on Reconciliation and Penance* (Washington, D.C.: United States Catholic Conference, 1984), 16; Congregation for the Doctrine of the Faith, *Instruction on Christian Freedom and Liberation*, 42, 74.

35. In the words of the 1971 Synod of Bishops: "Participation constitutes a right which is to be applied in the economic and in the social and political field," *Justice in the World*, 18.

36. *Pastoral Constitution*, 26.

37. Pope John Paul II, Address at the General Assembly of the United Nations (October 2, 1979), 13, 14.

38. See Pope Pius XII, 1941 Pentecost Address, in V. Yzermans, *The Major Addresses of Pope Pius XII, vol. I* (St. Paul: North Central, 1961), 32–33.

39. *Peace on Earth*, 8–27. See *On Human Work*, 18–19. *Peace on Earth* and other modern papal statements refer explicitly to the "right to work" as one of the fundamental economic rights. Because of the ambiguous meaning of the phrase in the United States, and also because the ordinary way people earn their living in our society is through paid employment, the NCCB has affirmed previously that the protection of human dignity demands that the right to useful employment be secured for all who are able and willing to work. See NCCB, *The Economy: Human Dimensions* (November 20, 1975), 5, in NCCB, *Justice in the Marketplace*, 470. See also Congregation for the Doctrine of the Faith, *Instruction on Christian Freedom and Liberation*, 85.

40. *The Development of Peoples*, 14.

41. Martha H. Good, "Freedom From Want: The Failure of United States Courts to Protect Subsistence Rights," *Human Rights Quarterly* 6 (1984): 335–365.

42. *Pastoral Constitution*, 43.

43. *Mater et Magistra*, 65.

44. On the recent use of this term see: Congregation for the Doctrine of the Faith, *Instruction on Christian Freedom and Liberation*, 46–50, and 66–68; *Evangelization in Latin America's Present and Future, Final Document of the Third General Conference of the Latin American Episcopate* (Puebla, Mexico, January 27–February 13, 1979), esp. part VI, ch. 1, "A Preferential Option for the Poor," in J. Eagleson and P. Scharper, eds., *Puebla and Beyond* (Maryknoll, N.Y.: Orbis Books, 1979), 264–267; Donal Dorr, *Option for the Poor: A Hundred Years of Vatican Social Teaching* (Dublin: Gill and Macmillan/Maryknoll, N.Y.: Orbis Books, 1983).

45. *Octogesima Adveniens*, 23.

46. Address to Bishops of Brazil, 6.9, *Origins* 10:9 (July 31, 1980): 135.

47. Pope John Paul II, Address to Workers at Sao Paulo, 4, *Origins* (July 31, 1980): 138; Congregation for the Doctrine of the Faith, *Instruction on Christian Freedom and Liberation*, 66–68.

48. *Pastoral Constitution*, 47.

49. Address on Christian Unity in a Technological Age (Toronto, September 14, 1984) in *Origins* 14:16 (October 4, 1984): 248.

50. *On Human Work*, 3.

51. Ibid., 5, 6.

52. Ibid., 6, 10.

53. *Quadragesimo Anno*, 79. The meaning of this principle is not always accurately understood. For studies of its interpretation in Catholic teaching see: Calvez and Perrin, *Catholic Social Principles* (Milkwaukee: Bruce, 1950), 328–342; Johannes Messner, "Freedom as a Principle of Social Order: An Essay in the Substance of Subsidiary Function," *Modern Schoolman* 28 (1951): 97–110; Richard E. Mulcahy, "Subsidiarity," *New Catholic Encyclopedia*, vol. 13 (New York: McGraw-Hill, 1966), 762; Franz H. Mueller, "The Principle of Subsidiarity in Christian Tradition," *The Christian Vision of Economic Life Catholic Sociological Review* 4 (October 1943): 144–157; Oswald von Nell-Breuning, "Zur Sozialreform, Erwagungen zum Subsidiaritatsprinzip," *Stimmen der Zeit* 157, Bd. 81 (1955–56): 1–11; id., "Subsidiarity," *Sacramentum Mundi* (New York: Herder and Herder, 1970), 6, 114–116; Arthur Fridolin Utz, *Formen und Grenzen des Subsidiaritatsprinzips* (Heidelberg: F. H. Kerle Verlag, 1956); id., "The Principle of Subsidiarity and Contemporary Natural Law," *Natural Law Forum* 3 (1958): 170–183; id., *Grundsatze der Sozialpolitik: Solidaritat und Subsidiaritat in der Alterversicherung* (Stuttgart: Sewald Verlag, 1969).

54. *Pastoral Constitution*, 31.

55. *On Human Work*, 16.

56. *Rerum Novarum*, 62; see also 9.

57. *On Human Work*, 19.

58. Ibid., 20.

59. Ibid.

60. Ibid.

61. Pope John Paul II, Address to Business Men and Economic Managers (Milan, May 22, 1983) in *L'Osservatore Romano*, weekly edition in English (June 20, 1983): 9:1.

62. Thomas Aquinas, *Summa Theologiae*, IIa, IIae, q. 66.

63. As Pope John Paul II has stated: "This gigantic and powerful instrument—the whole collection of the means of production that in a sense are considered synonymous with 'capital'—is the result of work and bears the signs of human labor." *On Human Work*, 12.

64. *Rerum Novarum*, 10, 15, and 36.

65. *Mater et Magistra*, 109.

66. *Rerum Novarum*, 65, 66; *Mater et Magistra*, 115.

67. *On the Development of Peoples*, 23.

68. Pope John Paul II, *Opening Address at the Puebla Conference* (Puebla, Mexico, January 28, 1979), in John Eagleson and Philip Scharper, eds. *Peubla and Beyond*, 67.

69. *On Human Work*, 14.

70. Ibid., 17.

71. *Divini Redemptoris*, 49.

72. *Peace on Earth*, 60–62.

73. Vatican Council II, *Declaration on Religious Freedom* (*Dignitatis Humanae*), 6. See John Courtney Murray, *The Problem of Religious Freedom*, Woodstock Papers, no. 7 (Westminster, Md.: Newman Press, 1965).

74. *Peace on Earth*, 63–64; *Quadragesimo Anno*, 80. In *Rerum Novarum* Pope Leo XIII set down the basic norm which determines when government intervention is called for: "If, therefore, any injury has been done to or threatens either the common good or the interests of individual groups, which injury cannot in any other way be repaired or prevented, it is necessary for public authority to intervene" *Rerum Novarum*, 52. Pope John XXIII synthesized the Church's understanding of the function of governmental intervention this way:'The State, whose purpose is the realization of the common good in the temporal order, can by no means disregard the economic activity of its citizens. Indeed it should be present to promote in suitable manner the production of a sufficient supply of material goods, . . . contribute actively to the betterment of the living conditions of workers, . . . see to it that labor agreements are entered into according to the norms of justice and equity, and that in the environment of work the dignity of the human being is not violated either in body or spirit," *Mater et Magistra*, 20–21.

75. *Quadragesimo Anno*, 80.

76. Preface for the Feast of Christ the King, *The Sacramentary of the Roman Missal*.

77. *Octogesima Adveniens*, 26–35.

78. *Pastoral Constitution*, 39.

79. Ibid.

80. *Octogesima Adveniens*, 42.

A New American Experiment

CHAPTER

Partnership for the Public Good
(nos. 295–325)

295. For over two hundred years the United States has been engaged in a bold experiment in democracy. The founders of the nation set out to establish justice, promote the general welfare, and secure the blessings of liberty for themselves and their posterity. Those who live in this land today are the beneficiaries of this great venture. Our review of some of the most pressing problems in economic life today shows, however, that this undertaking is not yet complete. Justice for all remains an aspiration; a fair share in the general welfare is denied to many. In addition to the particular policy recommendations made above, a long-term and more fundamental response is needed. This will call for an imaginative vision of the future that can help shape economic arrangements in creative new ways. We now want to propose some elements of such a vision and several innovations in economic structures that can contribute to making this vision a reality.

296. Completing the unfinished business of the American experiment will call for new forms of cooperation and partnership among those whose daily work is the source of the prosperity and justice of the nation. The United States prides itself on both its competitive sense of initiative and its spirit of teamwork. Today a greater spirit of partnership and teamwork is needed; competition alone will not do the job. It has too many negative consequences for family life, the economically vulnerable, and the environment. Only a renewed commitment by all to the common good can deal creatively with the realities of international interdependence and economic dislocations in the domestic economy. The virtues of good citizenship require a lively sense of participation in the commonwealth and of having obligations as well as rights within it.[1] The nation's economic health depends on strengthening these virtues among all its people, and on the development of institutional arrangements supportive of these virtues.[2]

297. The nation's founders took daring steps to create structures of participation, mutual accountability, and widely distributed power to ensure the political

rights and freedoms of all. We believe that similar steps are needed today to expand economic participation, broaden the sharing of economic power, and make economic decisions more accountable to the common good. As noted above, the principle of subsidiarity states that the pursuit of economic justice must occur on all levels of society. It makes demands on communities as small as the family, as large as the global society and on all levels in between. There are a number of ways to enhance the cooperative participation of these many groups in the task of creating this future. Since there is no single innovation that will solve all problems, we recommend careful experimentation with several possibilities that hold considerable hope for increasing partnership and strengthening mutual responsibility for economic justice.

A. COOPERATION WITHIN FIRMS AND INDUSTRIES

298. A new experiment in bringing democratic ideals to economic life calls for serious exploration of ways to develop new patterns of partnership among those working in individual firms and industries.[3] Every business, from the smallest to the largest, including farms and ranches, depends on many different persons and groups for its success: workers, managers, owners or shareholders, suppliers, customers, creditors, the local community, and the wider society. Each makes a contribution to the enterprise, and each has a stake in its growth or decline. Present structures of accountability, however, do not acknowledge all these contributions or protect these stakes. A major challenge in today's economy is the development of new institutional mechanisms for accountability that also preserve the flexibility needed to respond quickly to a rapidly changing business environment.[4]

299. New forms of partnership between workers and managers are one means for developing greater participation and accountability within firms.[5] Recent experience has shown that both labor and management suffer when the adversarial relationship between them becomes extreme. As Pope Leo XIII stated, "Each needs the other completely: capital cannot do without labor, nor labor without capital."[6] The organization of firms should reflect and enhance this mutual partnership. In particular, the development of work patterns for men and women that are more supportive of family life will benefit both employees and the enterprises they work for.

300. Workers in firms and on farms are especially in need of stronger institutional protection, for their jobs and livelihood are particularly vulnerable to decisions of others in today's highly competitive labor market. Several arrangements are gaining increasing support in the United States: profit sharing by the workers in a firm; enabling employees to become company stockholders;

granting employees greater participation in determining the conditions of work; cooperative ownership of the firm by all who work within it; and programs for enabling a much larger number of Americans, regardless of their employment status, to become shareholders in successful corporations. Initiatives of this sort can enhance productivity, increase the profitability of firms, provide greater job security and work satisfaction for employees, and reduce adversarial relations.[7] In our 1919 Program for Social Reconstruction, we observed "the full possibilities of increased production will not be realized so long as the majority of workers remain mere wage earners. The majority must somehow become owners, at least in part, of the instruments of production."[8] We believe that this judgment remains generally valid today.

301. None of these approaches provides a panacea, and all have certain drawbacks. Nevertheless we believe that continued research and experimentation with these approaches will be of benefit. Catholic social teaching has endorsed on many occasions innovative methods for increasing worker participation within firms.[9] The appropriateness of these methods will depend on the circumstances of the company or industry in question and on their effectiveness in actually increasing a genuinely cooperative approach to shaping decisions. The most highly publicized examples of such efforts have been in large firms facing serious financial crises. If increased participation and collaboration can help a firm avoid collapse, why should it not give added strength to healthy businesses? Cooperative ownership is particularly worthy of consideration in new entrepreneurial enterprises.[10]

302. Partnerships between labor and management are possible only when both groups possess real freedom and power to influence decisions. This means that unions ought to continue to play an important role in moving toward greater economic participation within firms and industries. Workers rightly reject calls for less adversarial relations when they are a smokescreen for demands that labor make all the concessions. For partnership to be genuine it must be a two-way street, with creative initiative and a willingness to cooperate on all sides.

303. When companies are considering plant closures or the movement of capital, it is patently unjust to deny workers any role in shaping the outcome of these difficult choices.[11] In the heavy manufacturing sector today, technological change and international competition can be the occasion of painful decisions leading to the loss of jobs or wage reductions. While such decisions may sometimes be necessary, a collaborative and mutually accountable model of industrial organization would mean that workers not be expected to carry all the burdens of an economy in transition. Management and investors must also accept their share of sacrifices, especially when management is thinking of closing a plant or transferring capital to a seemingly more lucrative or competitive activity. The capital at the disposal

of management is in part the product of the labor of those who have toiled in the company over the years, including currently employed workers.[12] As a minimum, workers have a right to be informed in advance when such decisions are under consideration, a right to negotiate with management about possible alternatives, and a right to fair compensation and assistance with retraining and relocation expenses should these be necessary. Since even these minimal rights are jeopardized without collective negotiation, industrial cooperation requires a strong role for labor unions in our changing economy.

304. Labor unions themselves are challenged by the present economic environment to seek new ways of doing business. The purpose of unions is not simply to defend the existing wages and prerogatives of the fraction of workers who belong to them, but also to enable workers to make positive and creative contributions to the firm, the community, and the larger society in an organized and cooperative way.[13] Such contributions call for experiments with new directions in the U.S. labor movement.

305. The parts played by managers and shareholders in U.S. corporations also need careful examination. In U.S. law, the primary responsibility of managers is to exercise prudent business judgment in the interest of a profitable return to investors. But morally this legal responsibility may be exercised only within the bounds of justice to employees, customers, suppliers, and the local community. Corporate mergers and hostile takeovers may bring greater benefits to shareholders, but they often lead to decreased concern for the well-being of local communities and make towns and cities more vulnerable to decisions made from afar.

306. Most shareholders today exercise relatively little power in corporate governance.[14] Although shareholders can and should vote on the selection of corporate directors and on investment questions and other policy matters, it appears that return on investment is the governing criterion in the relation between them and management. We do not believe this is an adequate rationale for shareholder decisions. The question of how to relate the rights and responsibilities of shareholders to those of the other people and communities affected by corporate decisions is complex and insufficiently understood. We, therefore, urge serious, long-term research and experimentation in this area. More effective ways of dealing with these questions are essential to enable firms to serve the common good.

▪▪ B. LOCAL AND REGIONAL COOPERATION

307. The context within which U.S. firms do business has direct influence on their ability to contribute to the common good. Companies and indeed whole industries are not sole masters of their own fate. Increased cooperative

efforts are needed to make local, regional, national, and international conditions more supportive of the pursuit of economic justice.

308. In the principle of subsidiarity, Catholic social teaching has long stressed the importance of small and intermediate-sized communities or institutions in exercising moral responsibility. These mediating structures link the individual to society as a whole in a way that gives people greater freedom and power to act.[15] Such groups include families, neighborhoods, church congregations, community organizations, civic and business associations, public interest and advocacy groups, community development corporations, and many other bodies. All these groups can play a crucial role in generating creative partnerships for the pursuit of the public good on the local and regional level.

309. The value of partnership is illustrated by considering how new jobs are created. The development of new businesses to serve the local community is key to revitalizing areas hit hard by unemployment.[16] The cities and regions in greatest need of these new jobs face serious obstacles in attracting enterprises that can provide them. Lack of financial resources, limited entrepreneurial skill, blighted and unsafe environments, and a deteriorating infrastructure create a vicious cycle that makes new investment in these areas more risky and therefore less likely.

310. Breaking out of this cycle will require a cooperative approach that draws on all the resources of the community.[17] Community development corporations can keep efforts focused on assisting those most in need. Existing business, labor, financial, and academic institutions can provide expertise in partnership with innovative entrepreneurs. New cooperative structures of local ownership will give the community or region an added stake in businesses and even more importantly give these businesses a greater stake in the community.[18] Government on the local, state, and national levels must play a significant role, especially through tax structures that encourage investment in hard hit areas and through funding aimed at conservation and basic infrastructure needs. Initiatives like these can contribute to a multilevel response to the needs of the community.

311. The Church itself can work as an effective partner on the local and regional level. First-hand knowledge of community needs and commitment to the protection of the dignity of all should put Church leaders in the forefront of efforts to encourage a community-wide cooperative strategy. Because churches include members from many different parts of the community, they can often serve as mediator between groups who might otherwise regard each other with suspicion. We urge local church groups to work creatively and in partnership with other private and public groups in responding to local and regional problems.

■■ C. PARTNERSHIP IN THE DEVELOPMENT OF NATIONAL POLICIES

312. The causes of our national economic problems and their possible solutions are the subject of vigorous debate today. The discussion often turns on the role the national government has played in creating these problems and could play in remedying them. We want to point to several considerations that could help build new forms of effective citizenship and cooperation in shaping the economic life in our country.

313. First, while economic freedom and personal initiative are deservedly esteemed in our society, we have increasingly come to recognize the inescapably social and political nature of the economy. The market is always embedded in a specific social and political context. The tax system affects consumption, saving, and investment. National monetary policy, domestic and defense programs, protection of the environment and worker safety, and regulation of international trade all shape the economy as a whole. These policies influence domestic investment, unemployment rates, foreign exchange, and the health of the entire world economy.

314. The principle of subsidiarity calls for government intervention when small or intermediate groups in society are unable or unwilling to take the steps needed to promote basic justice. Pope John XXIII observed that the growth of more complex relations of interdependence among citizens has led to an increased role for government in modern societies.[19] This role is to work *in partnership with* the many other groups in society, helping them fulfill their tasks and responsibilities more effectively, not replacing or destroying them. The challenge of today is to move beyond abstract disputes about whether more or less government intervention is needed, to consideration of creative ways of enabling government and private groups to work together effectively.

315. It is in this light that we understand Pope John Paul II's recommendation that "society make provision for overall planning" in the economic domain.[20] Planning must occur on various levels, with the government ensuring that basic justice is protected and also protecting the rights and freedoms of all other agents. In the Pope's words:

> "In the final analysis this overall concern weighs on the shoulders of the state, but it cannot mean one-sided centralization by the public authorities. Instead what is in question is a just and rational coordination within the framework of which the initiative of individuals, free groups, and local work centers and complexes must be safeguarded."[21]

316. We are well aware that the mere mention of economic planning is likely to produce strong negative reaction in U.S. society. It conjures up images of

centralized planning boards, command economies, inefficient bureaucracies, and mountains of government paperwork. It is also clear that the meaning of "planning" is open to a wide variety of interpretations and takes very different forms in various nations.[22] The Pope's words should not be construed as an endorsement of a highly centralized form of economic planning, much less a totalitarian one. His call for a "just and rational coordination" of the endeavors of the many economic actors is a call to seek creative new partnership and forms of participation in shaping national policies.

317. There are already many forms of economic planning going on within the U.S. economy today. Individuals and families plan for their economic future. Management and labor unions regularly develop both long- and short-term plans. Towns, cities, and regions frequently have planning agencies concerned with their social and economic future. When state legislatures and the U.S. Congress vote on budgets or on almost any other bill that comes before them, they are engaged in a form of public planning. Catholic social teaching does not propose a single model for political and economic life by which these levels are to be institutionally related to each other. It does insist that reasonable coordination among the different parts of the body politic is an essential condition for achieving justice. This is a moral precondition of good citizenship that applies to both individual and institutional actors. In its absence no political structure can guarantee justice in society or the economy. Effective decisions in these matters will demand greater cooperation among all citizens. To encourage our fellow citizens to consider more carefully the appropriate balance of private and local initiative with national economic policy, we make several recommendations.

318. *First, in an advanced industrial economy like ours, all parts of society, including government, must cooperate in forming national economic policies.* Taxation, monetary policy, high levels of government spending, and many other forms of governmental regulation are here to stay. A modern economy without governmental interventions of the sort we have alluded to is inconceivable. These interventions, however, should help, not replace, the contributions of the other economic actors and institutions and should direct them to the common good. The development of effective new forms of partnership between private and public agencies will be difficult in a situation as immensely complex as that of the United States in which various aspects of national policy seem to contradict one another.[23] On the theoretical level, achieving greater coordination will make demands on those with the technical competence to analyze the relationship among different parts of the economy. More, practically, it will require the various subgroups within our society to sharpen their concern for the common good and moderate their efforts to protect their own short-term interests.

319. *Second, the impact of national economic policies on the poor and the vulnerable is the primary criterion for judging their moral value.* Throughout this letter we

have stressed the special place of the poor and the vulnerable in any ethical analysis of the U.S. economy. National economic policies that contribute to building a true commonwealth should reflect this by standing firmly for the rights of those who fall through the cracks of our economy: the poor, the unemployed, the homeless, the displaced. Being a citizen of this land means sharing in the responsibility for shaping and implementing such policies.

320. *Third, the serious distortion of national economic priorities produced by massive national spending on defense must be remedied.* Clear-sighted consideration of the role of government shows that the government and the economy are already closely intertwined through military research and defense contracts. Defense-related industries make up a major part of the U.S. economy and have intimate links with both the military and civilian government; they often depart from the competitive model of free-market capitalism. Moreover, the dedication of so much of the national budget to military purposes has been disastrous for the poor and vulnerable members of our own and other nations. The nation's spending priorities need to be revised in the interests of both justice and peace.[24]

321. We recognize that these proposals do not provide a detailed agenda. We are also aware that there is a tension between setting the goals for coherent policies and actually arriving at them by democratic means. But if we can increase the level of commitment to the common good and the virtues of citizenship in our nation, the ability to achieve these goals will greatly increase. It is these fundamental moral concerns that lead us as bishops to join the debate on national priorities.

▪▪ D. COOPERATION AT THE INTERNATIONAL LEVEL

322. If our country is to guide its international economic relationships by policies that serve human dignity and justice, we must expand our understanding of the moral responsibility of citizens to serve the common good to the entire planet. Cooperation is not limited to the local, regional, or national level. Economic policy can no longer be governed by national goals alone. The fact that the "social question has become worldwide"[25] challenges us to broaden our horizons and enhance our collaboration and sense of solidarity on the global level. The cause of democracy is closely tied to the cause of economic justice. The unfinished business of the American experiment includes the formation of new international partnerships, especially with the developing countries, based on mutual respect, cooperation and a dedication to fundamental justice.

323. The principle of subsidiarity calls for government to intervene in the economy when basic justice requires greater social coordination and regulation

of economic actors and institutions. In global economic relations, however, no international institution provides this sort of coordination and regulation. The U.N. system, including the World Bank, the International Monetary Fund, and the General Agreement on Tariffs and Trade, does not possess the requisite authority. Pope John XXIII called this institutional weakness a "structural defect" in the organization of the human community. The structures of world order, including economic ones, "no longer correspond to the objective requirements of the universal common good."[26]

324. Locked together in a world of limited material resources and a growing array of common problems, we help or hurt one another by the economic policies we choose. All the economic agents in our society, therefore, must consciously and deliberately attend to the good of the whole human family. We must all work to increase the effectiveness of international agencies in addressing global problems that cannot be handled through the actions of individual countries. In particular we repeat our plea made in *The Challenge of Peace* urging "that the United States adopt a stronger supportive leadership role with respect to the United Nations."[27] In the years following World War II, the United States took the lead in establishing multilateral bodies to deal with postwar economic problems. Unfortunately, in recent years this country has taken steps that have weakened rather than strengthened multilateral approaches. This is a short-sighted policy and should be reversed if the long-term interests of an interdependent globe are to be served.[28] In devising more effective arrangements for pursuing international economic justice, the overriding problem is how to get from where we are to where we ought to be. Progress toward that goal demands positive and often difficult action by corporations, banks, labor unions, governments, and other major actors on the international stage. But whatever the difficulty, the need to give priority to alleviating poverty in developing countries is undeniable; and the cost of continued inaction can be counted in human lives lost or stunted, talents wasted, opportunities foregone, misery and suffering prolonged, and injustice condoned.

325. Self-restraint and self-criticism by all parties are necessary first steps toward strengthening the international structures to protect the common good. Otherwise, growing interdependence will lead to conflict and increased economic threats to human dignity. This is an important long-term challenge to the economic future of this country and its place in the emerging world economic community.

Endnotes

1. *Octogesima Adveniens*, 24.

2. For different analyses along these lines with quite different starting points see Martin Carnoy, Derek Shearer and Russell Rumberger, *A New Social Contract* (New York: Harper and Row, 1983); Amatai Etzioni, *An Immodest Agenda: Reconstructing America Before the 21st*

Century (New York: McGraw-Hill, 1983); Charles E. Lindblom, *Politics and Markets* (New York: Basic Books, 1977), esp. 346–348; George C. Lodge, *The New American Ideology* (New York: Alfred A. Knopf, 1975); Douglas Sturm, "Corporations, Constitutions and Covenants," *Journal of the American Academy of Religion*, 41 (1973): 331–55; Lester Thurow, *The Zero-Sum Society* (New York: Basic Books, 1980), esp. ch. 1; Roberto Mangabeira Unger, *Knowledge and Politics* (New York: Free Press, 1975); George F. Will, *Statecraft as Soulcraft: What Government Does* (New York: Simon and Schuster, 1982), esp. ch. 6.

3. *Pastoral Constitution*, 68. See *Mater et Magistra*, 75–77.

4. Charles W. Powers provided a helpful discussion of these matters in a paper presented at a conference on the first draft of this letter sponsored by the Harvard University Divinity School and the Institute for Policy Studies, Cambridge, Massachusetts, March 29–31, 1985.

5. See John Paul II, "The Role of Business in a Changing Workplace," 3, *Origins* 15 (February 6, 1986): 567.

6. *Rerum Novarum*, 28. For an analysis of the relevant papal teachings on institutions of collaboration and partnership, see John Cronin, *Catholic Social Principles: The Social Teaching of the Catholic Church Applied to American Economic Life* (Milwaukee: Bruce, 1950), ch. VII; Oswald von Nell-Breuning, *Reorganization of Social Economy: The Cosical Encyclical Developed and Explained*, trans. Bernard W. Dempsey (Milwaukee: Bruce, 1936), chs. X–XII; Jean-Yves Calvez and Jacques Perrin, *The Church and Social Justice*, trans. J. R. Kirwan (Chicago: Regnery, 1961), ch. XIX.

7. Michael Conte, Arnold S. Tannenbaum and Donna McCulloch, *Employee Ownership*, Research Report Series, Institute for Social Research (Ann Arbor, Mich.: University of Michigan, 1981); Robert A. Dahl, *A Preface to Economic Democracy* (Berkeley, Calif.: University of California Press, 1985); Harvard Business School, "The Mondragon Cooperative Movement," case study prepared by David P. Ellerman (Cambridge, Mass.: Harvard Business School, n.d.); Robert Jackall and Henry M. Levin, eds., *Worker Cooperatives in America* (Berkeley, Calif.: University of California Press, 1984); Derek Jones and Jan Svejnar, eds., *Participatory and Self-Managed Firms: Evaluating Economic Performance* (Lexington, Mass.: D.C. Heath, 1982); Irving H. Siegel and Edgar Weinberg, *Labor-Management Cooperation: The American Experience* (Kalamazoo, Mich.: W.E. Upjohn Institute for Employment Research, 1982); Stuart M. Speiser, "Broadened Capital Ownership—The Solution to Major Domestic and International Problems," *Journal of Post-Keynesian Economics VIII* (1985): 426–434; Jaroslav Vanek, ed., *Self-Management: Economic Liberation of Man* (London: Penguin, 1975); Martin L. Weitzman, *The Share Economy* (Cambridge, Mass.: Harvard University Press, 1984).

8. *Program of Social Reconstruction in Justice in the Marketplace*, 381.

9. *Mater et Magistra*, 32, 77, 85–103; *On Human Work*, 14.

10. For examples of worker-owned and operated enterprises supported by the Campaign for Human Development's revolving loan fund see CHD's *Annual Report* (Washington, D.C.: United States Catholic Conference).

11. *Quadragesimo Anno* states the basic norm on which this conclusion is based: "It is wholly false to ascribe to property alone or to labor alone whatever has been obtained through the combined effort of both, and it is wholly unjust for either, denying the efficacy of the other, to arrogate to itself whatever has been produced" (53).

12. *On Human Work*, 12.

13. Ibid., 20. This point was well made by John Cronin twenty-five years ago: "Even if most injustice and exploitation were removed, unions would still have a legitimate place. They are the normal voice of labor, necessary to organize social life for the common good. There is positive need for such organization today, quite independently of any social evils

which may prevail. Order and harmony do not happen; they are the fruit of conscious and organized effort. While we may hope that the abuses which occasioned the rise of unions may disappear, it does not thereby follow that unions will have lost their function. On the contrary, they will be freed from unpleasant, even though temporarily necessary, tasks and able to devote all their time and efforts to a better organization of social life," *Catholic Social Principles*, 418. See also AFL-CIO Committee on the Evolution of Work, *The Future of Work* (Washington, D.C.: AFL-CIO, 1983).

14. For a classic discussion of the relative power of managers and shareholders see A.A. Berle and Gardiner C. Means, *The Modern Corporation and Private Property* (New York: Macmillan, 1932).

15. Peter L. Berger and Richard John Neuhaus, *To Empower People: The Role of Mediating Structures in Public Policy* (Washington, D.C.: American Enterprise Institute, 1977).

16. United States Small Business Administration, *1978 Annual Report* (Washington, D.C.: Government Printing Office, 1979).

17. For recent discussion from a variety of perspectives see: Robert Friedman and William Schweke, eds., *Expanding the Opportunity to Produce: Revitalizing the American Economy Through New Enterprise Development: A Policy Reader* (Washington, D.C.: Corporation for New Enterprise Development, 1981); Jack A. Meyer, *Meeting Human Needs: Toward a New Public Philosophy* (Washington, D.C.: American Enterprise Institute, 1982); Committee for Economic Development, *Jobs for the Hard-to-Employ: New Directions for a Public-Private Partnership* (New York: Committee for Economic Development, 1978); Gar Alperovitz and Jeff Faux, *Rebuilding America: A Blueprint for the New Economy* (New York: Pantheon Books, 1984).

18. Christopher Mackin, *Strategies for Local Ownership and Control: A Policy Analysis* (Somerville, Mass.: Industrial Cooperative Association, 1983).

19. *Mater et Magistra*, 59 and 62.

20. *On Human Work*, 18.

21. Ibid.

22. For examples and analysis of different meanings of economic planning see Naomi Caiden and Aaron Wildavsky, *Planning and Budgeting in Poor Countries* (New York: Wiley, 1974); Robert Dahl and Charles E. Lindblom, *Politics, Economics and Welfare: Planning and Politico-Economic Systems Resolved Into Basic Social Processes* (Chicago: University of Chicago Press, 1976); Stephen S. Cohen, *Modern Capitalist Planning: The French Model* (Berkeley: University of California Press, 1977); Albert Waterston, *Development Planning: Lessons of Experience* (Baltimore: Johns Hopkins Press, 1965); *Rebuilding America*, chs. 14, 15.

23. For example, many students of recent policy point out that monetary policy on the one hand and fiscal policies governing taxation and government expenditures on the other have been at odds with each other, with larger public deficits and high interest rates as the outcome. See Alice M. Rivlin, ed., *Economic Choices 1984* (Washington, D.C.: The Brookings Institution, 1984), esp. ch. 2.

24. *The Challenge of Peace*, 270–271.

25. *On the Development of Peoples*, 3.

26. *Peace on Earth*, 134–135.

27. *The Challenge of Peace*, 268.

28. See Robert O. Keohane and Joseph S. Nye Jr., "Two Cheers for Multilateralism," *Foreign Policy* 60 (Fall 1985): 148–167.

A Commitment to the Future

CHAPTER

(nos. 326–365)

326. Because Jesus' command to love our neighbor is universal, we hold that the life of each person on this globe is sacred. This commits us to bringing about a just economic order where all, without exception, will be treated with dignity and to working in collaboration with those who share this vision. The world is complex and this may often tempt us to seek simple and self-centered solutions; but as a community of disciples we are called to a new hope and to a new vision that we must live without fear and without oversimplification. Not only must we learn more about our moral responsibility for the larger economic issues that touch the daily life of each and every person on this planet, but we also want to help shape the Church as a model of social and economic justice. Thus, this chapter deals with the Christian vocation in the world today, the special challenges to the Church at this moment of history, ways in which the themes of this letter should be followed up, and a call to the kind of commitment that will be needed to reshape the future.

A. THE CHRISTIAN VOCATION IN THE WORLD TODAY

327. This letter has addressed many matters commonly regarded as secular, for example, employment rates, income levels, and international economic relationships. Yet, the affairs of the world, including economic ones, cannot be separated from the spiritual hunger of the human heart. We have presented the biblical vision of humanity and the Church's moral and religious tradition as a framework for asking the deeper questions about the meaning of economic life and for actively responding to them. But words alone are not enough. The Christian perspective on the meaning of economic life must transform the lives of individuals, families, in fact, our whole culture. The Gospel confers on each Christian the vocation to love God and neighbor

in ways that bear fruit in the life of society. That vocation consists above all in a change of heart: a conversion expressed in praise of God and in concrete deeds of justice and service.

1. Conversion

328. The transformation of social structures begins with and is always accompanied by a conversion of the heart.[1] As disciples of Christ each of us is called to a deep personal conversion and to "action on behalf of justice and participation in the transformation of the world."[2] By faith and baptism we are fashioned into a "new creature"; we are filled with the Holy Spirit and a new love that compels us to seek out a new profound relationship with God, with the human family, and with all created things.[3] Renouncing self-centered desires, bearing one's daily cross, and imitating Christ's compassion, all involve a personal struggle to control greed and selfishness, a personal commitment to reverence one's own human dignity and the dignity of others by avoiding self-indulgence and those attachments that make us insensitive to the conditions of others and that erode social solidarity. Christ warned us against attachments to material things, against total self-reliance, against the idolatry of accumulating material goods and seeking safety in them. We must take these teachings seriously and in their light examine how each of us lives and acts towards others. But personal conversion is not gained once and for all. It is a process that goes on through our entire life. Conversion, moreover, takes place in the context of a larger faith community: through baptism into the Church, through common prayer, and through our activity with others on behalf of justice.

2. Worship and Prayer

329. Challenging U.S. economic life with the Christian vision calls for a deeper awareness of the integral connection between worship and the world of work. Worship and common prayer are the wellsprings that give life to any reflection on economic problems and that continually call the participants to greater fidelity to discipleship. To worship and pray to the God of the universe is to acknowledge that the healing love of God extends to all persons and to every part of existence, including work, leisure, money, economic and political power and their use, and to all those practical policies that either lead to justice or impede it. Therefore, when Christians come together in prayer, they make a commitment to carry God's love into all these areas of life.

330. The unity of work and worship finds expression in a unique way in the Eucharist. As people of a new covenant, the faithful hear God's challenging word proclaimed to them—a message of hope to the poor and oppressed—and

they call upon the Holy Spirit to unite all into one body of Christ. For the Eucharist to be a living promise of the fullness of God's Kingdom, the faithful must commit themselves to living as redeemed people with the same care and love for all people that Jesus showed. The body of Christ which worshipers receive in Communion is also a reminder of the reconciling power of his death on the Cross. It empowers them to work to heal the brokenness of society and human relationships and to grow in a spirit of self-giving for others.

331. The liturgy teaches us to have grateful hearts: to thank God for the gift of life, the gift of this earth, and the gift of all people. It turns our hearts from self-seeking to a spirituality that sees the signs of true discipleship in our sharing of goods and working for justice. By uniting us in prayer with all the people of God, with the rich and the poor, with those near and dear, and with those in distant lands, liturgy challenges our way of living and refines our values. Together in the community of worship, we are encouraged to use the goods of this earth for the benefit of all. In worship and in deeds for justice, the Church becomes a "sacrament," a visible sign of that unity in justice and peace that God wills for the whole of humanity.[4]

3. Call to Holiness in the World

332. Holiness is not limited to the sanctuary or to moments of private prayer; it is a call to direct our whole heart and life toward God and according to God's plan for this world. For the laity holiness is achieved in the midst of the world, in family, in community, in friendships, in work, in leisure, in citizenship. Through their competency and by their activity, lay men and women have the vocation to bring the fight of the Gospel to economic affairs, "so that the world may be filled with the Spirit of Christ and may more effectively attain its destiny in justice, in love, and in peace."[5]

333. But as disciples of Christ we must constantly ask ourselves how deeply the biblical and ethical vision of justice and love permeates our thinking. How thoroughly does it influence our way of life? We may hide behind the complexity of the issues or dismiss the significance of our personal contribution; in fact, each one has a role to play, because every day each one makes economic decisions. Some, by reason of their work or their position in society, have a vocation to be involved in a more decisive way in those decisions that affect the economic well-being of others. They must be encouraged and sustained by all in their search for greater justice.

334. At times we will be called upon to say no to the cultural manifestations that emphasize values and aims that are selfish, wasteful, and opposed to the Scriptures. Together we must reflect on our personal and family decisions and curb unnecessary wants in order to meet the needs of others. There are

many questions we must keep asking ourselves: Are we becoming ever more wasteful in a "throw-away" society? Are we able to distinguish between our true needs and those thrust on us by advertising and a society that values consumption more than saving? All of us could well ask ourselves whether as a Christian prophetic witness we are not called to adopt a simpler lifestyle, in the face of the excessive accumulation of material goods that characterizes an affluent society.

335. Husbands and wives, in particular, should weigh their needs carefully and establish a proper priority of values as they discuss the questions of both parents working outside the home and the responsibilities of raising children with proper care and attention. At times we will be called as individuals, as families, as parishes, as Church, to identify more closely with the poor in their struggle for participation and to close the gap of understanding between them and the affluent. By sharing the perspectives of those who are suffering, we can come to understand economic and social problems in a deeper way, thus leading us to seek more durable solutions.

336. In the workplace the laity are often called to make tough decisions with little information about the consequences that such decisions have on the economic lives of others. Such times call for collaborative dialogue together with prayerful reflection on Scripture and ethical norms. The same can be said of the need to elaborate policies that will reflect sound ethical principles and that can become a part of our political and social system. Since this is a part of the lay vocation and its call to holiness, the laity must seek to instill a moral and ethical dimension into the public debate on these issues and help enunciate the ethical questions that must be faced. To weigh political options according to criteria that go beyond efficiency and expediency requires prayer, reflection, and dialogue on all the ethical norms involved. Holiness for the laity will involve all the sacrifices needed to lead such a life of prayer and reflection within a worshiping and supporting faith community. In this way the laity will bridge the gap that so easily arises between the moral principles that guide the personal life of the Christian and the considerations that govern decisions in society in the political forum and in the marketplace.

4. Leisure

337. Some of the difficulty in bringing Christian faith to economic life in the United States today results from the obstacles to establishing a balance of labor and leisure in daily life. Tedious and boring work leads some to look for fulfillment only during time off the job. Others have become "workaholics," people who work compulsively and without reflection on the deeper meaning of life and their actions. The quality and pace of work should be

more human in scale enabling people to experience the dignity and value of their work and giving them time for other duties and obligations. This balance is vitally important for sustaining the social, political, educational, and cultural structures of society. The family, in particular, requires such balance. Without leisure there is too little time for nurturing marriages, for developing parent-child relationships, and for fulfilling commitments to other important groups: the extended family, the community of friends, the parish, the neighborhood, schools, and political organizations. Why is it one hears so little today about shortening the work week, especially if both parents are working? Such a change would give them more time for each other, for their children, and for their other social and political responsibilities.

338. Leisure is connected to the whole of one's value system and influenced by the general culture one lives in. It can be trivialized into boredom and laziness, or end in nothing but a desire for greater consumption and waste. For disciples of Christ, the use of leisure may demand being countercultural. The Christian tradition sees in leisure, time to build family and societal relationships and an opportunity for communal prayer and worship, for relaxed contemplation and enjoyment of God's creation, and for the cultivation of the arts which help fill the human longing for wholeness. Most of all, we must be convinced that economic decisions affect our use of leisure and that such decisions are also to be based on moral and ethical considerations. In this area of leisure we must be on our guard against being swept along by a lack of cultural values and by the changing fads of an affluent society. In the creation narrative God worked six days to create the world and rested on the seventh (Gn 2:1–4). We must take that image seriously and learn how to harmonize action and rest, work and leisure, so that both contribute to building up the person as well as the family and community.

▦ B. CHALLENGES TO THE CHURCH

339. The Church is all the people of God, gathered in smaller faith communities, guided and served by a pope and a hierarchy of bishops, ministered to by priests, deacons, religious, and laity, through visible institutions and agencies. Church is, thus, primarily a communion of people bonded by the Spirit with Christ as their Head, sustaining one another in love, and acting as a sip or sacrament in the world. By its nature it is people called to a transcendent end; but, it is also a visible social institution functioning in this world. According to their calling, members participate in the mission and work of the Church and share, to varying degrees, the responsibility for its institutions and agencies.[6]

At this moment in history, it is particularly important to emphasize the responsibilities of the whole Church for education and family life.

1. Education

340. We have already emphasized the commitment to quality education that is necessary if the poor are to take their rightful place in the economic structures of our society. We have called the Church to remember its own obligation in this regard and we have endorsed support for improvements in public education.

341. The educational mission of the Church is not only to the poor but to all its members. We reiterate our 1972 statement: "Through education, the Church seeks to prepare its members to proclaim the Good News and to translate this proclamation into action. Since the Christian vocation is a call to transform oneself and society with God's help, the educational efforts of the Church must encompass the twin purposes of personal sanctification and social reform in the light of Christian values."[7] Through her educational mission the Church seeks: to integrate knowledge about this world with revelation about God; to understand God's relationship to the human race and its ultimate destiny in the Kingdom of God; to build up human communities of justice and peace; and to teach the value of all creation. By inculcating these values the educational system of the Church contributes to society and to social justice. Economic questions are, thus, seen as a part of a larger vision of the human person and the human family, the value of this created earth, and the duties and responsibilities that all have toward each other and toward this universe.

342. For these reasons the Church must incorporate into all levels of her educational system the teaching of social justice and the biblical and ethical principles that support it. We call on our universities, in particular, to make Catholic social teaching, and the social encyclicals of the popes a part of their curriculum, especially for those whose vocation will call them to an active role in U.S. economic and political decision making. Faith and technological progress are not opposed one to another, but this progress must not be channeled and directed by greed, self-indulgence, or novelty for its own sake, but by values that respect human dignity and foster social solidarity.

343. The Church has always held that the first task and responsibility for education lies in the hands of parents: they have the right to choose freely the schools or other means necessary to educate their children in the faith.[8] The Church also has consistently held that public authorities must ensure that public subsidies for the education of children are allocated so that parents can freely choose to exercise this right without incurring unjust burdens. This parental right should not be taken from them. We call again for equitable sharing in public benefits for those parents who choose private and religious schools for their children. Such help should be available especially for low-income parents. Though many of these parents sacrifice a great deal for their children's education, others are effectively deprived of the possibility of exercising this right.

2. Supporting the Family

344. Economic life has a profound effect on all social structures and particularly on the family. A breakdown of family life often brings with it hardship and poverty. Divorce, failure to provide support to mothers and children, abandonment of children, pregnancies out of wedlock, all contribute to the amount of poverty among us. Though these breakdowns of marriage and the family are more visible among the poor, they do not affect only that one segment of our society. In fact, one could argue that many of these breakdowns come from the false values found among the more affluent—values which ultimately pervade the whole of society.

345. More studies are needed to probe the possible connections between affluence and family and marital breakdowns. The constant seeking for self-gratification and the exaggerated individualism of our age, spurred on by false values often seen in advertising and on television, contribute to the lack of firm commitment in marriage and to destructive notions of responsibility and personal growth.[9]

346. With good reason, the Church has traditionally held that the family is the basic building block of any society. In fighting against economic arrangements that weaken the family, the Church contributes to the well-being of society. The same must be said of the Church's teaching on responsible human sexuality and its relationship to marriage and family. Economic arrangements must support the family and promote its solidity.

3. The Church As Economic Actor

347. Although all members of the Church are economic actors every day in their individual lives, they also play an economic role united together as Church. On the parish and diocesan level, through its agencies and institutions, the Church employs many people; it has investments; it has extensive properties for worship and mission. *All the moral principles that govern the just operation of any economic endeavor apply to the Church and its agencies and institutions; indeed the Church should be exemplary.* The Synod of Bishops in 1971 worded this challenge most aptly: "While the Church is bound to give witness to justice, she recognizes that anyone who ventures to speak to people about justice must first be just in their eyes. Hence, we must undertake an examination of the modes of acting and of the possessions and lifestyle found within the Church herself."[10]

348. Catholics in the United States can be justly proud of their accomplishments in building and maintaining churches and chapels, and an extensive system of schools, hospitals, and charitable institutions. Through sacrifices and

personal labor our immigrant ancestors built these institutions. For many decades religious orders of women and men taught in our schools and worked in our hospitals with very little remuneration. Right now, we see the same spirit of generosity among the religious and lay people even as we seek to pay more adequate salaries.

349. We would be insincere were we to deny a need for renewal in the economic life of the Church itself and for renewed zeal on the part of the Church in examining its role in the larger context of reinforcing in U.S. society and culture those values that support economic justice.[11]

350. We select here five areas for special reflection: (1) wages and salaries, (2) rights of employees, (3) investments and property, (4) works of charity, and (5) working for economic justice.

351. We bishops commit ourselves to the principle that those who serve the Church—laity, clergy, and religious—should receive a sufficient livelihood and the social benefits provided by responsible employers in our nation. These obligations, however, cannot be met without the increased contributions of all the members of the Church. We call on all to recognize their responsibility to contribute monetarily to the support of those who carry out the public mission of the Church. Sacrificial giving or tithing by all the People of God would provide the funds necessary to pay these adequate salaries for religious and lay people; the lack of funds is the usual underlying cause for the lack of adequate salaries. The obligation to sustain the Church's institutions—education and health care, social service agencies, religious education programs, care of the elderly, youth ministry, and the like—falls on all the members of the community because of their baptism; the obligation is not just on the users or on those who staff them. Increased resources are also needed for the support of elderly members of religious communities. These dedicated women and men have not always asked for or received the stipends and pensions that would have assured their future. It would be a breach of our obligations to them to let them or their communities face retirement without adequate funds.

352. Many volunteers provide services to the Church and its mission which cannot be measured in dollars and cents. These services are important to the life and vitality of the Church in the United States and carry on a practice that has marked the history of the Church in this country since its founding. In this tradition, we ask young people to make themselves available for a year or more of voluntary service before beginning their training for more specific vocations in life; we also recommend expanding voluntary service roles for retired persons, we encourage those who have accepted this challenge.

353. All church institutions must also fully recognize the rights of employees to organize and bargain collectively with the institution through whatever

association or organization they freely choose.[12] In the light of new creative models of collaboration between labor and management described earlier in this letter, we challenge our church institutions to adopt new fruitful modes of cooperation. Although the Church has its own nature and mission that must be respected and fostered, we are pleased that many who are not of our faith, but who share similar hopes and aspirations for the human family, work for us and with us in achieving this vision. In seeking greater justice in wages, we recognize the need to be alert particularly to the continuing discrimination against women throughout Church and society, especially reflected in both the inequities of salaries between women and men and in the concentration of women in jobs at the lower end of the wage scale.

354. Individual Christians who are shareholders and those responsible within church institutions that own stocks in U.S. corporations must see to it that the invested funds are used responsibly. Although it is a moral and legal fiduciary responsibility of the trustees to ensure an adequate return on investment for the support of the work of the Church, their stewardship embraces broader moral concerns. As part owners, they must cooperate in shaping the policies of those companies through dialogue with management, through votes at corporate meetings, through the introduction of resolutions, and through participation in investment decisions. We praise the efforts of dioceses and other religious and ecumenical bodies that work together toward these goals. We also praise efforts to develop alternative investment policies, especially those which support enterprises that promote economic development in depressed communities and which help the Church respond to local and regional needs.[13] When the decision to divest seems unavoidable, it should be done after prudent examination and with a clear explanation of the motives.

355. The use of church property demands special attention today. Changing demographic patterns have left many parishes and institutions with empty or partially used buildings. The decline in the number of religious who are teaching in the schools and the reduction in the number of clergy often result in large residences with few occupants. In this regard, the Church must be sensitive to the image the possession projects, namely, that it in the use of its resources. This image can be overcome only by clear public accountability of its financial holdings, of its properties and their use, and of the services it renders to its members and to society at large. We support and encourage the creative use of these facilities by many parishes and dioceses to serve the needs of the poor.

356. The Church has a special call to be a servant of the poor, the sick, and the marginalized, thereby becoming a true sign of the Church's mission—a mission shared by every member of the Christian community. The Church now serves many such people through one of the largest private human services delivery systems in the country. The networks of agencies, institutions, and programs

provide services to millions of persons of all faiths. Still we must be reminded that in our day our Christian concerns must increase and extend beyond our borders, because everyone in need is our neighbor. We must also be reminded that charity requires more than alleviating misery. It demands genuine love for the person in need. It should probe the meaning of suffering and provoke a response that seeks to remedy causes. True charity leads to advocacy.

357. Yet charity alone is not a corrective to all economic social ills. All citizens, working through various organizations of society and through government, bear the responsibility for those who are in need. The Church, too, through its members individually and through its agencies, must work to alleviate injustices that prevent some from participating fully in economic life. Our experience with the Campaign for Human Development confirms our judgment about the validity of self-help and empowerment of the poor. The campaign, which has received the positive support of American Catholics since it was launched in 1970, provides a model that we think sets a high standard for similar efforts. We bishops know of the many faithful in all walks of life who use their skills and their compassion to seek innovative ways to carry out the goals we are proposing in this letter. As they do this, they *are* the Church acting for economic justice. At the same time, we hope they will join together with us and their priests to influence our society so that even more steps can be taken to alleviate injustices. Grassroots efforts by the poor themselves, helped by community support, are indispensable. The entire Christian community can learn much from the way our deprived brothers and sisters assist each other in their struggles.

358. In addition to being an economic actor, the Church is a significant cultural actor concerned about the deeper cultural roots of our economic problems. As we have proposed a new experiment in collaboration and participation in decision making by all those affected at all levels of U.S. society, so we also commit the Church to become a model of collaboration and participation.

C. The Road Ahead

359. The completion of a letter such as this one is but the beginning of a long process of education, discussion and action; its contents must be brought to all members of the Church and of society.

360. In this respect we mentioned the twofold aim of this pastoral letter: to help Catholics form their consciences on the moral dimensions of economic decision making and to articulate a moral perspective in the general societal and political debate that surrounds these questions. These two purposes help us to reflect on the different ways the institutions and ministers of the Church can assist the laity in their vocation in the world. Renewed emphasis on Catholic social teaching in our schools, colleges, and universities; special

seminars with corporate officials, union leaders, legislators, bankers, and the like; the organization of small groups composed of people from different ways of life to meditate together on the Gospel and ethical norms; speakers' bureaus; family programs; clearinghouses of available material; pulpit aids for priests; diocesan television and radio programs; research projects in our universities—all of these are appropriate means for continued discussion and action. Some of these are done best on the parish level, others by the state Catholic conferences, and others by the National Conference of Catholic Bishops. These same bodies can assist the laity in the many difficult decisions that deal with political options that affect economic decisions. Where many options are available, it must be the concern of all in such debates that we as Catholics do not become polarized. All must be challenged to show how the decisions they make and the policies they suggest flow from the ethical moral vision outlined here. As new problems arise, we hope through our continual reflection that we will be able to help refine Catholic social teaching and contribute to its further development.

361. We call upon our priests, in particular, to continue their study of these issues, so that they can proclaim the gospel message in a way that not only challenges the faithful but also sustains and encourages their vocation in and to the world. Priestly formation in our seminaries will also have to prepare candidates for this role.

362. We wish to emphasize the need to undertake research into many of the areas this document could not deal with in depth and to continue exploration of those we have dealt with. We encourage our Catholic universities, foundations, and other institutions to assist in these necessary projects. The following areas for further research are merely suggestive, not exhaustive: the impact of arms production and large military spending on the domestic economy and on culture; arms production and sales as they relate to Third World poverty; tax reforms to express the preferential option for the poor; the rights of women and minorities in the work force; the development of communications technology and its global influences; robotics, automation, and reduction of defense industries as they will affect employment; the economy and the stability of the family; legitimate profit versus greed; securing economic rights; environmental and ecological questions; future roles of labor and unions; international financial institutions and Third World debt; our national deficit; world food problems; "full employment" and its implementation; plant closings and dealing with the human costs of an evolving economy; cooperatives and new modes of sharing; welfare reform and national eligibility standards; income support systems; concentration of land ownership; assistance to Third World nations; migration and its effects; population policies and development; the effects of increased inequality of incomes in society.

D. Commitment to a Kingdom of Love and Justice

363. Confronted by this economic complexity and seeking clarity for the future, we can rightly ask our selves one single question: How does our economic system affect the lives of people—all people? Part of the American dream has been to make this world a better place for people to live in; at this moment of history that dream must include everyone on this globe. Since we profess to be members of a "catholic" or universal Church, we all must raise our sights to a concern for the well-being of everyone in the world. Third World debt becomes our problem. Famine and starvation in sub-Saharan Africa become our concern. Rising military expenditures everywhere in the world become part of our fears for the future of this planet. We cannot be content if we see ecological neglect or the squandering of natural resources. In this letter we bishops have spoken often of economic interdependence; now is the moment when all of us must confront the reality of such economic bonding and its consequences and see it as a moment of grace—a *kairos*—that can unite all of us in a common community of the human family. We commit ourselves to this global vision.

364. We cannot be frightened by the magnitude and complexity of these problems. We must not be discouraged. In the midst of this struggle, It is inevitable that we become aware of greed, laziness, and envy. No utopia is possible on this earth; but as believers in the redemptive love of God and as those who have experienced God's forgiving mercy, we know that God's providence is not and will not be lacking to us today.

365. The fulfillment of human needs, we know, is not the final purpose of the creation of the human person. We have been created to share in the divine life through a destiny that goes far beyond our human capabilities and before which we must in all humility stand in awe. Like Mary in proclaiming her *Magnificat*, we marvel at the wonders God has done for us, how God has raised up the poor and the lowly and promised great things for them in the Kingdom. God now asks of us sacrifices and reflection on our reverence for human dignity—in ourselves and in others—and on our service and discipleship, so that the divine goal for the human family and this earth can be fulfilled. Communion with God, sharing God's life, involves a mutual bonding with all on this globe. Jesus taught us to love God and one another and that the concept of neighbor is without limit. We know that we are called to be members of a new covenant of love. We have to move from our devotion to independence, through an understanding of interdependence, to a commitment to human solidarity. That challenge must find its realization in the kind of community we build among us. Love implies concern for all—especially the poor—and a continued search for those social and economic structures that permit everyone to share in a community that is a part of a redeemed creation (Rom 8:21–23).

Endnotes

1. *Reconciliation and Penance*, 13.

2. *Justice in the World*, 6.

3. *Medellin Documents: Justice* (1968), 4.

4. *Dogmatic Constitution on the Church*, 1; *Pastoral Constitution*, 42 and 45; *Constitution on the Liturgy*, 26; *Decree on the Church's Missionary Activity*, 5; *Liturgy and Social Justice*, ed. by Mark Searle, (Collegeville, Minn: Liturgical Press, 1980); National Conference of Catholic Bishops, *The Church at Prayer* (Washington, D.C.: United States Catholic Conference, 1983).

5. *Dogmatic Constitution on the Church*, 36.

6. *Justice in the World*, 41.

7. National Conference of Catholic Bishops, *To Teach as Jesus Did, A Pastoral Message on Education* (Washington, D.C.: United States Catholic Conference, 1972), 7.

8. Cf. Vatican Council II, *Declaration on Christian Education*, 3, 6. See also, *Charter of the Rights of the Family*, 5b; *Instruction on Christian Freedom and Liberation*, 94.

9. Pope John Paul II, *On the Family* (Washington, D.C.: United States Catholic Conference, 1981), 6. See also Robert N. Bellah, Richard Madsen, William M. Sullivan, Ann Swidler, Steven M. Tipton, *Habits of the Heart: Individualism and Commitment in American Life* (Berkeley: University of California Press, 1985); *The Family Today and Tomorrow: The Church Addresses Her Future* (Braintree, Mass.: Pope John XXIII Medical-Moral Research and Education Center, 1985).

10. *Justice in the World*, 40.

11. *Dogmatic Constitution on the Church*, 8.

12. National Conference of Catholic Bishops, *Health and Health Care* (Washington, D.C.: United States Catholic Conference, 1981), 50.

13. See ch. IV of this pastoral letter.

FOUNDATIONAL ISSUES
OF ECONOMIC JUSTICE

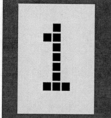

■ Economic Justice and the New Challenges of Globalization

David Hollenbach, SJ

■ INTRODUCTION

When the US Catholic bishops drafted *Economic Justice for All* (*EJA*) in the mid-1980s, the situation of the developing world, especially its poorest people, was very much on their minds. The chair of the drafting committee, Archbishop Rembert Weakland, had been Abbot Primate of the Benedictine order, a role that had given him firsthand experience of the needs of people in all five continents. Bishop William Weigand, also a member of the drafting committee, had served as a pastor in Cali, Colombia, for nearly ten years and had a deep concern for the plight of the poor in Latin America. Bishop Peter Rosazza's pastoral work in inner-city New Haven, Connecticut, had exposed him to the economic forces pushing many poor men and women in Central America and the Caribbean to seek a better life by migrating to the United States.

Thus is it not surprising that early in the drafting process the bishops decided to make the international economic links between the United States and the developing world one of the practical areas to be addressed by *EJA*, along with poverty and unemployment in the United States, and eventually adding agriculture as well. Several of the hearings so influential in shaping the document focused on these international links, one with economists from diverse parts of the developing world and the other with bishops from South and Central America. Though the pastoral letter's discussion of poverty and unemployment in the United States probably received most of the public discussion and debate during the drafting process, the letter's international emphasis was equally important in the eyes of the drafting committee and perhaps more important in stimulating response in the global Catholic Church. The letter was published in German, French, Italian, Spanish, and Portuguese and was widely discussed abroad, especially in Europe and Latin America. The pastoral letter drew on vigorous developments in Latin American theology that stressed the Church's special duty to work with and for the poor.[1] It was a stimulus for similar efforts to address issues of economic justice by episcopal leadership in England, Germany, and Australia, among other countries.

In his 2009 memoir, Archbishop Weakland noted the strong stress on these international dimensions in *EJA*. When he noted topics not adequately treated in the document, however, the question of globalization topped his list of lacunae.[2] The phenomenon of globalization is one of the most important signs of the times in the early twenty-first century. It is a new reality that all countries of the global North and South must address as all peoples seek to chart their course into the future. The issue of globalization could be addressed more adequately if people called on a deepened understanding of the common good shared across borders. In particular, attention needs to be paid to how the common good and the closely linked notion of solidarity should shape the way all peoples view the pursuit of justice in a globalizing world.

This essay presents a four-part argument. First, a brief clarification of the meaning of globalization is offered. Second, key ideas in Catholic social thought about the links between the common good, solidarity, and justice that are relevant to the challenge of globalization are outlined. Third, suggestions for institutional agents that have responsibilities to respond to the demands of justice in the face of globalization are offered. Finally, a brief reflection is presented on how a solidarity-based understanding of justice would respond to some of the challenges of economic development that have arisen since the pastoral letter was written. This reflection notes the need to attend to both the capacities and the limits of markets to promote economic justice amid today's increasing globalization.

■ THE MEANING OF GLOBALIZATION

The increasing interdependence of the human family termed *globalization* has been subject to considerable intellectual and political controversy. In the midst of such controversies, globalization needs to be defined. Some years ago, Robert Keohane and Joseph Nye provided some useful precision by defining

---

[1] The "preferential option for the poor" is a theme that appears repeatedly in *Economic Justice for All*. See nos. 16, 52, 87, 88, 170, 186, 252, 260, 267, 274, 291, 336, and 362. The references in nos. 252, 260, 267, 274, and 291 all speak to international economic issues. This thematic emphasis on the option for the poor was clearly drawn from Latin American liberation theology. See the treatment by Gustavo Gutierrez, "Option for the Poor," in *Mysterium Liberationis: Fundamental Concepts of Liberation Theology*, ed. Ignacio Ellacuria and Jon Sobrino (Maryknoll, NY: Orbis Books, 1993), 235–50.

[2] Rembert G. Weakland, *A Pilgrim in a Pilgrim Church: Memoirs of a Catholic Archbishop* (Grand Rapids, MI: Eerdmans, 2009), 286.

globalization as the increase in networks of interdependence among people at multicontinental distances.[3] This description points to the fact that globalization involves complex networks of interdependence, not single strands of interconnection. Globalization is occurring on multiple levels of social life: economic (e.g., trade, finance, investment, production, and consumption), technological (e.g., new forms of electronic and wireless communication), environmental (e.g., climate change), cultural (e.g., the spread of Western dress and music to other parts of the world and the increasing interest by Western students in the study of non-Western cultures), political (e.g., the rise in importance of intergovernmental organizations both regionally, as with the European Union, and globally, as with the World Trade Organization [WTO]).[4]

These different dimensions of globalization have mixed consequences: some are good, some are bad, some helpful, some harmful. For example, the economic aspects of globalization have been accompanied by not only a decline in the global percentage of people living in poverty but also a continuation in large numbers of extremely poor people in certain regions. Recent figures from the World Bank tell us that in 2005 there were 1.4 billion people living in extreme poverty (on less than $1.25 per day), down from 1.9 billion in 1981. This is progress. Indeed more optimistic thinkers point to this decline in global poverty and argue that integration into global markets through trade and finance can lead to positive economic outcomes. This pro-globalization argument often invokes the example of the so-called East Asian tigers (Hong Kong, Taiwan, Singapore, and South Korea), places that grew rapidly in the last decades of the twentieth century as they became linked to global markets. More recently, China and Vietnam are offered as examples of how domestic free markets and links to the global marketplace can lead to rapid development. The identification of globalization with such desirable outcomes can give the term a strongly positive meaning.

Global markets, however, have certainly not had uniformly positive effects on developing countries. Though the number of poor people in the world has declined since the early 1980s, more than half the people of the African continent remain in poverty. This percentage has not improved since 1981.[5] The

---

[3] Robert O. Keohane and Joseph S. Nye, "Globalization: What's New? What's Not? (And So What?)" *Foreign Policy*, Spring 2000, 104–19, at 105.

[4] For an in-depth analysis of the diverse dimensions of globalization, see David Held, Anthony McGrew, David Goldblatt, and Jonathan Perraton, *Global Transformations: Politics, Economics, and Culture* (Stanford, CA: Stanford University Press, 1999). Similar, though not identical, dimensions of globalization are distinguished and analyzed in Joseph S. Nye and John D. Donahue, eds., *Governance in a Globalizing World* (Washington, DC: Brookings Institution Press, 2000), pt. 1, "Trends in Globalization."

[5] "World Bank Updates Poverty Estimates for the Developing World," press release, *http://econ. worldbank.org/WBSITE/EXTERNAL/EXTDEC/EXTRESEARCH/0,,contentMDK:21882162~pag ePK:64165401~piPK:64165026~theSitePK:469382,00.html*.

ment programs of the International Monetary Fund (IMF) and
of the 1980s and early 1990s constrained economic decisions
ents of developing countries through the conditions these
oans, debt relief, and other forms of financial assistance. This
ment, known as the Washington consensus, invoked the
d called for shrinking government and increasing open-
stically and internationally. In many African countries,
led to declining investment in education, health care,
such as roads. With less education and poorer health,
ents of the population of these counties were less able
and the lack of infrastructure linking rural agricul-
international markets meant they were left further
behind. kets can generate growth, people who are illiterate, sick, or
without the roads needed to participate in markets can be left altogether out of
the benefits. As Pope John Paul II put it, "if not actually exploited, they are to a
great extent marginalized; economic development takes place over their heads."[6]
Thus in some African countries the paradoxical result of integration into global
markets has been simultaneous growth in GDP and the number of poor people.
In hindsight, several economists who had been highly placed within the World
Bank wrote strong critiques of the policies followed by such international financial institutions in the 1980s and early 1990s.[7] In their view, these policies have
not alleviated and may even have contributed to inequality, poverty, and suffering in parts of the developing world. When such developments are identified
with globalization, the process surely gets a bad name.

These developments have led to significant new efforts to address the continuing reality of poverty. Millennium Development Goals, adopted by the governments of most of the world's countries at the UN General Assembly in 2000,
set targets that include halving extreme poverty, halting the spread of HIV/
AIDS, and providing universal primary education by 2015. These goals have
been taken up as policy objectives by both the World Bank and the IMF.[8] It
remains an open question, however, whether it is feasible to reach these goals,
especially in the aftermath of the global financial crisis that began in 2008 and
continues today.

---

[6] John Paul II, *Centesimus annus* (On the Hundredth Anniversary of *Rerum Novarum*), no. 33.

[7] See Joseph E. Stiglitz, *Globalization and Its Discontents* (New York: W.W. Norton, 2002); William Easterly, *The Elusive Quest for Growth: Economists' Adventures and Misadventures in the Tropics*
(Cambridge, MA: MIT Press, 2001).

[8] UN Millennium Declaration, September 18, 2000, *http://www.un.org/millennium/declaration/
ares552e.pdf*. The World Bank and IMF annually produce a Global Monitoring Report on the
implementation of Millennium Development Goals as a framework for accountability in global
development policy. See the World Bank's website on global monitoring at *http://web.worldbank.org/
WBSITE/EXTERNAL/EXTDEC/EXTGLOBALMONITOR/0,,menuPK:2185108~pagePK:64168
427~piPK:64168435~theSitePK:2185068,00.html*.

■■ CATHOLIC SOCIAL THOUGHT AND GLOBALIZATION

This mixture of positive and negative outcomes led John Paul II to state in 2001 that "globalization, *a priori*, is neither good nor bad. It will be what people make of it."[9] What people make of it, in turn, will be determined by the values that guide their decisions on specific economic choices, policies, and institutions. John Paul was clear that such decisions must simultaneously "be at the service of the human person" and "serve solidarity and the common good."[10]

The link between service of the human person and the promotion of solidarity and the common good is a central theme in Roman Catholic social thought. This link played a major role in shaping the moral argument in *EJA* and is central to more recent teachings of the Holy See on economic issues, particularly in Pope Benedict XVI's *Caritas in veritate* (Charity in Truth). Clarifying this link between human dignity and solidarity is important for the development of a normative, ethical approach to globalization.

To begin clarifying this link, note that human interdependence is a fact of life. Humans interact in a host of ways, both with those nearby and those at great distances. Ethical reflection begins by noting that some of these connections serve the human good and others lead to human harm. Thus in considering the impact of globalization, careful attention must be paid to the quality of economic interdependence across borders. John Paul II has distinguished the de facto interdependence that is inevitable in human life from a moral interdependence that respects the dignity of persons in a reciprocal way.

De facto interdependence can have negative or positive value from a moral point of view. Morally negative patterns of interdependence are marked by inequality or exclusion from resources necessary for the realization of human dignity. Such negative interdependence is evident between groups whose interactions are marred by domination or oppression, by conflict or war, or who are living under economic institutions that exclude some people from relationships that are prerequisite for decent lives. Morally positive interdependence, on the other hand, is marked by equality and reciprocity. Those who are interacting show respect for each other's equal human dignity and relate to each other in ways that reciprocally support each other's dignity and freedom. Thus Catholic social thought holds that morally positive forms of interdependence are patterns of interaction based on respect for the equal dignity of persons and that generate reciprocal connections enabling persons to share in

---

[9] John Paul II, "Address to the Pontifical Academy of Social Sciences," April 27, 2001, no. 2, *http://www.vatican.va/holy_father/john_paul_ii/speeches/2001/documents/hf_jp-ii_spe_20010427_pc-social-sciences_en.html*.

[10] Ibid.

the common good.[11] Such equal reciprocity or reciprocal equality can be called solidarity; this solidarity leads to forms of interdependence that are just. On the other hand, interconnections marked by inequalities that lead to the domination of one person or group by another or to the exclusion of some from active participation in the interaction are unjust; such patterns of domination or exclusion undermine the dignity, freedom, and agency of those who are in the subordinate positions or who are altogether excluded.

Therefore, if we adopt Nye and Keohane's definition of globalization as the "increase in networks of interdependence among people at multicontinental distances,"[12] the ethical assessment of globalization becomes a question of determining whether the strands in the network of interdependence are marked by equality and reciprocity or by inequalities that lead to domination and exclusion. Morally positive patterns of globalization will exhibit a solidarity among participants stemming from a reciprocal respect for their equal dignity. In John Paul II's words, such patterns are marked by "a solidarity which will take up interdependence and transfer it to the moral plane."[13] Benedict XVI has echoed John Paul's call to move global interdependence in a moral direction by steering it toward interactions based on "communion and the sharing of goods."[14] Benedict's rich theological concept of communion thus has direct ethical implications. It requires reciprocity in social relationships, and such reciprocity requires respect for the equal dignity of the partners to the relationship.

In the face of the differing aspects of globalization, therefore, one of the chief contributions of the Church's ministry will be to support movement from patterns of global interdependence marked by inequality, domination, and oppression to patterns based on equality, reciprocity, and solidarity. This will be a ministry that continues to pursue what *EJA* called "basic justice"—that form of justice that *"demands the establishment of minimum levels of participation in the life of the human community for all persons"* (no. 77, italics in the original). In negative terms, it will be a ministry that resists all forms of what *EJA* called "the ultimate injustice"—activity in which "a person or group [is] treated actively or abandoned passively as if they were nonmembers of the human race" (no. 77).[15] Inclusion and participation based on equality, therefore, are the basic marks of patterns of

---

[11] Catholic social thought thus overlaps with the normative standpoint of the recent "Manifesto for a Global Economic Ethic: Consequences for Global Businesses," issued June 6, 2009 at the UN under the auspices of the Global Ethics Foundation led by Hans Küng. The manifesto stresses "humanity" and "reciprocity" as its central ethical norms. See *http://www.unglobalcompact.org/docs/ news_events/9.1_news_archives/2009_10_06/Global_Economic_Ethic_Manifesto.pdf.*

[12] Keohane and Nye, "Globalization: What's New?" 105.

[13] John Paul II, *Sollicitudo rei socialis* (On Social Concern), no. 26, in David J. O'Brien and Thomas A. Shannon, eds., *Catholic Social Thought: The Documentary Heritage* (Maryknoll, NY: Orbis Books, 1992).

[14] Benedict XVI, *Caritas in veritate* (Charity in Truth), no. 42.

[15] In O'Brien and Shannon, eds., *Catholic Social Thought,* 576–7.

globalization that are just. These values should shape the social, economic, and political institutions of our globalizing world.

This is especially relevant to the assessment of the economic dimensions of globalization. For example, as the interconnections of global markets have had increasing impact on wider segments of the world's population, one can ask whether these markets have benefited all people in reciprocal and proportionally equal ways or whether some have benefited notably more than others. Many sub-Saharan African countries have experienced notable economic growth in very recent years, in part due to the intensification of global trade and transnational investment. Nevertheless, poverty in sub-Saharan Africa remains unacceptably high. As the World Bank has concluded, "Serious development challenges remain in Africa, where in 2008 about half of the population were living on $1.25 a day . . . and 645 out of every 100,000 African women died in childbirth."[16] The interconnection of these African countries with the developed world through trade and financial markets, therefore, has not adequately addressed poverty. Nor are sub-Saharan African countries equal and reciprocal participants in shaping the policies of the institutions that significantly influence world trade and finance, such as the WTO and the IMF. This has been called "globalization's democratic deficit," and it continues today despite some small increases in the voting power of developing countries at the World Bank.[17] In addition, though the current world financial crisis affects nearly all people in harmful ways, its effects have been more harmful in poor countries than in rich ones. The impact of the crisis is also internally unequal within developing countries. According to recent World Bank estimates, about 64 million more people were pushed into extreme poverty (i.e., they were living on less than $1.25 a day) in 2010 than had the crisis not occurred.[18] This crisis was caused by actions taken in the developed world, but once again the poorest paid the biggest price and bore a disproportionate burden of the negative consequences. These unequal effects on poor nations and on the poorest within them cannot be considered just.

---

[16] World Bank Annual Report 2011, "The Year in Review," 14, *http://web.worldbank.org/WBSITE/ EXTERNAL/EXTABOUTUS/EXTANNREP/EXTANNREP2011/0,,menuPK:8070643~pagePK:64 168427~piPK:64168435~theSitePK:8070617,00.html*.

[17] Joseph S. Nye, Jr., "Globalization's Democratic Deficit: How to Make International Institutions More Accountable," *Foreign Affairs* 80, no. 4 (July/August 2001): 2–6, and, on recent adjustments, the World Bank press release, "World Bank Reforms Voting Power, Gets $86 Billion Boost," *http:// web.worldbank.org/WBSITE/EXTERNAL/NEWS/0,,contentMDK:22556045~pagePK:34370~piPK: 34424~theSitePK:4607,00.html*.

[18] World Bank, *Global Economic Prospects 2010: Crisis, Finance, and Growth* (Washington, DC: International Bank for Reconstruction and Development/World Bank, 2010), xi, *http://siteresources. worldbank.org/INTGEP2010/Resources/GEP2010-Full-Report.pdf*.

▦ INSTITUTIONAL DIMENSIONS OF GLOBALIZATION

In light of these unequal and nonreciprocal effects of the global marketplace, Catholic social thought insists that although free markets can contribute to growth and advancement of human well-being, free markets alone are not enough to assure the attainment of justice in the global economic sphere. Neither the individualistic pursuit of self-interest, central to many models of free market capitalism, nor the subordination of personal initiative to society, characteristic of centrally planned economic systems, is ethically acceptable. Freedom and solidarity are interconnected and mutually dependent. Justice requires the inclusion of those being excluded from the benefits of global markets as well as assistance to those negatively affected by these markets. This ethical perspective has institutional implications.

In some circumstances, for example, markets will need social and political guidance. In light of the challenges raised by poverty and the current financial crisis, Pope Benedict XVI has stressed the need for more effective institutional mechanisms to regulate markets. In addressing the Pontifical Academy of Social Sciences recently, he declared, "the worldwide financial breakdown has . . . shown the error of the assumption that the market is capable of regulating itself, apart from public intervention and the support of internalized moral standards."[19] The ethical requirements of the common good and the dignity of the person must guide the decisions, policies, and institutions that shape global economic interactions for these interactions to be just. In particular, commitment to the common good and respect for the demands of human dignity together point to "the urgency of strengthening the governance procedures of the global economy, albeit with due respect for the principle of subsidiarity."[20] In other words, stronger global governance structures are needed to secure justice while respecting the need for national and local initiatives as well.

This Catholic willingness to consider limits on the free market includes the conviction that advancement of the global common good in an increasingly integrated world calls for stronger structures of transnational governance. John XXIII's 1963 encyclical *Pacem in Terris* (Peace on Earth) drew a strong conclusion about the inadequacy of the international political institutions of his day. He wrote that these institutions "are unequal to the task of promoting the common good of all peoples."[21] In response, John XXIII called for a "public authority, having worldwide power and endowed with the proper means for

---

[19] Benedict XVI, "Address to the Pontifical Academy of Social Sciences," April 30, 2010, *http://www.vatican.va/holy_father/benedict_xvi/speeches/2010/april/documents/hf_ben-xvi_spe_20100430_scienze-sociali_en.html.*

[20] Ibid.

[21] John XXIII, *Pacem in Terris* (Peace on Earth), no. 135.

the efficacious pursuit of its objective," namely, the worldwide common good. He gave particular endorsement to the United Nations (UN).[22] Benedict XVI went even farther in his recent encyclical *Caritas in veritate* (Charity in Truth), when he wrote that "In the face of the unrelenting growth of global interdependence, there is a strongly felt need, even in the midst of a global recession, for a reform of the *United Nations Organization*, and likewise of *economic institutions and international finance*, so that the concept of the family of nations can acquire real teeth."[23]

John XXIII's call for a "public authority" capable of enforcing the global common good and Benedict's desire that such authority have "real teeth" suggests the Catholic Church is envisioning something approximating a world government that would oversee the dynamics of global interaction in the interest of justice, much as national governments have responsibility for the domestic requirements of justice. Both popes, of course, carefully qualified their discussion with a call for full respect for the principle of subsidiarity, that is, respect for national and local initiative.

The contribution of subsidiarity would be clearer, however, if these Church teachings gave more attention to the fact that today's global order is being shaped by forces beyond nation-states or global organizations such as the UN. The dynamics of global interaction are increasingly the result of a complex network of institutions, some private and some public, some national, some regional, and some global. For example, the extent of poverty in developing countries is affected by the actions of private entrepreneurs and by global development and financial institutions such as the UN Development Program, the World Bank, and the IMF. The extent of poverty is also shaped by the activities of regional agencies (e.g., the African and Inter-American Development Banks), by country-to-country bilateral assistance, by direct foreign investment or loans from private corporations and banks, and by the activities of numerous nongovernmental organizations (NGOs) dedicated to promoting development. In this context, of particular note are the activities of church-related and other faith-based organizations such as Caritas Internationalis and World Vision and of secular development agencies like Oxfam. Some of these agencies seek not only to provide development assistance but also to influence development-related policies of governmental and private agencies.

The roles played by these diverse actors spotlight that nation-states and global institutions like the UN are far from the only actors significantly influencing development. Anne-Marie Slaughter notes that the emerging global order is composed of multiple agencies including government agencies that are horizontally networked with their counterparts in other countries, entire governments that are vertically networked into global and regional intergovernmental

---

[22] Ibid., nos. 135–8.

[23] Benedict XVI, *Caritas in veritate* (Charity in Truth), no. 67, italics in the original.

organizations, private companies, and religious communities and faith-based organizations—all of these are linked in various ways with governmental and intergovernmental agencies.[24] In *The Common Good and Christian Ethics,* I describe this emerging global scene as "a network of crisscrossing communities."[25]

This picture of global networks suggests that the institutional framework for greater justice in an interconnected world will not simply be a matter of establishing a new worldwide layer of governmental authority to control transnational economic actors. Despite their endorsement of the principle of subsidiarity, John XXIII's and Benedict XVI's calls for a "public authority" with global power and "real teeth" suggests that something like a world government would be the precondition for greater justice today. But just as national sovereignty should be limited when it leads to injustices, the multifarious actors that comprise today's global web suggest that the effective response would have to be made on multiple levels and by a variety of institutions. A more effective UN, though needed, will be but one of the factors that must contribute to more just global economic interaction based on equality and reciprocity. Other agencies that would have key roles to play include global and regional intergovernmental bodies such as the IMF, the World Bank, the European Union, and the African Development Bank. Private corporations and banks will also play crucial roles, as will nongovernmental development agencies, certainly including the Catholic Church and its development arms such as Caritas and Catholic Relief Services.

Because globalization is an ever-thickening web of transborder interconnections, the moral responsibility for economic justice falls on the many diverse actors spinning this web of interdependence. Respect for equality and reciprocity needs to occur throughout this growing, multidimensional web of transnational connections. This respect will not be achieved only by superimposing a new institutional layer of power or control above that of the nation-state. Perhaps some brief, concrete reflection will help illustrate this.

■ OVERCOMING POVERTY: PRACTICAL REFLECTIONS

Addressing a complex issue like global poverty is risky: if matters are oversimplified, the proposed solutions could be counterproductive. With the hope of avoiding such distortion, this chapter concludes with a few words about the consequences of the ethical position presented here for overcoming poverty,

---

[24] Anne-Marie Slaughter, *A New World Order,* 19–22 and 10. For a study of the emerging role of NGOs, see Margaret E. Keck and Kathryn Sikkink, *Activists beyond Borders: Advocacy Networks in International Politics* (Ithaca, NY: Cornell University Press, 1998).

[25] David Hollenbach, *The Common Good and Christian Ethics* (Cambridge: Cambridge University Press, 2002), 229.

particularly as it concerns aid programs and their relationship to good governance and peacemaking. In addition, a brief suggestion is made regarding the challenges that government, private corporations and banks, nongovernmental agencies, and the Catholic Church all face in responding to the reality of poverty in the world.

EJA strongly advocates assistance for the poor in the developing world. Indeed, *EJA* sees such assistance as a way to live the option for the poor so close to the heart of Gospel and states that it should be "*the central priority for policy choice*" in our interdependent world (no. 260, italics in the original). The bishops noted that although the United States had been a leader in development assistance in the years following World War II, by 1986 the United States was contributing a smaller percentage of its GNP to development assistance than almost all the other industrialized member-countries of the Organization of Economic Cooperation and Development. The bishops said this was "a grave distortion of the priority that development assistance should command" (*EJA*, no. 266).

Voices in the discussion of efforts to overcome poverty in the developing world today continue to support the pastoral letter's call for aid as an effective way to address global poverty. For example, Jeffrey Sachs, who advises the Secretary General of the United Nations on implementation of Millennium Development Goals, strongly supports increased aid from rich countries.[26] In 2002, heads of state from the world's nations gathered at Monterrey, Mexico, for a UN conference on financing development. A consensus was reached that developed countries should continue to set 0.7 percent of GNP as their target for development aid to poor countries.[27] Implementing this consensus would require a considerable increase in aid funds by the United States.

In recent years, however, the effectiveness of aid as a remedy for poverty has been challenged by a number of analysts. William Easterly, formerly of the World Bank, has argued that all of the grand development schemes of recent decades have failed, including those advocated by Sachs.[28] The most provocative challenge has come from Dambisa Moyo, a Zambian woman and a Harvard- and Oxford-trained economist who worked at Goldman Sachs for eight years. Moyo's provocative thesis is that, at least in Africa, not only has aid failed to alleviate poverty, it has worsened poverty. In her words, "the problem is that aid is not benign—it is malignant. No longer part of the potential solution, it is part of the problem—in fact aid *is* the problem."[29] Moyo argues that aid creates

---

[26] See Jeffrey Sachs, *The End of Poverty: Economic Possibilities for Our Time* (New York: Penguin, 2005). See also Sachs, "Hold the Rich Nations to Their Word," *Financial Times*, December 16, 2009, *http://www.ft.com/cms/s/0/e361fa90-e9e2-11de-ae43-00144feab49a.html.*

[27] Monterrey Consensus, no. 42, in *Financing Development: Building on Monterrey* (New York: United Nations, 2002), 8, *http://www.un.org/esa/ffd/documents/Building%20on%20Monterrey.pdf.*

[28] See William Easterly, *The White Man's Burden: Why the West's Efforts to Aid the Rest Have Done So Much Ill and So Little Good* (New York: Penguin, 2006).

[29] Dambisa Moyo, *Dead Aid: Why Aid Is Not Working and How There Is a Better Way for Africa* (New York: Farrar, Straus and Giroux, 2009), 47.

Dambisa Moyo

a cycle of corruption, giving corrupt leaders the resources they need to stay in power, which leads to continuing poverty and then further aid. Because aid puts large pots of money at the disposal of the government in power, it increases that government's incentive to use violence to hold power, and if one is out of power, to seize it, thus making civil war more likely. Aid also removes the incentive for creative initiative that would increase investment and trade and thereby enhance development. Thus, Moyo proposes that to overcome poverty in Africa, aid should be replaced by market-based initiatives involving trade, enhanced foreign direct investment, and support for micro-finance that enables poor people to participate in the market.[30]

Moyo's analysis contains elements of truth. For example, there is no doubt corruption is a major obstacle to development in many of the world's poorest countries, especially Africa, and that this corruption has been linked with civil conflict in some of these countries, and that such conflict only deepens poverty.

---

[30] See ibid., 145.

For example, Kenya's former anti-corruption minister, John Githango, faced threats to his life when he challenged the deep divisions in society that were rooted in economic differences between ethnic groups. These divisions led to governmental corruption and frequently erupted in tribal conflict as with the postelection violence in 2007.[31] However, Moyo's analysis overlooks the failure of market-oriented structural adjustment programs instituted by the World Bank and the IMF during the 1980s and early 1990s. Moyo also seems overly confident that in the face of the present global financial crisis, African countries will be increasingly attractive sites for direct foreign investment and will be able to enter into global trade markets if incentives to do so are increased by the end of aid. Indeed, Moyo's teacher at Oxford, Paul Collier, counters that in the context of the current financial crisis, "aid agencies look to be more important as sources of finance for investment than at any time in the past two decades."[32]

Moyo also fails to adequately credit the important positive role that aid aimed at alleviating the effects of HIV/AIDS has played in African countries, such as her own Zambia.[33] Without such aid, more people would now be suffering from AIDS and unable to contribute to any form of economic advancement. The same can be said of aid that effectively targets other health needs and that supports effective educational programs among the poor. People who are sick or illiterate are unlikely to be able to participate in markets in ways that advance development. They will simply be left out of whatever growth and development occurs. If the sick and illiterate are a sizable part of a population, as in many sub-Saharan countries, programs that directly address health and education would be needed. Aid programs that effectively address these needs will remain crucial.

Nevertheless, government-to-government bilateral aid will surely not be the only key to alleviating poverty in developing countries, such as those in sub-Saharan Africa. The political and economic situations in those countries have dimensions that cannot be effectively addressed by bilateral aid programs. International pressure to confront corruption and move toward good governance has

---

[31] See the powerful narrative of Githango's struggle against corruption in Kenya in Michaela Wrong, *It's Our Turn to Eat: The Story of a Kenyan Whistle Blower* (London: Fourth Estate, 2009).

[32] Paul Collier, "Time to Turn Off the Aid Tap? Review of *Dead Aid*, by Dambisa Moyo," *The Independent*, January 30, 2009, *http://www.independent.co.uk/arts-entertainment/books/reviews/dead-aid-by-dambisa-moyo-1519875.html*. For a fuller development of Collier's views, see his two recent books, *The Bottom Billion: Why the Poorest Countries Are Failing and What Can Be Done about It* (New York: Oxford University Press, 2007), and *Wars, Guns, and Votes: Democracy in Dangerous Places* (New York: Harper Perennial, 2009).

[33] See Michael Gerson's critique of Moyo's book, "'Dead Aid,' Dead Wrong," in the *Washington Post*, April 3, 2009, *http://www.washingtonpost.com/wp-dyn/content/article/2009/04/02/AR2009040203285.html*. Gerson worked in the White House as chief speechwriter and as a senior policy advisor for George W. Bush.

rightly become a central concern of the World Bank and the IMF.[34] Good governance, of course, is not guaranteed by the presence of multiparty elections. When a large percentage of the population of a developing country is poor and illiterate, the manipulation of elections through patronage and distortion of information is relatively easy. Under such conditions, free elections do not guarantee accountable government. A lack of accountability will enable a government to use its power to serve the economic interests of its leaders rather than the poor majority. Thus, development and overcoming poverty require actions by donor countries and the international community to reinforce genuine political accountability. Without such accountability, aid is not likely to benefit the people it is aimed at helping. Private agencies like Oxfam are also concerned with ensuring that their programs support only those development initiatives that are "owned" and controlled by the people they aim to assist.[35] Involving greater numbers of poor people in the marketplace through microloans is supported by groups as diverse at the Grameen Bank and Catholic Relief Services.[36]

Public and private aid, therefore, should aim to increase participation of poor people in the economic and political life of their society. In countries with widespread corruption, this means placing conditions on aid to prevent it from ending up in the pockets of the ruling elite. Through such conditions, donor countries and the international community can exert political and economic pressure to make governments more transparent and accountable. For example, continued corruption in Kenya, vividly revealed by what many believe to have been the stealing of the December 2007 election, continues to impede that country's development. The United States and World Bank have both been exerting considerable political and economic pressure on the Kenyan government to clean up its act and should continue to do so.[37]

The Kenyan case also illustrates why working to prevent internal conflicts and civil war must become a central goal in development strategy. Following the 2007 Kenyan election, violent conflicts broke out along ethnic and class lines in numerous parts of the country. These conflicts were rooted in the belief of some ethnic communities, particularly the Luo, that other ethnic groups, particularly the Kikuyu, had been using their control of political power to their own

---

[34] See World Bank, *Global Monitoring Report: Millennium Development Goals, Strengthening Mutual Accountability, Aid, Trade, and Governance* (2006), *http://siteresources.worldbank.org/INTGLOBAL MONITORING2006/Resources/2186625-1145565069381/GMR06Complete.pdf*.

[35] See Oxfam America, *Ownership in Practice: The Key to Smart Development*, research report, September 21, 2009, *http://www.oxfamamerica.org/publications/ownership-in-practice-the-key-to-smart-development*.

[36] See the CRS microloan webpage at *http://crs.org/microfinance*.

[37] See US Secretary of State Hilary Rodham Clinton, "Remarks with Kenyan Foreign Minister Moses Wetangula," Nairobi, Kenya, August 5, 2009, *http://www.state.gov/secretary/rm/2009a/08/126890.htm*.

economic advantage. Ethnic tensions in Kenya are complex, but the postelection violence there is a clear example of how civil conflict and lack of economic development can be closely linked in poor nations.[38] Work for development in such contexts can thus require political and diplomatic efforts to address the roots of conflict in order to prevent it.

Private corporations and banks conducting business in developing countries have a responsibility to ensure their activity does not deepen corruption or enhance the wealth and power of elites in ways that hurt and oppress the poor majority. The UN Global Compact, initiated by Secretary General Kofi Annan in 2000, affirms that private corporations, as the primary agents driving globalization, should support human rights and oppose corruption. When corporations do this, they "can help ensure that markets, commerce, technology and finance advance in ways that benefit economies and societies everywhere."[39] Though the implementation of this compact is far from adequate, it signals that the responsibility to address the economic impact of globalization on the poor falls on corporations as well as governments.

Development policy today thus needs to address issues ranging from the strictly economic (such as GNP growth, increased investment, and access to credit) to the political (such as good governance, the prevention of war, and access to health care and education among poor people). Pursuing desired outcomes in these areas will require the engagement of many different actors: governments (through bilateral assistance and governmental funding of private initiatives), intergovernmental organizations (through the activities pursued by agencies such as the World Bank, the UN Development Program, and the Inter-American Development Bank), private commercial and financial corporations, and nongovernmental and faith-based organizations (such as Oxfam and CRS).

The challenge of alleviating poverty in the developing world today can be envisioned as calling to a variety of actors, private and public, to make diverse contributions to the overall development project, contributions including governmental grants and loans, investments that avoid exploitation, and projects by secular and church-based development NGOs. This can lead to envisioning the development challenge as a grid, in which the rows are the health, educational, financial, investment, credit, political, and other needs of particular developing societies and the columns are the actors that can help respond to these needs. Promoting development that will alleviate poverty, therefore, calls for each set of needs to be addressed by one or more relevant actors. No one actor can address every need; rather, each actor has specific responsibilities to contribute in responding to needs.

---

[38] See Collier, *Wars, Guns, and Votes*, esp. ch. 5, "Wars: The Political Economy of Destruction."

[39] "Overview of the UN Global Compact," *http://www.unglobalcompact.org/aboutthegc/index.html.*

◫ CONCLUSION

Seeking justice for the poor in our globalizing world raises challenges not only for governments and intergovernmental bodies, but for all actors who benefit from or affect the way global activity impacts poor people. That includes virtually all of us. The responsibilities we have to help raise up poor people will depend on our capacity and power to do so. In all cases, acting on such responsibility should seek to move toward greater equality and reciprocity and away from conditions of inequality and domination. Since the challenge of alleviating poverty is complex, responding to it calls for numerous partnerships among private, governmental, and intergovernmental bodies. It also calls for individuals dedicated to exercising leadership for greater global justice in the many spheres where aiding poor people is possible and necessary.

Globalization thus means that the challenge of *EJA* today is somewhat different than it was when the bishops issued their letter twenty-five years ago. But this challenge remains as demanding and controversial today as it was when the document first appeared.

FOCUS QUESTIONS

1. What are some of the key moral challenges raised by the growing reality of economic globalization?

2. Why do the bishops see a strong interconnection between the dignity of the human person and the solidarity and interdependence that form communities?

3. Is it appropriate to set limits on the free market in the name of moral standards of justice? Why or why not?

4. Is aid to poor, developing countries by rich, developed countries effective? Is it morally required?

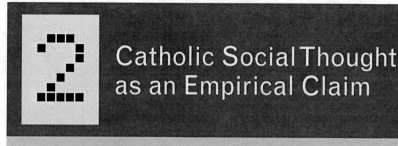

2 Catholic Social Thought as an Empirical Claim

Daniel K. Finn

■ INTRODUCTION

The US bishops' 1986 pastoral letter *Economic Justice for All* (*EJA*) contributes to a long line of official Catholic Church teachings on the economy. As a part of that tradition, *EJA* is radically novel in but one way: it is the result of an open consultation with economists, other social scientists, and a wide variety of others in the drafting process. After writing a first draft, the committee of bishops responsible for *EJA* held a series of public meetings around the United States to receive testimony from a wide variety of citizens. Church authorities in Rome later discouraged the US bishops from such a public reliance on consultation because it appeared to them to undermine the bishops' teaching authority—as it might seem the bishops didn't know what to teach until they consulted with laity.[1] On the other hand, nearly everyone agreed afterward that the consultation not only strengthened the document but arguably turned it into the most publically discussed text in the history of the US Catholic Church.

From a similar desire to learn from diverse perspectives, Pope John Paul II consulted some two dozen world-renowned economists prior to publishing his statement on economics, *Centesimus annus* (On the Hundredth Anniversary of *Rerum Novarum*), in 1991. Thus, not only the US bishops but the pope himself endorsed a fuller dialogue between theology and economics as an essential step in developing the tradition of Catholic social thought and making it relevant to the contemporary context.

Convinced that this consultative approach is fruitful, the Institute for Advanced Catholic Studies began the True Wealth of Nations research project.[2]

---

[1] Oral conversation between the author and the chair of the bishops' committee, Archbishop Rembert Weakland.

[2] *The True Wealth of Nations: Catholic Social Thought and Economic Life*, ed. Daniel K. Finn (Oxford: Oxford University Press, 2010).

This project hosts a careful and sophisticated conversation across the boundary between theology and economics and includes not just theologians and economists but other humanists and social scientists. Two particular elements characterize this effort: a focus on *prosperity* and a *basic empirical proposition*; namely, that "the economic and cultural criteria identified in the tradition of Catholic social thought provide an effective path to sustainable prosperity for all."[3]

First, while economists are very much at home speaking of wealth as the goal of economic life, theologians are more accustomed to focus on well-being. It is difficult to have a conversation between these groups about the morality of economic life when the goals each seeks differ from those of the other. Misunderstandings arise almost immediately. But the notion of prosperity bridges the gap between the two disciplines because prosperity not only entails economic wealth but also stretches economists' perspectives beyond economic wealth toward notions of well-being and stretches theologians' perspectives to specify dimensions of well-being in economic life.

Prosperity is helpfully described as the opposite of what occurs in Thomas Hobbes' state of nature, in which life is famously described as "solitary, poor, nasty, brutish, and short." Real prosperity is the opposite of all of these characteristics, not just the second.[4] Life is truly prosperous when it is communal, flourishing, hospitable, humane, and long-lived.

The second element (the basic empirical element) is grounded in the claim of Catholic social thought that individuals and nations should conduct their economic lives in certain ways and that the morally right thing to do is that which most contributes to human fulfillment. This is an empirical claim: that implementing Catholic social thought will actually be better for people. Just as with the use of the word *prosperity*, this empirical claim allows theologians and economists to participate in a common research project and in so doing stretches both groups. Because this is an empirical claim about the impact of Catholic social thought, it presses economists to consider causal factors beyond those easily measured. And because it is an empirical claim and not simply a moral claim, it stretches theologians to grapple with whether implementing Catholic social thought would indeed improve the economy.

■■ THE HISTORICAL IMPACT OF CATHOLIC SOCIAL THOUGHT

Any assessment of what Catholic social thought can do to put a nation on a path to sustainable prosperity for all must first explore what the tradition has already

---

[3] The True Wealth of Nations Project, basic statement, *http://www.ifacs.com/programs/wealth/report/index.html*.

[4] The Catholic Bishops of England and Wales, "The Common Good and the Catholic Churches' Social Teaching," conference statement, 1996.

accomplished. Two European scholars, husband and wife Stefano and Vera Negri Zamagni, have examined the late-medieval cultural preparation for modern economic markets and the remarkable impact of Catholic social thought on the rise of Christian democracy in Western Europe in the twentieth century.

The birth of the market economy often is traced to sixteenth- or seventeenth-century Britain, a premise for which the fullest expressions are perhaps articulated by Adam Smith and others in the late eighteenth century. Stefano Zamagni, however, argues that the market economy began much earlier, in late-medieval Italy, when Franciscan friars began rethinking economic life. Because of their embrace of poverty, Zamagni argues, Franciscans were uniquely able to envision an economic system that would better help ordinary people, that is, the poor. Starting with the work of Giovanni Olivi in the thirteenth century, capital was understood as a sum of money assigned to a business that contains "a seed of gain."[5] The understanding was that someone employing such resources and taking a risk can often generate new wealth with that seed money.

The Franciscans developed many of the institutions of modern economic life on which we now depend. Theirs were the first banks (pawn banks), allowing the poor to make economic use of their assets. Franciscan Luca Pacioli invented double-entry bookkeeping. And Franciscans were responsible for numerous other structural changes, including institutions called the *commendam* (forerunner of today's limited liability corporation), bills of exchange, and the first stock exchanges.

Zamagni recounts an economic and civic rebirth that, long before the Industrial Revolution, included technological change, the rise of small manufacturing (mostly textiles), and the development of larger economic institutions. This economic organization Zamagni refers to as "the civil economy," a system that flourished in the thirteenth, fourteenth, and fifteenth centuries that was able, he argues, to integrate novel economic organizational structures with a fundamental morality that kept economic life subservient to humanity's higher goals. According to Zamagni, this civil economy was indeed a market economy as it included three "governing principles" that define markets: the division of labor, accumulation and development, and freedom of enterprise (including creativity, risk-taking, entrepreneurial coordination of the work of many others, and competition among economic agents). This, Zamagni argues, was indeed a competitive market, for it exhibited the three elements necessary for economic competition: freedom of every interacting person, rational pursuit of interests, and well-defined rules enforced by an authority outside the economic game.

Zamagni emphasizes, however, this competition was done with the common good in mind, joining profitability with virtue, a dynamic frequently stressed by

---

[5] Stefano Zamagni, "Catholic Social Thought, Civil Economy, and the Spirit of Capitalism," in *True Wealth*, 65.

the Franciscan theorists of the day. Thus, Zamagni argues, the economic problems experienced today are largely attributable to the fact that we have capitalist markets, not civil markets. The unique characteristic of capitalist markets, he argues, is an intellectual commitment not to the *common* good but to the *total* good, as occurs in utilitarianism. The unfortunate part of focusing on the total good, according to Zamagni, is that per capita economic income becomes the measure of economic success, even if sizable proportions of the population remain in dire poverty.

Intellectually, the consensus of Italy's civil economic era was first challenged by the political "realism" of Machiavelli and later Hobbes and, economically speaking, was then even more fundamentally undermined by the analysis of classical political economists, from Adam Smith to David Ricardo to John Stuart Mill. Thus, Zamagni proposes, the intellectual task is to sharpen the awareness of the conflicting philosophical premises and political consequences of these two conceptions of market: civil and capitalist. Part of the challenge, and the cause of the resistance of mainstream economics to change over the last two centuries, he believes, has been the intellectual mistake represented in economists' view of *rationality* and *interest*. Here Zamagni recounts the well-known story of how a person's interests become only self-interest, and any efforts to help others become interpreted as simply another form of self-interest and thus indistinguishable from outright selfishness, at least as understood within an economic framework.

Catholic social thought has consistently offered alternate interpretations of human life and economic interaction. Zamagni's research serves as a reminder that human life and economic interaction were not always interpreted as they are by today's economists and that the hope of reestablishing a more humane, yet vibrant, economic life will best be served by attending to core concepts stemming from the history of Catholic social thought.

Vera Negri Zamagni outlines the history of the political impact of Catholic social thought in the late nineteenth century.[6] Americans today tend to be largely ignorant of the history Negri Zamagni articulates. Put briefly, the development of center-left "Christian democratic" political parties across Europe in the twentieth century (e.g., the German Christian Democratic Union) and their subsequent dominance in many nations following World War II were heavily dependent upon the participation of Catholics in the political process, people who self-consciously implemented the principles of Catholic social thought in creating economies with a more humane face. This remains a challenge in the United States, in that many conservative Americans today think the European economy works badly—a view shared by only a minority of Europeans, who tend to rate their quality of life above that of

---

[6] Vera Negri Zamagni, "The Political and Economic Impact of Catholic Social Thought since 1891: Christian Democracy and Christian Labor Unions in Europe," in *True Wealth*, 95–115.

Americans.[7] But if this American perception is inaccurate, it nonetheless suggests the political challenge faced by North American Catholics who want to transform the US economy in light of Catholic social thought. Having traced some of the early implementations of Catholic social thought in economics, we now turn to what this tradition advocates in terms of economic justice.

■■ WHAT DOES CATHOLIC SOCIAL THOUGHT RECOMMEND?

Catholic social thought is notoriously complicated, not in the difficulty of any single idea used, but in the complex, nearly organic, relationship of its parts. There is no single concept logically superior to all others from which all others are deductively derived. Rather, there is an intricate interrelationship among concepts, with ideas providing support for other notions and also drawing their cogency from those other notions. Hans von Balthasar, one of the most prominent Catholic theologians of the twentieth century, describes this characteristic of Catholic thought as its "symphonic nature." That is, in the intellectual analysis of the common good and in anyone's efforts to further the common good, the various elements entailed depend upon one another for their meaning, harmony, and effect. Albino Barrera, OP, an economist and theologian, provides an organizing principle and summary of what Catholic social thought recommends for a responsible economic life.[8] Barrera begins with one of the most basic ideas in Catholic social thought, the common good. He notes that the common good itself is a complex idea, one that seems to have no universally accepted definition. Barrera begins, where many do, with the notion of the common good as articulated in *Gaudium et spes* (The Church in the Modern World). There, the *common good* is defined as "the sum total of social conditions which allow people, either as groups or as individuals, to reach their fulfillment more fully and more easily."[9]

Documents by popes or councils of bishops are not written in an academic style, in which definitions are tight and all questions are answered. Thus, further simplification is needed. Barrera accomplishes this by focusing not on the common good (which encompasses all spheres of social life) but on "the economic common good." In other words, the minimum conditions necessary in *economic life* for human flourishing. In the Catholic tradition, *the* common

---

[7] For an independent annual rating of quality of life, see, for example, the "Quality of Life Index," which regularly ranks several European nations above the United States, *http://internationalliving. com/2010/02/quality-of-life-2010/*.

[8] Albino Barrera, "What Does Catholic Social Thought Recommend for the Economy? The Economic Common Good as a Path to True Prosperity," in *True Wealth*, 13–36.

[9] *Gaudium et spes*, par. 26.

good is God, but the term *common good* is used analogically in Catholic social thought to refer to what Barrera calls "the functional integrity of the person and community."[10]

Barrera specifies the scope of the minimum economic conditions for human flourishing with the help of the scriptural notion of *sedeq* (righteousness or justice). Drawing on scholarship concerning this central theme of biblical theology, Barrera identifies four dimensions of divine righteousness that the Hebrew tradition calls people to participate in: *sedeq* as an innate quality of God, *sedeq* as the appropriate order of God's plan in creation and law, *sedeq* as God's saving act, and *sedeq* "as an empowering divine gift to humans to continue the work of God and as a Divine invitation for people to be righteous themselves."[11]

From this analysis of the biblical notion of *sedeq*, Barrera ascribes three particular characteristics to the notion of the common good:

1. The common good is part of a divinely created order and serves this order. Thus, the requirements of the common good are not a matter of whim or opinion but of an objective order: humans will actually be happier when the common good is achieved.

2. The pursuit of the common good is a means by which humans partake of the divine activity that sustains the order of creation. Thus, the obligations of the common good are not some sort of difficult imposition from the outside, but a divine gift through which believers participate in God's governance.

3. The common good is founded on the proper ordering of the goods of human life, material and immaterial.

Barrera clarifies this commitment to the economic common good by identifying four more specific intermediate means: pursuit of an overarching common good, integral human development for oneself, integral human development for others, and care of the earth. Developing this line of thought further, he points to three social principles of modern Catholic social thought: the gift of self, the gift of each other, and the gift of earth. For him, each of these is critical to the notion of integral human development that is so central to the notion of a fulfilling human life in modern Catholic social thought. Barrera then identifies the other fundamental concepts widely employed in Catholic social thought. Subsidiarity becomes an expression of the gift of the self, solidarity relates to the gift of each other, and universal destination of goods and stewardship is rooted in the gift of the earth.

From this framework comes an explanation of why Catholic social thought so often includes a both/and dimension, because it so often affirms the best

---

[10] Barrera, "What Does Catholic Social Thought Recommend" 16.

[11] Ibid.

elements of conflicting political positions held by liberals and conservatives. Several examples will help. Catholic social thought both affirms the right to private property and insists on obligations based in the universal destination of goods. It relies on the private sector and also government as agents of development. It encourages freedom of enterprise and private initiative yet calls for safeguards to protect the interests of workers and the poor. It praises both market and nonmarket mechanisms for allocating resources within the economy. It insists on both efficiency and equity as goals in political economy, attending to the allocative and distributive dimensions of the price mechanism. Last, Catholic social thought recognizes the importance of government in guaranteeing economic rights even though integral human development is primarily the obligation of the individual.[12]

An example may be helpful in indicating the richness of this approach in deciding whether any particular nation has or has not implemented the recommendations of this tradition. Catholic social thought insists that everyone's needs be met and that this is ordinarily done through each worker's gainful employment. One might then measure the degree to which a nation has implemented what Catholic social thought recommends concerning one particular issue—say, the proper role of government in securing economic rights—by examining a number of proxies: in this case, the codification of economic rights in legislation; the presence of unemployment insurance, food stamps, housing and energy assistance; the provision of trade adjustment assistance in the face of the effects of international trade; the percentage of population without health insurance; the presence of job training and placement programs; as well as universal education and subsidized college education. Similarly, one might test whether the recommendations of Catholic social thought for justice between generations (whether those alive today or yet to be born) have been implemented by looking at the size of national and state debts, of personal debts at death, and at unfunded liabilities for Medicare, Social Security, and pensions, both public and private.

Any attempt at an econometric testing of the basic proposition that the implementation of the economic principles of Catholic social thought promotes sustainable prosperity for all would have to employ such measures to discern the degree to which a nation had in fact implemented the recommendations of Catholic social thought. Clearly, it remains true that no one should hold the illusion that an econometric test could be fully adequate, in that these proxies are only approximate, and other forms of evidence, both scientific and humanistic, are critical in assessing the validity of the claim.

---

[12] Ibid., 26

■ WHAT IS SUSTAINABLE PROSPERITY FOR ALL?

By identifying four goods essential to prosperity, economist Andrew Yuengert attempts to summarize what Catholic social thought holds as "sustainable prosperity for all."

As with Barrera's project, Yuengert faces a constant challenge in distinguishing means from ends. Whereas Barrera faces the problem of specifying the means that Catholic social thought recommends independent of the goals sought, Yuengert faces the problem of specifying the ends in a way that clearly separates them from the means. For example, although universal access to health care might seem to be a goal of Catholic social thought, in fact it is a means to the health of real persons. Health might result from any number of health-care and health-insurance systems and there should be no a priori assumption that there is but one morally correct way to organize either of these. Thus, the health of persons, not the presence of a particular health-care guarantee, must be part of the definition of prosperity.

Similarly, the Catholic tradition speaks of a large number of social institutions necessary for human prosperity. But, Yuengert argues (along with French political theorist Jacques Maritain, who helped draft the Universal Declaration of Human Rights), "the common good is common because it is received in persons."[13] Thus Yuengert proceeds to specify the nature of prosperity primarily as the fulfillment of individual persons. Part of that fulfillment certainly comes from an individual's participation in social institutions, but Yuengert further narrows the meaning of sustainable prosperity for all to the concrete experiences of persons themselves.

Beginning with a standard Christian understanding of human nature, Yuengert then highlights five dimensions of the belief that humans are created in the image of God:

1. The human person is a self-conscious subject, not merely an object.

2. Every person enjoys human freedom.

3. Each person possesses a fundamental human dignity.

4. Persons are not only individual but also inescapably social.

5. The human person is both matter and spirit.

Noting that this sustainable prosperity cannot be measured simply in terms of income, Yuengert concludes by identifying four kinds of goods requisite to any truly prosperous community, relying on an ethic of virtue in this articulation.

---

[13] Andrew M. Yuengert, "What Is 'Sustainable Prosperity for All' in the Catholic Social Tradition?" in *True Wealth*, 39.

The goods of personal character come first, including the cardinal virtues of temperance, fortitude, prudence, and justice. Thus, no matter how wealthy a nation, if its people are not virtuous, Yuengert would not ascribe prosperity to it.

Second are the goods of personal initiative, extending from the initiation of a new family to the creation of new firms, new ideas and technologies, new community initiatives, and so on. Yuengert argues that it is unlikely that a nation without a thriving sense of personal initiative would be either wealthy or virtuous. But if such were possible, it would not be truly prosperous without, in a Catholic view, a strong sense of individual initiative.

For Yuengert, the third set of goods in any prosperous society is consistent social relations: a rich network of such relations is necessary for a communion of persons to emerge. Recognizing, as Catholic social thought does, the importance of social relations pushes to a stress point the earlier distinction in this essay between the social means of prosperity and the ends of prosperity. That is, in Yuengert's analysis, community and political and economic institutions constitute important means of prosperity, but it is the engagement and enjoyment of those relationships by individual persons that constitute the end of prosperity. Nonetheless, if one were to attempt to measure such realities, far more than the subjective reports of individuals would be necessary, since social entities are humanly good in the Catholic tradition, and thus are responsibly considered ends within human life and not just means.

This insight is analogous to the widely recognized idea that one does not become happy by striving to be happy. One doesn't become fulfilled by striving for fulfillment. Catholics and many others assert that one comes to true happiness—fulfillment—by living out a full and virtuous human life and, having done so, one's reaction is to be happy about it, to feel fulfilled. Similarly here, persons who engage in social institutions only to gain certain psychological returns are understood as never attaining the appropriate goal. Rather, each person in numerous ways invests in social organizations—from family to civic organizations to government at various levels—in ways that hold those social entities as valuable in themselves. According to Yuengert, it is only out of such dedicated service to the common good that individuals attain a sense of fulfilling social relationships.

Material goods are certainly among the goods necessary in any truly prosperous society. Here, the Catholic vision requires that each person order these goods to their ultimate end in God. Thus, Yuengert points out, a crass consumerism must be rejected. Nonetheless, the tradition also recognizes the richness that material goods can provide and simultaneously insists that distributive justice be attentive to the achievement of appropriate levels of material goods by all persons.

Clearly, there is an intricate relationship among Yuengert's four sets of goods—virtues, personal initiative, social relations, and material goods—that is essential to any Catholic insight into true prosperity. There is no common metric for measuring these four such that a person or society as a whole could do without one if the other three were sufficiently strong. This position returns to the insight about Thomas Hobbes' view of the state of nature: life in a truly prosperous nation is *not* solitary, poor, nasty, brutish, or short.

Yuengert reminds his readers of a remarkable turn of attention on the part of many mainstream economists in the last quarter century, in which economists examine a number of the dimensions of true prosperity that lie beyond the notion of economic wealth. Perhaps best-known among these efforts is the work of Amartya Sen on "the capabilities approach" to human development. Sen's insights have since been woven into the UN Development Program's Human Development Index.[14] Similarly, there is a large and growing field called "happiness economics," which is responding to the empirical fact that beyond a certain level of income, more income increases the subjective perception of human happiness only temporarily and one's level of happiness soon drops back to that prior to the increase in income. This challenges the traditional economic commitment to rising economic living standards as the goal for economic life.

■■ SOCIAL CAPITAL AND CATHOLIC SOCIAL THOUGHT

The analysis of economic life developed by contemporary Catholic social thought can be improved by the inclusion of the notion of social capital. John Coleman, SJ, provides an insightful inquiry into the notion of "social capital," both as it arose in sociology and as it has come to be employed more broadly in economics and beyond. Coleman concludes that not only does the social scientific notion of social capital have much to contribute to Catholic social thought but also that Catholic social thought can be used to widen and deepen social scientists' grasp of social realities implicit in the notion of social capital.

The social capital literature within sociology is founded on the premise that "relationships matter." That is, social networks of themselves are a valuable asset in a society's capacity to produce wealth and well-being for its people. Coleman proceeds by drawing on the history of this notion as articulated in the work of American economist Glenn Loury, French sociologist Pierre Bourdieu, and American sociologists James Coleman and Robert Putnam. Each of these theorists uniquely employs a notion of social capital to illuminate economic and social realities. Each theory has its strengths and weaknesses. For example, Bourdieu gives a strong leftist interpretation of social capital and applies it to both production and reproduction of class divisions in society, overlooking

---

[14] Amartya K. Sen, *Commodities and Capabilities* (Oxford: Oxford University Press, 1985).

more positive features of social capital, even among the poor in their attempts to provide for themselves. Coleman corrects this error in applying the notion to non-elite groups but misses the important contribution that Bourdieu makes in linking social capital to the functions of power in society.

Putnam's distinction between "bonding" social capital (strengthening relationships within a group) and "bridging" social capital (strengthening ties with persons outside of one's group) provides a helpful addition to this analysis. Nonetheless, Putnam also falls short in that he discusses largely the positive effects of social capital without recognizing that it has been similarly important in the smooth operation of organized crime or the Nazi Party in interwar Germany.

Coleman goes on to remind us that the use of notions of trust in the work of Francis Fukuyama represents an important integration of the sociological notion of social capital into economic analysis. Fukuyama, certainly, has reminded everyone of the importance of shared norms and trust in those apparently self-interested relationships of contract and rationality within economics. Without reciprocity, moral obligation, duty, and trust, the economic system would itself collapse. As Coleman puts it, "rational utility maximization is not enough to give a full or satisfactory account of why successful economies prosper or unsuccessful ones stagnate and decline."[15]

Coleman reviews the importance of social capital to not only societal development but also the life and growth of profit-making firms. This awareness of the importance of this notion of social capital has also been demonstrated in the recent work of the World Bank and its articulation of its development agenda, a change that holds out real hope for improving the lives of the world's poorest people.

The notion of social capital has not yet been integrated into Catholic social thought; indeed, the phrase has yet to appear in any papal documents on economic life. Yet Coleman argues there are large areas of common concern in the articulation of Catholic social thought and the thinking that undergirds the notion of social capital in social science literature. Catholic social thought holds the view of humans as profoundly relational and has spoken clearly for the last two centuries about the importance of civil society. This, Coleman argues, speaks positively about the potential for integrating the notions of social capital into Catholic social thought.

In sum, Coleman identifies three distinct but interrelated elements in the notion of social capital: a structural element, a cognitive element, and a moral/affective element.[16] Catholic social thought has emphasized both the structural element (in the importance of social groups independent of both the market and the state) and the moral/affective element (in the importance of trust and

---

[15] John A. Coleman, "Wealth Creation, Social Virtues, and Sociality: Social Capital's Role in Creating and Sustaining Wealth," in *True Wealth*, 211.

[16] Ibid., 219.

the other social virtues). However, Coleman argues it is in the cognitive realm that Catholic social thought has the most to gain in adopting this notion of social capital. Social capital is essential for the creation and sustenance of wealth and well-being and this concept can provide Catholic social thought a conceptual framework for understanding that relationship. At the same time, however, Coleman contends the Catholic idea of the common good is "much more nuanced and subtle than the thinner social capital concept."[17]

One of the reasons for a rightful concern about too easy an integration of the social capital notion into Catholic social thought is that the social virtues, trust, and human sociology cannot in the Catholic tradition be thought of as simply means to an end, as a utilitarian view of social capital might imply. Rather Catholic social thought understands these as goods in their own right. Still an integration of these ideas with careful distinctions holds promise, he argues, for not only strengthening the capacity of Catholic social thought to articulate more precisely the moral dimension of the economy but also providing a more vivid and nuanced characterization of human sociality than exists today in much of the social capital literature in social science.

▪▪ CONCLUSION

The US bishops' pastoral letter *Economic Justice for All* arose from a process that the bishops implicitly recommended to all Catholics: to listen to the voices of both science and theology in any attempt to say what the tradition of Catholic social thought means for economic life today. This challenge is a difficult one, in part because the tradition arose in centuries past, when people thought quite differently about daily life than most people do today.

Mary Hirschfeld has noted that because the Catholic tradition employs many notions generated by Thomas Aquinas and others of centuries ago, such insights sometimes cannot be adequately characterized by a simple "translation" from Latin into English. The presumption in translation is that the same conceptual framework is available on both sides of the translation fence and one simply needs to find the proper words in a second language to articulate that which the first language had to say. The difference provided by seven centuries of intellectual ferment is that there are not easily available contemporary concepts that capture many of the ideas that form the foundations of Catholic social thought.

Thus, the True Wealth of Nations project follows on the US bishops' efforts to encourage, as this volume does, the careful study of both the theological and economic analyses necessary for an adequate application of the tradition of Catholic social thought to economic life today.

---

[17] Ibid.

FOCUS QUESTIONS

1. The True Wealth of Nations research project begins with the claim that "the economic and cultural criteria identified in the tradition of Catholic social thought provide an effective path to sustainable prosperity for all." Why is this claim helpful as a starting point for theologians and economists who aim to dialogue about morality and economic life?

2. Name five means and five ends that Catholic social thought recommends for the economy.

3. How is the notion of "social capital" related to trust? In what way could this notion (which is an analogy based on the economic idea of "capital") deepen moral reflection on the economy?

4. What difference would it make in debates today about the morality of capitalism if Stefano Zamagni is correct in arguing that the market economy first began in late-medieval Italy and not in seventeenth-century England?

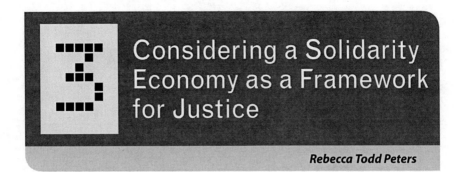

3. Considering a Solidarity Economy as a Framework for Justice

Rebecca Todd Peters

■ INTRODUCTION

Bill Curtis cut cloth for thirty years for Broyhill Industries in North Carolina, the heart of the US furniture market.[1] Furniture making, which is centered in the Piedmont area of North Carolina, has been a major employer in the state since the early 1900s, providing as many as ninety thousand jobs at the peak of manufacturing in 1990.[2] However, cheap wages overseas and limited environmental regulation have contributed to a major outsourcing of jobs, including Curtis' job, which was outsourced to China in 2005.[3] With jobs in the furniture industry drying up, Curtis decided to retool his employment skills and began studying information technology at Caldwell Community College. When Google announced they were opening a data center in Lenoir, Curtis was hopeful his new skills might land him a job in the information economy that was replacing the blue-collar work he had always known. In October 2007, Curtis completed his three-year training program and was ready for his interview with Google.[4] Unfortunately, at 55, he was competing with many younger, more tech-savvy applicants who had grown up with computers. After several months of searching for an IT job, Curtis took a part-time job as a corrections officer where

---

[1] Frank Langfitt, "Laid-Off Furniture Workers Try to Leap to Google," *All Things Considered,* National Public Radio, December 16, 2009, *http://www.npr.org/templates/story/story.php?storyId=121516133&ps=rs.*

[2] North Carolina in the Global Economy, "Furniture," *http://www.soc.duke.edu/NC_GlobalEconomy/furniture/overview.shtml.*

[3] Frank Langfitt, "High-Tech Dreams Dissipate for Furniture Workers," *All Things Considered,* National Public Radio, December 17, 2009, *http://www.npr.org/templates/story/story.php?storyId=121567306&ps=rs.*

[4] Ibid.

he earned $26,000 annually, which was not enough to pay his bills. After his wife, Janet, lost her furniture job in the recession, he picked up a second part-time job at Walmart for $9 an hour.[5]

■■ THE LOSS OF LIVING WAGES AND BENEFITS

Furniture represents just one of many industries that offered the kind of mid-range factory work that built the working class in the United States. Much of the work in textiles, furniture, steel, automobile, and other manufacturing sectors was not only repetitive but backbreaking, exhausting work. However, for most people, it paid the bills. Blue-collar manufacturing jobs that paid workers a reasonable wage, offered health-care benefits, and provided pension plans were a significant part of what built a healthy and wealthy US economy in the twentieth century. Even before the 2008 economic crisis, adherents of the current form of economic globalization, known as neoliberalism, argued that the current restructuring and retooling of the US economy is simply the market at work. From a neoliberal perspective, the unionized jobs in auto, textile, and other industries that once offered living wages and decent benefits are now inefficient relics of an old world order. Businesses simply don't have to pay what they used to in wages, not in a globalized economy—not when they can outsource parts manufacturing or even open assembly plants in developing countries where wages are far lower. Why pay a US furniture worker like Bill Curtis $14 an hour when they can pay a Chinese worker less than a dollar?[6] The logic of the system is impeccable—when production costs are lowered, profits are raised.

The changes that accompany increased global economic integration, however, raise deep moral concerns. The massive outsourcing of jobs in the last thirty years has brought increasing economic divides within and between first-world countries. Census data shows that income inequality in the United States has risen consistently in the last forty years, with increasing numbers of affluent and poor and a shrinking middle class.[7] In 2008, there were 39.8 million people living in poverty in the United States, roughly 13.2 percent of the population.[8]

---

[5] Ibid.

[6] In 2004, furniture workers in the United States earned $14.24 per hour; their Chinese counterparts, meanwhile, made just $.69 an hour. North Carolina in the Global Economy, "Furniture," *http://www.soc.duke.edu/NC_GlobalEconomy/furniture/overview.shtml*.

[7] Sean F. Reardon and Kendra Bischoff, "Growth in the Residential Segregation of Families by Income, 1970–2009," Stanford University, November 2011, *http://graphics8.nytimes.com/packages/pdf/national/RussellSageIncomeSegregationreport.pdf*.

[8] Carmen DeNavas-Walt, Bernadette D. Proctor, Jessica C. Smith, "Income, Poverty and Health Insurance Coverage in the United States: 2008," US Census Bureau, September 2009.

According to US Census Bureau data, 57 percent of those living in poverty were working full- or part-time. It is difficult, if not impossible, for people working in low-wage service jobs (often the only jobs available to low-skilled workers) to pull themselves above the poverty line. Increasingly, middle- and upper-middle-class families struggling with job loss are also finding it difficult to feed their families.[9] The number of people struggling to put food on their tables (a situation known as "food insecurity") rose from 11 percent of the population in 2007 to 14.5 percent in 2010.[10] But not only are increasing numbers of US families facing basic challenges in the globalized economy, the Earth's delicate ecosystems are also struggling for survival.

■■ NEOLIBERAL ECONOMICS AND ENVIRONMENTAL SUSTAINABILITY

From an environmental perspective, the industrial global economy and the consumer lifestyles that support it are not sustainable. Environmentalist Mathis Wackernagel calculates the ecological footprint[11] of the human species outstretched the carrying capacity of Earth in the late 1970s and by 2003, exceeded it by 25 percent.[12] Environmentalists claim that it is possible to exceed Earth's carrying capacity for a limited time before human behavior depletes Earth's reservoir of natural resources like water, oil, coal, fish, wildlife, soil, and its capacity to assimilate chlorinated chemicals and carbon dioxide. More important, since Wackernagel's calculations are based on actual use of these resources, these numbers will rise as more countries develop their industrial capacity and increase their consumption levels. Projections warn that it would take 5.3 more planets to sustain the entire world living at current levels of US consumption.[13]

---

[9] Pam G. Dempsey, "Food Insecurity Grows in East Central Illinois," CU-Citizen Access, May 14, 2011, *http://cu-citizenaccess.org/content/hunger-heartland-local-residents-struggle-eat.*

[10] US Department of Agriculture, "Food Security in the United States: Key Statistics and Graphics," updated September 7, 2011, *http://www.ers.usda.gov/Briefing/FoodSecurity/stats_graphs. htm#very_low.*

[11] Wackernagel developed the concept of the ecological footprint to measure the amount of land area necessary to support a particular lifestyle. His calculations are based on Earth's annual productivity and regenerative capacity. *State of the World 2004* (New York: W.W. Norton and Co., 2004), 291–2.

[12] *Living Planet Report 2006* (Gland, Switzerland: World Wildlife Fund, 2006), 2.

[13] Projections are from the Global Footprint Network, which specializes in measuring the ecological footprint of various societies. *Chinadependence: The Second UK Interdependence Report* (London: New Economics Foundation), 21, *http://www.neweconomics.org/gen/uploads/fmq2gmn5w2dn2qemwoor0m 4505102007192709.pdf.*

NEOLIBERALISM AND THE GLOBAL ECONOMY

The hyper-consumerism of twenty-first-century capitalism is, to some extent, a product of economic globalization and the ability of first-world consumers to stretch their dollars further by purchasing cheaper goods made in countries where wages are lower. Although the human community could manage economic globalization in many ways, since the early 1980s the dominant model for creating a single, integrated global economy has been neoliberalism. Also referred to as supply-side economics, the Washington consensus, trickle-down economics, or laissez-faire economics, neoliberalism argues for deregulation, privatization, and increased international trade in setting economic policy. In general, neoliberals dislike government involvement in the marketplace and argue that free-enterprise solutions are superior to government solutions.

The other school of thought that holds weight in the United States is that of social-equity liberals or welfare liberals who argue that government often has an important role to play in stimulating the economy (particularly during economic downturns) and in regulating the economy. Social-equity liberals have supported environmental regulations that check the power of industries to pollute and labor regulations that have created better working conditions in the United States than in the developing world.

Both neoliberalism and social-equity liberalism are rooted in an economic theory known as neoclassical economics.[14]

The creation of a single, integrated global economy—the goal of neoliberalism—requires increased consumer appetites for goods produced in foreign markets. While consumption in many parts of the world is certainly rising, US citizens, who comprise 5.2 percent of the world's population, account for 31.5 percent of the world's consumer spending,[15] consume one-third of the world's paper products,[16] and one-quarter of the world's coal, oil, and natural gas.[17] In the changing cultural context of an increasingly integrated global

---

[14] For a more nuanced analysis of neoliberalism and social-equity liberalism as well as two alternative theories of globalization, see Rebecca Todd Peters, *In Search of the Good Life: The Ethics of Globalization* (New York: Continuum, 2004).

[15] *State of the World 2004* (New York: W.W. Norton and Co., 2004), 6.

[16] Ibid., 9.

[17] Ibid., 11.

economy, much attention is placed on the economic consequences of neoliberal policies; however, it is also important to ask deep questions about the moral consequences of a neoliberal approach to globalization, production, and the world's social and environmental health and well-being. While neoclassical economic theory claims to be value-free, its emphasis on increasing profits and maximizing efficiency often come at the expense of the health of people and the environment. Considering the moral consequences of neoliberal economic globalization can begin by examining the long-term consequences for the health of the US economy and thinking about considerations that go beyond economic consequences. Manufacturing jobs have decreased by 20 percent since the implementation of the North American Free Trade Agreement (NAFTA) in 1994, and these jobs have largely been replaced by low-wage service jobs without benefits.[18] Government projections point to the greatest US growth in jobs related to computers, food preparation and service, customer service, security, medical assistance, and personal and home care—all jobs that often offer neither a living wage nor benefits.[19] While labor market shifts are nothing new, enthusiasm for shifts that threaten the stability of a nation's workforce ought to be met with caution.

From a moral perspective, it is also important to consider the kinds of jobs that are available in an economy and what kind of life these jobs allow people to create. Economists, social scientists, and politicians urge US citizens to prepare for an ongoing shift from an industrial to a postindustrial information economy. This shift is the direct result of neoliberal economic policies and attitudes regarding consumption, an approach that drives companies to seek the cheapest labor available. As people consider their support for such policies, they need to consider what these shifts mean for the quality of jobs available in the United States and the kinds of lives people can build when working these jobs. One of the moral considerations in constructing the global economy should be whether people are able to engage in meaningful work and provide for their families. People should also consider the environmental effects of the increase in transportation needed to ship goods made in one country and sold in another—not to mention the effects of the lax environmental laws that govern too many manufacturing facilities in developing countries.

With the increasing integration of cultures and societies that accompanies globalization, people must seek long-term solutions for the deep social problems shaping the world. Traditional indicators of economic health and progress, such as rising GDP and stock market values, do not necessarily translate into

---

[18] Public Citizen, "Debunking USTR Claims in Defense of NAFTA: The Real NAFTA Score 2008, *http://www.citizen.org/documents/NAFTA_USTR_Debunk_web.pdf*.

[19] Public Citizen, "The Ten Year Track Record of the North American Free Trade Agreement: U.S. Workers' Jobs, Wages and Economic Security," *NAFTA at Ten Series, http://www.citizen.org/documents/NAFTA_10_jobs.pdf*.

solutions for poverty, disease, obesity, illiteracy, unemployment, infant mortality, starvation, violence, and many other ills of the world. These social problems raise moral questions about how humans could organize economic structures in ways that contribute to the common good. These problems require long-term solutions that can only come when all sectors of the world (political, social, and economic) work together to make a difference.

The moral challenge that neoliberal globalization poses for Christians in the first world is how to act faithfully without expectation of gratitude, recognition, or commendation (Mt 6:1–4). The challenge of following Christ is to act without regard for personal recognition and with the knowledge that redressing injustice is what God calls Christians to do. If people want a different form of globalization and a world order marked by social justice and sustainability, then it is necessary to look for new ways of being in the world and new economic models that offer a path to achieve that goal. This chapter explores the ways a solidarity economy might offer such a pathway.

■ CONSIDERING A SOLIDARITY ECONOMY

The reality of neoliberal globalization is that people in the developed world are able to buy clothing, food, electronics, home goods, toys, and countless other products at shamefully low prices because they are made by people in the developing world who work for extraordinarily low wages. In a world where the structures of globalization privilege people in the developed world at the expense of their brothers and sisters in the developing world, *solidarity* is a way for first-world Christians to define their obligation to the distant other, to their global neighbor whom they do not know but to whom they are connected through the interdependence of God's created order. In this context, solidarity can be defined as a relationship between people or groups of people who are different from one another but who share mutual respect and a willingness to work together to address issues of social injustice. Solidarity describes a new vision of society built on shared bonds between people that call for loyalty, compassion, and companionship; bonds rooted in the *agape* (self-sacrificing) love of the Christian tradition. Learning how to live in solidarity with others is an expression of the call to "love your neighbor as yourself" (Mt 22:39). Observers of human nature note that it is far easier to practice this teaching when we know or like or feel kin to our neighbor in some way. However, Jesus teaches in the parable of the Good Samaritan that he expects people to see their neighbor even in those they do not know and might not like (Lk 10:25–37). Embracing solidarity as a moral norm means people must evaluate their individual and collective actions in terms of how they affect their neighbors—those next door and those across the globe.

First-world Christians, many of whom struggle with theological questions of privilege, blessings, and justice amid global poverty and inequality, need to develop a theology that helps them change both their own behavior and the unjust structures of the world around them. A theology of solidarity offers a new foundation upon which to build an ethic that calls Christians into covenant relationship and partnership with their brothers and sisters from the developing world. A theology of solidarity offers hope and the promise that sustainability is a more faithful and fulfilling life for Christians than consumption and the accumulation of wealth.

Solidarity in the Christian Tradition

The starting point for a theology of solidarity is the life and work of Jesus Christ. As the son of a carpenter raised in humble circumstances, Jesus sought commoners from his culture as partners in his ministry. He taught in accessible public spaces and was sought after by people who were on the margins of his society. He associated with and ministered to prostitutes, tax collectors, lepers, people with mental and physical infirmities and disease, adulterers, soldiers, fishermen, foreigners, children, widows, rich and poor alike. Jesus walked a path of solidarity with the people of his society. He preached a message of radical social transformation in which the blind would see, the lame would walk, lepers would be healed, the deaf would hear, the dead would live again, and the poor would have good news (Mt 11:4–5, 15:30–31; Lk 7:21–22). In this promise of a reversal of the social order of his day, Jesus offered a message of hope and good news to those who were oppressed and marginalized by the social, economic, and religious structures of his day. In proclaiming the meek would inherit the earth (Mt 5:5) and woe to the rich, the satisfied, and the happy (Lk 6:24–25), Jesus challenged the justice of the present social order and questioned the validity of the most powerful leaders of his day. He came with a vision for a new world order and practiced what he preached, living a life of deep solidarity with many who were "other" in his society. His commitment to an alternative worldview and uncompromising attitude toward seeing God's will done on earth as it is heaven was a radical witness to a life of solidarity, a witness that can serve as a model for solidarity as a contemporary Christian ethic.

To the extent that solidarity denotes a deep relationship of affection and mutuality between individuals or groups of people, it reflects the guiding normative value of love that has shaped Christian theology and practice from its earliest days. In both its *agape* (selfless love) and *philia* (love of friends and family) form, love is a dominant theme in the New Testament and the early Christian Church. The idea of solidarity in the social and political sense in which it is used by philosophers, social scientists, and politicians began to emerge in Christian thought in the late nineteenth century as both the Protestant and

Catholic churches struggled alongside their secular counterparts to discern appropriate responses to the changing social and political world wrought by the Industrial Revolution.

Within Protestant churches in the late nineteenth and early twentieth centuries, the Social Gospel movement in the United States and the Christian Socialist movement in Europe raised concerns about the growing tensions between the rising individualism in capitalist society and the reality of human interdependence even in the modern world. The exploitation and suffering of workers and people living in poverty prompted Protestant ministers, leaders, and laypeople to develop a theology of justice and compassion that supported the needs and interests of exploited workers by advocating public policy reforms including the minimum wage, worker safety standards, reasonable work weeks, and the end of child labor. In 1908 the Federal Council of Churches endorsed the Social Creed of the Churches, which detailed a social agenda for Protestants based on their faith commitments to justice and equality. While the Social Gospelers did not articulate solidarity as a foundation for their theology or movement, their work in partnership with marginalized and oppressed workers to improve their social situation and increase justice in society nonetheless reflects solidarity at heart.

The shift from the Middle Ages to the world of the Enlightenment also caused the Roman Catholic Church to rethink its role and position in society, particularly in the political realm. While papal authority and the magisterium had a long history of collusion regarding the political power and governance in Europe, the emerging democracies of the nineteenth century required Roman Catholics to rethink the relationship between politics and religion. In 1891 with the publication of *Rerum novarum* (The Condition of Labor), Pope Leo XIII signaled a new approach to the modern world that put to rest the ancient alliances between throne and altar.[20] *Rerum novarum* established the papacy's commitment to a just social order by declaring allegiance to the poor and needy in society and by reminding Roman Catholics of their Christian obligation to charity. Leo XIII did not leave responsibility for the poor solely to charity, however. He called for social reforms that would redress growing inequalities in society. Much like the Social Gospelers, without using the term *solidarity*, Roman Catholics called Christians to develop ministries and acts of social justice that would build social solidarity. *Rerum novarum* marked the beginning of what is now known as modern Catholic social teaching, or "the application of the word of God to people's lives and the life of society."[21]

---

[20] Steinar Stjernø, *Solidarity in Europe: The History of an Idea* (Cambridge: Cambridge University Press, 2004), 64.

[21] John Paul II, *Sollicitudo rei socialis* (On Social Concern), 1987, as quoted in Robert Ellsberg, "Introduction," in *The Logic of Solidarity: Commentaries on Pope John II's Encyclical "On Social Concern,"* eds. Gregory Baum and Robert Ellsberg (Maryknoll, NY: Orbis Books, 1989), ix.

This commitment to charity and social justice continued throughout the twentieth century. In 1961 Pope John XXIII introduced the idea of solidarity into papal discourse as he called for government assistance for people in need and government action to reduce economic inequality in societies and the world at large.[22] Philosopher Steinar Stjernø argues that the Roman Catholic concept of solidarity is rooted in compassion, in collective action to help the poor and underprivileged, and in recognition of the need to move beyond individual charity to fully address the inequality that threatens the world.[23] Solidarity finally becomes a central theme of Roman Catholic social teaching with the contributions of Pope John Paul II, who links the idea of solidarity with other key principles of Catholic social thought including the common good, love, justice, and subsidiarity. John Paul II focuses on solidarity as a concept that defines human relationships as bonds of family and friendship that then form the basis for the development of societies that actually care for their citizens—especially those who are the most marginalized and in need of assistance.

Solidarity in Economic Justice for All

The US bishop's pastoral on the economy, *Economic Justice for All* (*EJA*), offered a critique of the excesses of capitalism and argued for a stronger moral foundation for US economic policy and practice.[24] One of the foundational values that undergirded the bishops' critique and their vision of a more just future was that of *solidarity*, a term used thirty-five times in *EJA*. The pastoral advocates developing a "'New American Experiment'—to implement economic rights, to broaden the sharing of economic power, and to make economic decisions more accountable to the common good" (no. 21).

The term *solidarity* is used in several different ways in the document, each of which merits further examination. This examination reveals direct descriptions of what constitutes solidarity as well as implied definitions discernible through the rejection of that which is *not* representative of solidarity.[25] Most references to the term in the pastoral are fairly vague and assume a common understanding of what is meant by *solidarity*. However, ten times—almost one-third of the

---

[22] Stjernø, *Solidarity in Europe*, 68.

[23] Ibid.

[24] United States Catholic Bishops, *Economic Justice for All: Pastoral Letter on Catholic Social Teaching and the U.S. Economy* (Washington, DC: United States Catholic Conference, 1986).

[25] In his definition of *solidarity* in the *New Dictionary of Catholic Social Thought*, Matthew Lamb points out that Catholic social teaching on solidarity has largely been pastoral and there are "few systematic analyses of the scientific, philosophical, and theological implications" of solidarity. Lamb's observation appropriately describes the use of the term in *EJA* where *solidarity* is frequently used to describe the aspirations of human communities and behaviors but is never systematically defined. Lamb, "Solidarity," in *New Dictionary of Catholic Social Thought*, ed. Judith A. Dwyer (Collegeville, MN: Liturgical Press, 1994), 910.

references—the phrase "social solidarity" is used instead of merely "solidarity," although there does not appear to be anything particularly distinct that separates *social solidarity* from the simple use of the term *solidarity*. Nevertheless, despite the vague way in which the term is used, it is possible to discern four distinct ways in which the bishops use the term *solidarity*: (1) sixteen times it is used as a description of human community (nos. 33, 66, 67, 74, 105, 116, 185, 196, 248, 251, 252, 258, 322, 328, 342, 365); (2) eight times, as an action or practice (pastoral message, no. 24, *EJA* nos. 5, 73, 88, 102, 119 [twice], 250); (3) five times, as a principle or value (nos. 2, 13, 80, 83, 187); and (4) four times, as a relationship (nos. 28, 64, 79, 80). Furthermore, with regard to the first two uses of *solidarity*, there are a few places in which the bishops offer some substantive content, which begins to flesh out what they mean when they use the term.[26]

The first and most prominent way *solidarity* is used (43 percent of the time) is as a noun describing a particular type or quality of human community. Examples of what communities look like that possess solidarity include references to "social friendship and civic commitment that make human moral and economic life possible" (no. 66), "community . . . that recognize[s] the moral bonds among all people" (no. 258), and several references that imply a connection between the experience of solidarity and human dignity (nos. 196, 252, 322, 328, 342). Additionally, there is one explicit reference that links increasing employment opportunities to solidarity (no. 196). As referenced earlier, something can also be learned about what solidarity is by juxtaposing it against those things that can disrupt, destroy, or make solidarity difficult to achieve, namely, sin (nos. 33, 67), inequality (nos. 74, 185), violations of the freedom to associate (no. 105), individualism and greed (no. 248), and attachment to material things (no. 328).

Almost one-fourth of the uses of the term refer to solidarity in ways that suggest action, such as making a commitment (nos. 24, 55), confronting attitudes and behaviors that institutionalize justice (no. 55), a "drive for solidarity" (no. 73), or an action with the power to heal the suffering of poverty (no. 88). Some of these uses also highlight particular actions that people take that express solidarity, like affirmative action programs in education and employment (no. 73), industriousness (no. 102), volunteering to work for justice (for those people who are not poor), and working to build up communities (for those people who are poor) (no. 119). Each of these uses implies that solidarity is not intrinsic to human identity but a historical possibility that must be sought out and cultivated, requiring action on the part of human beings. One bold statement claims that people acting in solidarity will experience the power and presence of Christ (no. 55).

Based on the ways the term *solidarity* is used in *EJA*, the following three uses of solidarity could contribute to ethical discourse: (1) as a virtue that individuals should possess and express in their interactions with others (particularly

---

[26] It is worth noting that two of the thirty-five references appear in titles or subtitles and so it is impossible to classify how they are being used.

the poor), (2) as a principle that should guide not only individual behavior but the development of public policy, and (3) as an ideal vision for how the human community can work together toward the common good. The latter two uses of *solidarity* offer important foundations for the development of a solidarity economy. If the principle of solidarity was central to the development of public policy (including economic policy), it could contribute to the development of an alternative vision of economic life rooted in the common good.

■ CONTRIBUTIONS OF SOLIDARITY TO A MORE JUST ECONOMY

We live in a world of stark disparities between wealth and poverty. In 2010, 12.5 million households were millionaires.[27] Their combined wealth was US $121.8 trillion, more than eight times the US GDP.[28] On the other end of the spectrum, according to World Bank calculations, in 2008 nearly 1.4 billion people lived in "extreme poverty," living on less than $1.25 a day, with another 1.1 billion living on less than $2.00 a day.[29] In 2009, it was reported that approximately 17,000 children were dying from hunger and preventable hunger-related diseases every day.[30]

An ethic of solidarity offers a moral foundation for building a new set of economic, political, and social relations that respond to the very real needs of a planet in crisis and a human community in which half of the population lives in poverty. When solidarity is understood as the voluntary action of individuals and groups working together and reaching across lines of difference toward a common good, it represents a different paradigm for human behavior and relationships than either individualism or collectivism, the moral foundations of capitalism and communism. A moral norm of solidarity as the basis for economic policy and trade would include two key theological principles as its starting point: the sacredness of life and the interdependence between human community and the natural world. If economic policy were to begin from this starting point, it would be much more difficult to craft policies that exploit or harm people and the environment. Furthermore, these theological principles would translate into economic policies that hold a different set of assumptions about the nature of economics and markets than those now guiding free market capitalism. One

---

[27] Boston Consulting Group, "Shaping a New Tomorrow: How to Capitalize on the Momentum of Change," May 31, 2011, *http://www.bcg.com/media/PressReleaseDetails.aspx?id=tcm:12-77753*.

[28] Ibid. In 2010, US GDP was $14.6 billion, according to World Bank data, *http://data.worldbank. org/country/united-states*.

[29] "2008 World Development Indicators: Poverty Data, a Supplement to World Development Indicators 2008 (Washington, DC: World Bank, 2008), 10.

[30] CNN, "U.N. Chief: Hunger Kills 17,000 Kids Daily," November 17, 2009, *http://edition.cnn. com/2009/WORLD/europe/11/17/italy.food.summit/*.

assumption that needs to shift is to begin to think about economics and markets as public tools that can be used to shape society in particular ways. Economies and markets are social tools that facilitate human exchange within and across cultures. When these tools are organized solely by private interests for private gain, it is usually workers and the environment that suffer. This need not be the case. Public-private partnerships, worker-owned businesses, and increased attention to the social well-being of people and the health of the planet could help to reshape how people understand the purpose of markets in society. Recognizing that economic and social policies are integrally related and that policies must balance attention to individuals and to the common good would also help shift attitudes toward the purpose of markets. It would also more accurately reflect the intimate connection between economics and social life. Finally, a shift from the assumption that the primary purpose of the economy is to grow and produce profits, toward an understanding that the economy is intended to increase the general well-being of humanity and the earth, would mark another significant step toward the development of a solidarity economy.[31]

The idea of a solidarity economy represents a radically new foundation for political, economic, and social arrangements. Ultimately, a solidarity economy would stem from a different social narrative than the cultural myths of rugged individualism and self-sufficiency that shape the contemporary US political economy, which lays the responsibility for success solely on individuals. This does not mean a norm of solidarity absolves individuals from being responsible, but it recognizes that the human condition of interdependence requires the development of structures in society within which people are able to function responsibly. Creating stable social networks that provide for the development of thriving communities is an achievable goal. A solidarity economy must stand on a social narrative of community and compassion and a radical mutuality that recognizes and affirms the interdependence of human life and the natural world. An ethic of solidarity offers new avenues for thinking about creative ways of shaping economic behavior, avenues that are based on the goal of a human community rooted in the Christian ethical principles of social justice and sustainability.

∷ SOCIAL JUSTICE AS THE PROPHET PRINCIPLE

The acceptance of the profit motive as an adequate guiding force behind economic exchange and business development lends itself to the creation of an economy that thrives on greed, graft, unlimited growth, duplicity, and exploitation.

---

[31] This is informed by Paul Hawken's idea that "the promise of business is to increase the general well-being of humankind through service, a creative invention and ethical philosophy." *The Ecology of Commerce* (New York: Harper Business, 1993), 1.

Ironically, each of these problems has been cited in recent years as a condition that has prevented the free market from functioning properly. But each of these problems is a symptom of a deeper flaw at the core of neoclassical economics and the capitalist market system it generates. The Hobbesian view of human nature at the heart of neoclassical economics—that humans are self-interested wealth maximizers—is one of individualism, selfishness, and ultimately cruelty. While the economic system based on this worldview allows a fabulously good life for the world's elite, it leaves most of the world's population living in poverty and offers inadequate financial tools and structures that are now in a state of collapse.

In recent years as social ethicists and theologians have argued for a broader set of social goals and goods to be achieved through economic activity, neoclassical economists have responded that it is not the job of an economy to pursue social goals. When economists claim the primary task of business and markets is to make a profit and generate wealth, this claim is built on a particular theoretical construct about the role and purpose of the economy. Economic structures are also moral structures that reflect particular understandings of what it means to be human and to live a good life. If economies and markets are tools created by humans to help organize society, then it is possible to construct economies in many ways with many goals.

The prophetic tradition that exists within the Jewish, Christian, and Muslim belief systems offers wisdom for imagining an alternate vision of how to shape the moral foundations of the economy. The prophetic tradition is marked by a commitment to structuring society in ways that reflect God's concern for the well-being of all people and the created order. This commitment, also referred to as social justice, is the foundation of the Exodus, in which Moses, Miriam, and Aaron led God's people out of slavery. It is the heart of the message of the prophets, who constantly remind the people that God wants them to care for the marginalized in their midst, most often represented by poor people, widows, orphans, and foreigners. Social justice is also the foundation of the ministry of Jesus, who calls out for the rearrangement of the social order in which he is to bring good news to poor people, release to captives, sight for the blind, and freedom to the oppressed (Lk 4:18). From Isaiah and Micah to Dorothy Day, Martin Luther King, Jr., and César Chávez, prophets call people to accountability before God and help them imagine what a new world might be like. Prophets are often figures who stand in solidarity with the poor and oppressed and who work to establish just social systems. Religious prophets challenge human communities to create social networks and economic systems that establish justice in the world, which is the foundation of the prophet principle: *human communities should seek to create social networks and economic systems that establish justice in the world.* Rather than profit and wealth accumulation, the prophet principle offers social justice as the ideal toward which people should strive in creating and shaping human communities and political economies.

■ SUSTAINABILITY AS THE CARETAKING PRINCIPLE

A wide range of environmentalists, theologians, and other cultural critics have questioned the sustainability of neoliberal globalization and the free market approach. The issue of the sustainability of the current global economic system is perhaps easiest to see with regard to the relationship between agriculture and Earth. The green revolution that began in the 1950s and lasted into the early 1980s, for example, increased world grain production by 250 percent but only at significant ecological cost.[32] The industrial models of agriculture first promoted by the green revolution remain dominant in the growing and profitable agribusiness sector. Industrial agriculture, also known as monocropping, focuses on maximizing output by increasing yield. This was largely achieved by harnessing the power of fossil fuels through "synthetic nitrogen fertilizers, petroleum based agrochemicals, diesel powered machinery, refrigeration, irrigation and an oil dependent distribution system."[33] Monocropping also contributes to soil degradation, which in turn leads to an increased reliance on fertilizers and irrigation. All this furthers the unsustainable agricultural practices that currently dominate the global economic order. In addition to considering the current economic relationship between agriculture and the Earth and the environmental exploitation of the current global economic system, it is also necessary to consider ways the entire economic system is currently oriented toward profit rather than sustainability.

From a theological perspective, orienting economic relations around the value of sustainability, rather than profit or exploitation, is consonant with a Christian understanding of stewardship and promoting the flourishing of creation. Virtually every faith tradition has a creation story that shapes its understanding of origins, humanity, and often relationships. In the Christian tradition, the creation story found in Genesis is a beautiful, lyrical tale of the care and concern that God put into shaping the world and all that is in it. A deep and abiding tradition in this story is the idea that God designated humankind to watch over and care for creation. From this reading of the story, the idea of stewardship is not one of domination, but of caretaking. Basing economic relationships on the principle of caretaking and developing sustainable businesses offers an alternative to greed, exploitation, and the obsession with maximizing profits that characterize capitalist markets. It's not that profits are bad per se. But when profits eclipse sustainability as the primary engine driving economic policy and practices, then economic relationships are driven by greed rather than

---

[32] Dale Allen Pfeiffer, "Eating Fossil Fuels," *http://www.fromthewilderness.com/free/ww3/100303_eating_oil.html*.

[33] Jay Tomczak, "Implications of Fossil Fuel Dependence for the Food System," *Energy Bulletin*, *http://www.energybulletin.net/17036.html*.

a fundamental concern for the sustainability of Earth and humanity's responsibility as stewards of God's creation.

If justice and sustainability become basic market principles, certain other assumptions of economic theory will also have to change:

1. Private property and individual rights will need to be balanced and mediated by recognition of the importance of healthy and sustainable communities.

2. Recognition that unfettered markets are a theoretical abstraction will encourage refocussing of public policy debates on how government can best facilitate justice, care, and sustainability.

3. The definition of *efficiency* will need to be expanded to include care of people and the planet, as well as profit.

▪▪ EXAMPLES OF A SOLIDARITY ECONOMY

The neoliberal vision of a global free market economy is currently the dominant paradigm for economic policy and globalization.[34] Within this context it is difficult to imagine what an alternative economy might look like. Nevertheless, even amid the dominance of neoliberalism, there are vibrant examples of businesses, communities, and workers who organize their economic life in ways that embrace sustainability and social justice and challenge dominant assumptions of neoliberalism and free market capitalism. From fair trade to worker co-ops, from community-supported agriculture to local currencies, people in the United States and around the world are struggling to set up alternative economic structures (e.g., businesses, currencies, and markets) that embody the values of a solidarity economy and many of the alternative assumptions identified in this chapter.

While people often associate the idea of economic systems with monetary economies, the reality is, economic systems are human ways to order the exchange of goods and services. Not all economic systems require money. For instance, in extended networks of families and friends, people are engaged in a *gift economy*, meaning they do things for one another without expecting anything in return. When friends invite one another over for dinner or offer to watch one another's children, these activities are a form of exchange of goods and services exercised within a framework of friendship and family, a form of exchange that reflects deep moral bonds of love, compassion, and a genuine concern for one another's well-being. This form of exchange mitigates the expectation of quid pro quo in which people track one another's actions and expect a corresponding deed in return. This type of reciprocity models an altruistic behavior rooted in what economist Nancy Folbre terms "the invisible heart." Folbre coined this term in opposition to Adam Smith's term "the invisible hand," which has been used in neoclassical economics

---

[34] For further discussion of ethical paradigms alternative to neoliberal globalization, see Peters, *In Search of the Good Life.*

to describe the aggregate effect on the marketplace of individuals acting primarily out of individual self-interest.[35] Folbre's term is intended to highlight that many daily actions and transactions between people are motivated by care and compassion, rather than self-interest as modern economists claim.

Religious communities in which individuals and families donate money in tithes and offerings toward the collective goal of running a church and contributing to the well-being of a community are another example of an alternative economy. When people pool their resources, they can hire pastors, musicians, secretaries, janitors, day care workers, and other personnel to work with a congregation toward achieving the common goals of their mission and ministry. Churches, synagogues, mosques, and other centers of religious communities provide many services including fellowship, spiritual guidance, counseling, child care, youth activities, opportunities for community activism and volunteerism, worship, prayer, and countless other tangible and intangible benefits. No one, however, is *charged* for these services. Even more significantly, people are not asked how much they contribute when they walk in the door of a religious institution; the services provided are expected to be shared freely with all interested members of the community. In these communities, tithing is voluntary and anonymous. Such faith communities and the ways they organize themselves socially and economically represent *collective economics* in which a group of people organize their relationships and economic affairs in a way that stresses the common good over individual needs and desires.

In *barter economies*, goods and services are exchanged without any money needing to change hands. A new social movement known as "time banking" is a contemporary barter economy model in which people trade goods or services with others in their community. For instance, if someone provides an hour of English tutoring, they might later redeem an hour of babysitting from someone else in the network. Time banks make a number of socially valuable contributions to local economies and communities. They promote community building by encouraging citizens to get to know their neighbors in new ways through reciprocal relationships of trust, which form around the exchange of child care, running errands, household projects, tutoring, and so on. Time banks can also increase community respect and individual self-worth by encouraging community members to identify their assets and talents and valuing these as meaningful contributions to society. When previously devalued tasks or activities such as tutoring, chauffeuring, or grocery shopping are recognized as valuable contributions to the functioning of a local community, it can help people reconsider ideas regarding the value and definition of *work* and the meaning of *community*. More than eighty-five time banks in the United States are registered with TimeBanks USA, a nonprofit dedicated to supporting and promoting the time-banking movement.[36]

---

[35] Nancy Folbre, *The Invisible Heart: Economics and Family Values* (New York: New Press, 2001).

[36] Information taken from the member directory, *http://www.timebanks.org/directory.htm.*

In addition to these examples of nonmonetary economies, solidarity economies also have room for monetary exchanges, and profits are still an essential aspect to be considered. However, within a solidarity economic framework, maximizing profits is not the only consideration. Workers, the environment, and the local community are all recognized as stakeholders that contribute to the health and vitality of any business enterprise, and none of these are created in pursuit of wealth. Creativity, ingenuity, and entrepreneurial instincts are central to imagining alternative economic strategies that uphold the values of a solidarity economy. One strategy is to emphasize worker democracy by establishing a cooperative business in which all workers have a say in how to allocate profits. In some cases the profits (or a portion of them) are reinvested in the business to help with routine maintenance, grow capacity, increase publicity, or for other strategic investments that would ensure the health and vitality of the business. In other cases a portion of the profits might be set aside as a social capital fund that workers can use to improve the quality of their lives. This is a common practice with the organization Fair Trade USA, which runs an intensive fair trade certification program. To receive the Fair Trade certification label, participating businesses must set aside 12 percent of retail sales in a fund governed by a workers' committee to be used for the social development of workers and their families. In Ecuador, flower farmers have used these "social premium" funds for computer training classes for workers and their children, for small loans to help workers build homes, to hire a company dentist, to start an English language program for children, and to start a hot water program for the community.[37] Each of these programs not only provides significant material improvement in the lives of the workers but also stems from a larger business philosophy in which workers are treated with dignity and respect and paid wages and benefits that significantly improve the quality of their lives. Worker cooperatives provide more than 100 million jobs internationally, a figure 20 percent higher than that for multinational corporations.[38] These cooperatives exist in developed countries as well, with the Mondragon in the Basque region of Spain as the most highly touted example. Over the past fifty years, the Mondragon community has built a network of more than 250 cooperative businesses that employ more than 80,000 workers.[39] With profits of €1.78 million, Mondragon is the eleventh largest business in Spain.[40]

Worker co-ops, however, are not the only possibility for organizing business enterprises in a solidarity economy. Economist David Korten notes the deep

[37] For details, see Jon Tevlin, "To Ecuador, with Love," *Utne Reader*, July–August 2008.

[38] Emily Kawano, "Crisis and Opportunity: The Emerging Solidarity Economy Movement," in *Solidarity Economy I: Building Alternatives for People and Planet*, ed. Emily Kawano, Thomas Neal Masterson, and Jonathan Teller-Elsberg (Amherst, MA: Center for Popular Economics, 2010), 17.

[39] *Corporate Profile 2010*, http://www.mondragon-corporation.com/mcc_dotnetnuke/Portals/0/documentos/eng/Corporative-Profile/Corporative-Profile.html.

[40] Ibid. Gross earnings found at http://www.mondragon-corporation.com/language/en-US/ENG/Economic-Data/Most-relevant-data.aspx.

changes needed in our economic system cannot come from individual businesses acting responsibly: "[T]hey require building a new economy comprised of responsible, locally-rooted businesses that function within a framework of community values and accountability."[41] The Business Alliance for Local Living Economies (BALLE) is a network of locally owned, socially responsible businesses that work together to support one another and build vibrant local communities. BALLE is composed of more than eighty community networks in the United States and Canada, representing more than twenty-two thousand small, local businesses.[42] The principles that guide their work include sharing prosperity, which they accomplish by seeking to "provide meaningful living wage jobs, create opportunities for broad-based business ownership, engage in fair trade, and expect living returns from our capital."[43]

▓ CONCLUSION

The global economic crisis that began in 2008 represents a failure of society to recognize that the reigning economic model is a system laden with values placing profit and economic gain over sustainability and economic justice. Economic activity and the theory that undergirds it are a human creation intended to serve the needs of human societies. Economic activity is a basic human behavior and as such is also an expression of moral behavior. Economic systems are human constructions; they can be built in ways that reflect and respect the values of human communities. A new economic model—one that self-consciously understands how values are embedded in the political economy—is needed. Such an economic model would not focus on growth and trade as primary indicators of success, but on the health and well-being of workers and the environment, reducing infant mortality, starvation relief, health-care delivery, feeding the most impoverished people, and controlling HIV/AIDS for all people, rich and poor. This new economic model need not eschew profit or growth or efficiency, but it should put these goals in perspective. It must balance these goals with other moral considerations, such as sustainability, justice, and the social well-being of people and communities. From an ethical perspective that seeks to promote justice and human well-being, the human community can no longer afford to follow a model of economic theory that lacks these values. Constructing a solidarity economy based on the principles of justice and sustainability is possible.

---

[41] From remarks made by David Korten at the 2007 US Social Forum and transcribed in "Beyond Reform vs. Revolution: Economic Transformation in the U.S.," in *Solidarity Economy: Building Alternatives for People and Planet*, ed. Jenna Allard, Carl Davidson, and Julie Matthaei (Chicago: Change-Maker Publications, 2008), 103. Korten serves on the board of BALLE.

[42] BALLE, *http://www.livingeconomies.org/aboutus*.

[43] BALLE, *http://www.livingeconomies.org/aboutus/mission-and-principles*.

Such a market system would mediate against the exploitation of workers and harm to the environment. Furthermore, the engines of a solidarity economy could function to develop new economic structures and delivery systems that promote economic stability and health in vulnerable communities and populations domestically and internationally.

FOCUS QUESTIONS

1. What are some of the moral challenges that neoliberal globalization poses to Christian ethical demands for social justice?

2. What are new and different ways you can imagine organizing the economy so that all people's needs are met (workers, consumers, and producers)?

3. How do you and your family engage in noncapitalistic economic behavior or economic systems?

4. In what ways might an ethic of solidarity help address problems in the global economic order?

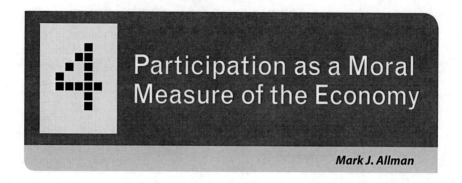

■ INTRODUCTION

The importance of the economy to politics, business, and people's everyday lives is indisputable. But how do we gauge the health of the economy? How do we know if it is doing well or poorly? There is no shortage of economic indicators; the following list provides just a few examples:

- Gross Domestic Product (GDP)—a measure of the total output of goods and services in a country
- Stock Market Indices (e.g., Dow Jones Industrial Average, NASDAQ-100, Standard and Poor's Fortune 500)—measures of the value of publically traded companies based on selected groups of stocks
- Consumer Confidence Index—monthly assessment of how US consumers feel about the US economy and their spending habits
- Consumer Price Index—change in prices of goods and services representing typical purchases by US urban consumers
- Unemployment Rate—percentage of unemployed workers
- Housing Starts—number of new homes being built in a month, often considered an economic bellwether

None of these measures alone provides a comprehensive picture of the economy, but all assume the economy's health is best measured with econometrics. In other words, these measures assume a statistical analysis of the relationship between economic variables (e.g., interest rates, trade volume, capital flows, labor costs, inflation rates, etc.) provides the best picture of how the economy is doing.

Econometrics is essential to economics, but other measures are needed to complement these data-driven assessments. Economics has never been just about money. On the first day of my business ethics course, I ask students two questions:

1. What is the purpose of a corporation?
2. What is the purpose of the economy?

Most students answer the first question by saying something along the lines of, "To maximize the return on shareholder investment" or "To make money." In answer to the second, a typical response is, "To help people exchange goods and services so they can get the things they want and need."

Their answers to the first question tend to focus on profit while responses to the second focus on people. It is with the second question that economics begins to sound more like theology, philosophy, psychology, and sociology. The primary object of study in economics after all is not money but people. The measure of an economy is not best gauged by GDP, unemployment rates, or the Dow Jones alone. An economy is best measured in terms of what it does to, with, and for people, and as such economics is really about ethics and justice. This chapter explores *participation* as a metric for how well the economy is functioning. Two approaches to participation are examined: Catholic social teaching and the work of the economist Amartya Sen. Fostering wider and deeper participation in social, political, and economic arenas is both an end (a goal) and a means (a way of achieving) of social justice.

▪▪ PARTICIPATION

To begin, a preliminary understanding of participation is helpful. Human beings are social animals that self-actualize or self-realize through their actions—we come to realize who we are by what we do. Actions express and confirm both one's personal values and one's commitment to social norms. In other words, we become fully or authentically human through our actions. Participation is a particular kind of human action, namely, an action that is performed "together with others" (e.g., a dialogue, a cooperative effort, an encounter with friends and strangers) and that is carried out with a varying degree of intentionality and proximity (i.e., acting directly or indirectly).[1] In its simplest form, to participate is to have a say in, to exercise control over, or minimally to be consulted about actions and decisions that affect one's life and community. Alienation and apathy are two of the greatest threats to participation. Alienation is caused by social institutions and systems that systematically marginalize individuals and groups and hamper their ability to exercise control over their lives, while apathy involves feelings of either powerlessness ("What difference can I make, I'm only one person?"), or a diminished sense of responsibility for one's own welfare (a sense of entitlement) or that of others ("I don't have to worry about those in need, that's someone else's job, like the government or the church").

---

[1] Karol Wojtyla (Pope John Paul II), *The Acting Person*, trans. A. Potcki (Dordrecht, Holland: D. Reidel Publishing, 1979), 261.

As an ethical principle, participation contends that the greatest social injustice is not the deprivation of basic necessities (food, clothing, shelter) but the exclusion of large portions of human society from participating in the discussion about and the execution of policies that affect them. Participation, as both a means and an end of economic justice, figures prominently in Catholic social thought and in the works of Amartya Sen. It is to these two that we now turn.

▪▪ PARTICIPATION IN CATHOLIC SOCIAL TEACHING

Catholic social teaching refers to a collection of writings by popes and bishops over several centuries that explores the social, political, and economic implications of the Christian faith. Since 1891, with the publication of Pope Leo XIII's encyclical *Rerum novarum* (The Condition of Labor), nearly every pope has issued at least one major social encyclical (an official letter by a pope to a particular group of bishops or to all bishops) on the most pressing social, political, or economic issues of their day (e.g., workers' rights, global poverty, nuclear weapons, critiques of Marxism and capitalism). When one reads the corpus of Catholic social teaching, certain ethical principles (or major themes) regularly appear: dignity of the human person, human rights, the common good, solidarity, preferential option for the poor and vulnerable, peace, family, subsidiarity, and the role of government.[2] Participation is one of the major themes and recurring principles in Catholic social teaching, but this has not always been the case.

In the early modern period (1500–1800 CE), discussions of participation focused on the moral and practical legitimacy of democracy as a form of political participation. The Catholic Church's cautious reception of popular political participation was fueled by the historical experience of the French Revolution (in which more than two thousand priests and vowed religious were killed), the fear of the loss of political power through the separation of church and state (including the removal of public financial support for the Church), suspicion of religious freedom and calls to secularize education and marriage, and objections to democracy's apparent connections to modernism, rationalism, and moral relativism.[3] For the Catholic Church, democracy seemed to promise nothing but bloodshed, decadence, and loss of power.

---

[2] There is no shortage of proposed lists of key principles or themes in Catholic social teaching, and most are quite similar. The Catholic Church, however, does not maintain an official list of key themes, nor does it single out any particular principles as most important. The Office for Social Justice for the Archdiocese of St. Paul and Minneapolis maintains one of the best webpages on Catholic Social Teaching, *http://www.osjspm.org/catholic_social_teaching.aspx.*

[3] See Paul Sigmund, "Democracy," in *New Dictionary of Catholic Social Thought*, ed. Judith Dwyer (Collegeville, MN: Liturgical Press, 1994), 269–75, and Bryan J. Hehir, "Catholicism and Democracy: Conflict, Change, and Collaboration," in *Christianity and Democracy in Global Context*, ed. John Witte (Boulder, CO: Westview Press, 1993).

Leo XXIII (1878–1903) and Pius XII (1939–1958)

But the Church has slowly warmed to the notion of political participation. Writing during the social and political upheaval of the Industrial Revolution, Pope Leo XIII defended popular political participation, going so far as to say, "At certain times and under certain laws, such participation may not only be of benefit to the citizens, but may even be of *obligation*."[4] Thus Leo XIII found common ground between the aims of secular democracy and the mission of the Church. Pope Pius XII, having witnessed the great collapse of capitalism in the 1930s and World War II, declared that democracy can be morally legitimate so long as it does not devolve into tyranny of the majority or state absolutism.[5] By contemporary standards this hardly seems bold, but it does represent a significant shift for the Catholic Church, which for centuries modeled itself on hierarchical monarchy.[6] In its earliest form, the Catholic principle of participation was forged in response to both the objectification of workers during the Industrial Revolution and the political and economic recovery that followed World War II.

JACQUES MARITAIN

This chapter focuses on Catholic social teaching, but a larger body of literature called Catholic social thought also addresses questions of social justice. Catholic social thought includes not only statements by members of the magisterium (popes and bishops) but also contributions of theologians and laypeople. Most of this chapter focuses on Catholic social teaching, but popes and bishops do not think or write in isolation. They draw on the works of others. For example, the French philosopher and political theorist Jacques Maritain (1882–1973) drew on the medieval political theory of Thomas Aquinas in arguing that people have the right of self-governance because God invites people to participate in God's sovereignty.[7] In so doing, Maritain laid a foundation within the Catholic Church's tradition for embracing popular political participation (democracy) as not merely acceptable but as a fundamental right.

---

[4] *Immortale dei*, no. 36 (quoted by Sigmund, 271), italics added.

[5] Pius XII, "1944 Christmas Message," nos. 21–34 and 47–50 in AAS 37 (1945), *www.ewtn.com/library/PAPALDOC/P12XMAS.HTM*.

[6] Donal Dorr, *Option for the Poor: A Hundred Years of Catholic Social Teaching* (Maryknoll, NY: Orbis Books, 1992), 96–112.

[7] See Jacques Maritain, *Man and the State* (Chicago: University of Chicago Press, 1951; repr., Washington DC: Catholic University Press of America, 1998) and Christine Firer Hinze, *Comprehending Power in Christian Social Ethics* (Atlanta, GA: American Academy of Religion, 1995), 66–75.

Pope John XXIII (1958–1963)

Pope John XXIII was deeply concerned that the economic growth of the postwar period be "accompanied by a corresponding social progress, so that all classes of citizens can participate in the increased productivity."[8] In particular, he feared economic progress could result in the instrumentalization or objectification of workers:

> If the whole structure and organization of an economic system is such as to compromise human dignity, to lessen a man's sense of responsibility or to rob him of opportunity for exercising personal initiative, then such a system, we maintain, is altogether unjust, no matter how much wealth it produces, or how justly and equitably such wealth is distributed.[9]

Drawing on Leo XIII and Pius XII, John XXIII reiterated the demand that employees participate in ownership and management as well as enjoy some of the profits from the businesses in which they work.[10]

In his second social encyclical, *Pacem in terris* (Peace on Earth, 1963), John XXIII advanced a Christian understanding of human rights, addressing his encyclical not just to bishops or Catholics but to "all people of good will." For Christians, human rights are grounded in the inviolable dignity of the human person and in the social nature of human beings. Rights also include corresponding obligations. In particular, John XXIII singles out the right and duty to participate in the common good.[11] He casts this as primarily a political right and duty since participation in governance is how the common good is most often maintained.[12] In recasting participation as a human right and duty, participation charts a course between "liberal" and "conservative" political philosophies. "Liberal" participation emphasizes inclusive social structures, social welfare programs, and social safety nets that protect the poor and disenfranchised. However, with the right to participate comes responsibilities. In this vein, participation emphasizes more "conservative" values. These obligations are not simply those filled by government, social service agencies, or other organizations within civil society. They include individual responsibility and the individual exercise of freedom, ingenuity, and hard work. Thus any social structure or governmental organization that lessens individual autonomy or weakens the individual's sense of responsibility for his or her welfare

---

[8] *Mater et magistra*, no. 73.

[9] Ibid., no. 83, cf. nos. 84, 90, and 96.

[10] Ibid., nos. 32 and 91–2.

[11] *Pacem in terris*, no. 56.

[12] Ibid., no. 73, cf. nos. 74–5.

and to the common good must be seen as an assault on the duty to participate, as well.[13]

Vatican II (1962–1965)

The Second Vatican Council, a gathering of nearly all the Catholic bishops in the world, presented an opportunity for the Catholic Church to clarify its social justice tradition. As regards participation, it did so in two principal areas: global poverty and workers' rights. In its analysis of global poverty, the council observed that poverty often includes social and political exclusion on the local, national, and international levels:

> Nations on the road to progress, like those recently made independent, desire to participate in the goods of modern civilization, not only in the political field but also economically, and to play their part freely on the world scene. Still they continually fall behind while very often their dependence on wealthier nations deepens more rapidly, even in the economic sphere.[14]

This observation represents a shift from the classical solution to global poverty, which calls for growing the economy, following the rubric, "if you grow the pie, everyone gets a larger piece." This popular but simplistic approach to solving global poverty assumes that if poor nations follow the example of wealthy Western countries, they too will achieve prosperity and stability. This approach, however, fails to adequately consider that most Western economies achieved their status through colonization, slavery, and environmental exploitation, and that economies are cultural constructions and Western models may not easily translate to other parts of the world. This approach also assumes that the Western economic model inevitably leads to prosperity.[15]

The bishops adopted a sophisticated understanding of development (attempts to alleviate deep-seated and systematic poverty) that is not solely economic, but social and political as well:

> Economic development . . . must not be left to the sole judgment of a few men or groups possessing excessive economic power, or of the political community alone, or of certain especially powerful

---

[13] For more on the concept of responsibility, see John Haughey, "Responsibility for Human Rights: Contributions from Bernard Lonergan," *Theological Studies* 63, no. 4 (December 2002): 764–88; John Paul II, *Centesimus annus*, no. 48; and Michael Novak, "The Crisis of the Welfare State," in *Readings in Moral Theology No. 12: The Catholic Church, Morality, and Politics*, ed. Charles Curran and Leslie Griffin (New York: Paulist Press, 2001), 274–83.

[14] *Gaudium et spes*, no. 9.

[15] Dorr, *Option for the Poor*, 170–71.

nations. It is proper, on the contrary, that at every level the largest possible number of people have an active share in directing that development. . . . Growth must not be allowed merely to follow a kind of automatic course [mechanical evolution] resulting from the economic activity of individuals. Nor must it be entrusted solely to the authority of government. . . . Citizens, for their part, should remember that they have the right and the duty . . . to contribute according to their ability to the true progress of their own community.[16]

Regarding workers' rights, the bishops continued the Catholic Church's tradition of supporting labor unions as an effective mechanism for protecting workers' rights and promoting employee participation in business enterprises:

[T]he active participation of everyone in the running of an enterprise should be promoted. . . . However, decisions concerning economic and social conditions, on which the future of the workers and their children depends, are rather often made not within the enterprise itself but by outside institutions on a higher level. Hence the workers themselves should have a share also in controlling these institutions either in person or through freely elected delegates.[17]

Paul VI (1963–1978) and the World Synod of Bishops (1971)

Pope Paul VI, in his first encyclical after the council (*Populorum progressio/ On the Development of Peoples*, 1967), criticized the growing gap between rich and poor, new forms of colonialism, and the assumption that free trade automatically leads to full human development.[18] Four years later in *Octogesima adveniens* (A Call to Action, 1971), he asserted that the chief social injustice and assault upon human dignity facing the modern world is not the deprivation of basic needs (food, water, clothing, shelter, and health care) but the exclusion of large portions of society from active participation in shaping the social, economic, and political structures that affect them.[19] For Paul VI, despite the rapid changes in this period, "two aspirations persistently make themselves felt . . . the aspiration to equality and the aspiration to participation."[20]

---

[16] *Gaudium et spes*, no. 65, cf. nos. 69–71 and 85–7. Elsewhere, the bishops call for inclusive social, political, and cultural structures on global, national, and local levels as an effective response to the injustice of exclusion. In particular, they praise, "those national procedures which allow for the largest possible number of citizens to participate in public affairs with genuine freedom" (no. 31).

[17] Ibid., no. 68.

[18] See Dorr, *Option for the Poor*, 179–204.

[19] *Octogesima adveniens*, no. 17.

[20] Ibid., no. 22. He goes on to say, "The two aspirations, to equality and to participation, seek to promote a democratic type of society. Various models are proposed, some are tried out, none of them gives complete satisfaction, and the search goes on between ideological and pragmatic tendencies. The Christian has the duty to take part in this search and in the organization and life of the political society" (no. 24).

Paul VI framed his analysis of development in quantitative and qualitative terms. He was highly critical of attempts to alleviate poverty that focus on "merely quantitative economic growth"; for the poor also desire and deserve "to attain objectives of a qualitative order." When measuring "[t]he quality and the truth of human relations," he asserted, *the degree of participation and of responsibility* are no less significant and important for the future of society than the quantity and variety of the goods produced and consumed."[21] Thus, for Paul VI, development must be measured not only economically but also in terms of social and political participation.

Like John XXII before him, Paul VI claimed that the right to participate is an essential part of human dignity, but he also coupled this claim with a unique understanding of freedom. For Paul VI, freedom is not the ability to do as one wishes, freedom flows out of humanity's social nature and is expressed in the responsibility or duty to contribute to the common good.[22] In his earlier encyclical, he went so far as to unequivocally declare that those who enjoy the benefits of a "developed economy" have a responsibility to sacrifice some of their wealth in solidarity with the world's poor. Specifically, he said the responsibility of those who live in wealthier nations includes the willingness to give generously to charity, to pay higher taxes in support of foreign aid programs, to pay higher prices for imported goods, and, in some instances, to live in poorer countries as an act of solidarity and service.[23]

In the same year that *Octogesima adveniens* was published, the bishops of the world held a synod that resulted in a document titled *Justice in the World*. In it they declare:

> Action on behalf of justice and participation in the transformation of the world fully appear to us as a constitutive dimension of the preaching of the gospel, or in other words of the Church's mission for the redemption of the human race and its liberation from every oppressive situation.[24]

"Justice as participation" is the dominant concept in *Justice in the World*, such that one can speak of participation as a necessary condition for social justice and as a social, political, and economic right.[25] They also describe participation as a necessary condition for and a means to full human development. Thus any

---

[21] Ibid., no. 41 (italics added).

[22] "In *Mater et magistra* [no. 31], Pope John XXIII also stressed how much the admittance to responsibility is a basic demand of man's nature, a concrete exercise of his freedom and a path to his development." Ibid., no. 47.

[23] *Populorum progressio*, no. 47, cf. nos. 43–5 and 79.

[24] *Justice in the World*, no. 6.

[25] "Participation constitutes a right which is to be applied both in the economic and in the social and political fields." Ibid., no. 18.

social, political, or economic mechanisms, practices, or institutions that exclude people from playing an active role in their own development are a violation of their right to development and their right to participate as well as an assault on their human dignity.[26]

Economic Justice for All (1986)

Participation receives its most thorough explication in Catholic social teaching in the US bishops' pastoral letter *Economic Justice for All (EJA)*. In the letter, the bishops make four claims about the right to participate: (1) it is a demand of basic justice, (2) it is a key element in the preferential option for the poor, (3) it is essential to their "New American Experiment," and (4) it demands that greater participation be fostered on an international level.

The first assertion, that participation is essential to justice, is the letter's foundational principle. In the preface, participation is identified as one of the six principal themes of the document, "*All people have a right to participate in the economic life of society*. Basic justice demands that people be assured a minimum level of participation in the economy" (no. 15, italics in the original). The best definition of participation in all of Catholic social teaching is presented later in the document:

> [*B*]*asic justice demands the establishment of minimum levels of participation in the life of the human community for all persons.* The ultimate injustice is for a person or group to be treated actively or abandoned passively as if they were nonmembers of the human race. To treat people this way is effectively to say that they simply do not count as human beings. This can take many forms, all of which can be described as varieties of marginalization, or exclusion from social life. . . . Stated positively, justice demands that social institutions be ordered in a way that guarantees all persons the ability to participate actively in the economic, political, and cultural life of society. (nos. 77–8, italics in the original)

The US bishops speak of participation as a simultaneously social, political, and economic obligation, incumbent on the whole of society:

> *Social justice implies that persons have an obligation to be active and productive participants in the life of society and that society has a duty to enable them to participate in this way* . . . [which] also includes a duty to organize economic and social institutions so that people can contribute to society in ways that respect their freedom and the dignity of their labor. (nos. 71–2, italics in the original)

---

[26] Ibid., nos. 15–18.

The bishops offer three important caveats that qualify their understanding of participation as a basic demand of justice:

1. The right to social, political, and economic participation is grounded not in law or custom but in the social nature of the human person.
2. Political exclusion often takes such forms as "restriction of free speech, concentration of power in the hands of a few, or outright repression by the state," whereas economic exclusion occurs through poverty, unemployment, underemployment, and the cycle of poverty (no. 77).[27]
3. In calling for a basic or minimum level of participation, the bishops qualify their position by noting, "[t]he level of participation may legitimately be greater for some persons than for others" (no. 78).[28]

The second claim they make regarding participation is grounded in the biblical principle of the preferential option for the poor.[29] The preferential option for the poor does not simply aim at meeting the material needs of the poor (food, water, clothing, shelter, and health care). It seeks to increase "*active participation in economic life by those who are presently excluded or vulnerable*" (no. 91, italics in the original. See also nos. 185 and 187). In other words, this principle moves beyond charity to address the root causes of poverty:

> The principle of participation leads us to the conviction that the most appropriate and fundamental solutions to poverty will be those that enable people to take control of their own lives. For poverty is not merely the lack of adequate financial resources. It entails a more profound kind of deprivation, a denial of full participation in the economic, social and political life of society and an inability to influence

---

[27] In this paragraph they also point out, "These patterns of exclusion are created by free human beings. In this sense they can be called forms of social sin."

[28] Later in the document, in a sentiment that echoes John XXIII, the bishops clarify this claim, noting that they are not calling for a radically egalitarian society: "Catholic social teaching does not require absolute equality in the distribution of income and wealth. Some degree of inequality is not only acceptable, but may be considered desirable for economic and social reasons, such as the need for incentives and the provision of greater rewards for greater risks" (no. 185).

[29] The preferential option for the poor stems from biblical analysis (particularly of the words and actions of the Hebrew prophets) and the realization that a society's faithfulness to God and the covenant can be measured by how the poor are treated. It is a commitment to overcoming the injustices of oppression, exploitation, and marginalization and a commitment to the defense of human dignity and to combating unjust social structures. The bishops assert, "The prime purpose of this special commitment to the poor is to enable them to become active participants in the life of society. It is to enable all persons to share in and contribute to the common good" (no. 88). See Donal Dorr, "Preferential Option for the Poor," in *The New Dictionary of Catholic Social Thought*, ed. Judith Dwyer (Collegeville, MN: The Liturgical Press, 1994): 755–9. For a more detailed explication of the preferential option for the poor, see Dorr's *Option for the Poor*.

decisions that affect one's life. It means being powerless in a way that assaults not only one's pocketbook but also one's fundamental human dignity. Therefore, we should seek solutions that enable the poor to help themselves through such means as employment. Paternalistic programs which do too much for and too little with the poor are to be avoided. (no. 188)

Third, one of the more controversial parts of the letter is its call for a "New American Experiment." Toward the end of the document, the bishops reflect on the American democratic tradition and the demands of justice in the contemporary social, political, and economic arena:

> The nation's founders took daring steps to create structures of participation, mutual accountability, and widely distributed power to ensure the political rights and freedoms of all. We believe that similar steps are needed today to expand economic participation, broaden the sharing of economic power, and make economic decisions more accountable to the common good. (no. 297)

They characterize this experiment as an attempt in "collaboration and participation in decision making by all those affected at all levels of U.S. society" (no. 358). In other words, greater degrees of justice could be fostered within the economy by addressing structures of inclusion and exclusion, particularly employment, ownership of property, education, wages, and benefits. They make several suggestions for ways that greater participation in the economy could be fostered, including securing the rights to employment, healthy working conditions, decent benefits, and a living wage that allows for ownership of property—the gamut of human rights outlined in the UN *Universal Declaration of Human Rights* and Church teaching (nos. 79–81). Other special areas of concern that would cultivate greater participation include an education system that provides the necessary skills for success in society and the labor market, and widespread ownership of property, especially among minorities (nos. 114, 205, 225, 233, 235, 243).

The final claim made by the bishops is that the principle of participation extends beyond the domestic economy to the global economy. The bishops highlight the crucial role the United States plays in the global economy.

> In short nations separated by geography, culture, and ideology are linked in a complex commercial, financial, technological, and environmental network. These links have two direct consequences. First, they create hope for a new form of community among peoples, one built on dignity, solidarity, and justice. Second, this rising global awareness calls for greater attention to the stark inequities across

countries in the standards of living and control of resources. We must not look at the welfare of U.S. citizens as the only good to be sought. Nor may we overlook the disparities of power in the relationships between this nation and the developing countries. . . . What Americans see as a growing interdependence is regarded by many in the less-developed countries as a pattern of domination and dependence. (no. 13)

The bishops go on to declare that the most severe patterns of exclusion exist in the international arena:

Whole nations are prevented from fully participating in the international economic order because they lack the power to change their disadvantaged position. Many people within the less developed countries are excluded from sharing in the meager resources available in their homelands by unjust elites and unjust governments. (no. 77)

They also expand the definition of basic justice, which they originally applied to the US economy, to encompass the world (no. 258).

With *EJA*, participation rises to an unprecedented prominence within the corpus of Catholic social thought. Reflecting on the global economy, the bishops conclude:

In short, the international economic order, like many aspects of our own economy, is in crisis; the gap between rich and poor countries and between rich and poor people within countries is widening. The United States represents the most powerful single factor in the international economic equation. . . . To restructure the international order along lines of greater equity and participation and apply the preferential option for the poor to international economic activity will require sacrifices of at least the scope of those we have made over the years in building our own nation. . . . Only a renewed commitment by all to the common good can deal creatively with the realities of international interdependence and economic dislocations in the domestic economy. The virtues of good citizenship require a lively sense of participation in the commonwealth and of having obligations as well as rights within it. (nos. 290, 296)

Although the document incorporates a number of more traditional concepts concerning economic and social justice (solidarity, the preferential option for the poor, and the common good), participation serves as the organizing principle that informs the bishops' discernment of the demands of justice.

DAVID HOLLENBACH

David Hollenbach, SJ (1942–), holds the University Chair in Human Rights and International Justice at Boston College. He has developed one of the most comprehensive treatments of participation in the Catholic social thought tradition.[30] For Hollenbach, the tradition's understanding of justice rests on the assertion that human beings are social animals and to deny people the right to participate is a violation of their dignity as human persons. For Hollenbach, participation is the foundation of all human rights. Hollenbach served on the drafting committee for *EJA* and is credited for making participation a central feature in the document.

David Hollenbach

Used with permission David Hollenbach

John Paul II (1978–2005)

Long before he became pope, Pope John Paul II wrote *The Acting Person* (1969), which argues that action (and especially acting together with others) is a self-constituting behavior and an expression of the social nature of the human person.[31] In other words, persons come to know themselves and help to create their community by engaging in what John Paul II calls "you-and-I" and "we" relationships. This understanding of what it means to be human colors his works as pope. For example, in *Laborem exercens* (On Human Work, 1981), he defends the dignity of work (paid and unpaid) by describing it as the principal means by which one participates in society, a means of self-realization, and a participation in God's creative and redemptive activity.[32] In *Sollicitudo rei socialis* (On Social Concern, 1987), John Paul II asserts that attempts to alleviate global poverty must not focus exclusively on economic factors but must include cultural and political dimensions as well. He advocates for a concept of development as participation in which the level of participation of marginalized people becomes the criteria for determining the authenticity of development

---

[30] See David Hollenbach, *Claims in Conflict: Retrieving and Renewing the Catholic Human Rights* (Mahwah, NJ: Paulist Press, 1979); *Justice, Peace, and Human Rights: American Catholic Social Ethics in a Pluralistic World* (New York: Crossroads, 1988); and *The Common Good and Christian Ethics* (Cambridge: Cambridge University Press, 2002).

[31] See Meghan J. Clark, "Integrating Human Rights: Participation in John Paul II, Catholic Social Thought and Amartya Sen" *Political Theology* 8, no. 3 (2007): 299–317.

[32] *Laborem exercens*, nos. 1, 4, 6, 16, 24, and 25.

programs.[33] He also identifies literacy, education, food production and distribution, and political reform as appropriate indices for measuring levels of participation.[34]

John Paul II's most systematic treatment of participation is found in his 1991 encyclical *Centesimus annus* (On the Hundredth Anniversary of *Rerum Novarum*), written on the centenary anniversary of Leo XII's *Rerum novarum*. Here participation becomes both an *end of* and a *means to* justice. John Paul II frames his discussion of economic globalization in terms of marginalization (the antithesis of participation), which occurs on both the national and international levels.[35] Marginalization can be seen in the shift from subsistence agriculture to industrialization that often results in migration, urbanization, and an accompanying loss of traditional culture, which, in turn, leads to further estrangement on the family and community levels. Turning to political participation, John Paul II offers a qualified endorsement of democracy:

> The Church values the democratic system inasmuch as it ensures the participation of citizens in making political choices, guarantees to the government the possibility both of electing and holding accountable those who govern them and of replacing them through peaceful means when appropriate.[36]

John Paul II holds democracy in high esteem not as an end in itself but only to the degree that it enables political participation, includes measures of accountability and transparency, and functions in accord with human dignity.

Benedict XVI (2005–)

In his first encyclical, *Deus caritas est* (God Is Love, 2005), Pope Benedict XVI identifies working for "a just ordering of society" as the proper role or vocation of the laity (members of the Church who are not ordained). "As citizens of the State . . . they cannot relinquish their participation 'in the many different economic, social legislative and administrative and cultural areas, which are intended to promote organically and institutionally the *common good.*'"[37] He

---

[33] *Sollicitudo rei socialis*, no. 17. He elaborates on his notion of authentic development by criticizing the "naïve mechanistic optimism" of the Enlightenment, which saw development as "a straightforward, process, as if it were automatic and in itself limitless, as though given certain conditions, the human race were able to progress rapidly toward an undefined perfection of some kind" (no. 27).

[34] Ibid., no. 44.

[35] "The fact is that many people, perhaps the majority today, do not have the means which would enable them to take their place in an effective and humanly dignified way within a productive system. . . . They have no way of entering the network of knowledge and intercommunication which would enable them to see their qualities appreciated and utilized. Thus, if not actually exploited, they are to a great extent marginalized" (*Centesimus annus*, no. 33).

[36] Ibid., no. 46.

[37] *Deus caritas est*, no. 29. The internal quotes are from John Paul II, *Christifideles Laici* (December 30, 1988), no. 42.

reiterates this point in his second encyclical, *Caritas in Veritate* (Charity in Truth, 2009), in which he calls for increased "citizens' interest and participation in the *res publica* [public affairs]."[38] He applies the same principle to the international order, calling for "giving poorer nations an effective voice in shared decision-making . . . [which] seems necessary in order to arrive at a political, juridical and economic order which can increase and give direction to international cooperation for the development of all peoples in solidarity."[39] Practically speaking, Benedict XVI argues that this requires reform of the United Nations as well as of institutions of international finance (e.g., the World Trade Organization, the World Bank, and the International Monetary Fund).

Participation, as an ethical principle, has developed within Catholic social thought from the robust defense of workers' rights and cautious endorsements of democracy to ultimately declaring participation a human right and a constitutive dimension of justice and development. Within the larger framework of Catholic social thought, participation is the linchpin that connects solidarity to the common good. Solidarity is "not a feeling of vague compassion or shallow distress at the misfortunes of so many people, both near and far. On the contrary it is a firm and persevering determination to commit oneself to the common good."[40] Solidarity is more than a feeling, it is a commitment to serving the common good, in which the common good is understood to mean "the sum total of social conditions which allow people, either as groups or individuals, to reach their fulfillment more fully and more easily."[41] Participation joins solidarity and the common good. If solidarity is primarily expressed in action, then this action is a form of participation that involves acting together with others in service of the common good. This understanding of participation as both (1) a right and a duty and (2) a means and an end of justice is not exclusively religious or even Catholic. It has parallels in economics, principally in the work of Amartya Sen.

■■ AMARTYA SEN AND DEVELOPMENT AS PARTICIPATION

Economist and Nobel laureate Amartya Sen (1933–) has radically altered the field of development economics, which is concerned with alleviating global poverty. In particular, his "poverty as capabilities" approach serves as the principal

---

[38] *Caritas in Veritate*, no. 24.

[39] Ibid., no. 67.

[40] John Paul II, *Sollicitudo rei socialis*, no. 38. He goes on to say, "Solidarity helps us to see the 'other' whether a person, people or nation not just as some kind of instrument, with a work capacity and physical strength to be exploited at low cost and then discarded when no longer useful, but as our 'neighbor,' a 'helper' (cf. Gen. 2:18–20), to be made a sharer, on par with ourselves, in the banquet of life to which all are equally invited by God" (no. 39).

[41] *Gaudium et spes*, no. 26.

Amartya Sen

way that the United Nation's Human Development Programme measures poverty. While Sen's approach does not have any religious grounding, his analysis of economic justice is remarkably congruent with Catholic social teaching. Both insist participation is essential and intrinsic to (an end of) and instrumental to/causative of (a means to) authentic human development.

For Sen, modern economics is handicapped by its abandonment of welfare economics (which focuses on questions of well-being and ethics) and its overemphasis on engineering and logistics (which focus on how the economy functions). In particular, he is critical of engineering economics' unchallenged and narrow understanding of human motivation, in which humans are assumed to be acting rationally (and predictably) when they act out of self-interest. The idea that selfishness is a requirement of rationality is, according to Sen, "patently absurd."[42] He does not deny that self-interest influences human behavior, he objects to the claim that acting out of other motivations (e.g., a sense of duty or group loyalty) renders the human person irrational. According to Sen, this does

---

[42] Sen, *On Ethics and Economics* (Oxford: Blackwell, 1987), 16.

not accord with common human experience and fails to appreciate that people often act out of several motivations. Finally, Sen is critical of definitions and measures of well-being that focus solely on outcomes (wealth, possessions, etc.) because they ignore the importance of agency.

Agency, for Sen, is the ability and opportunity to form goals, commitments, and values.[43] Well-being and agency are intimately related, but not identical. Well-being cannot be measured using some universal calculus of happiness. Well-being involves personal values and desires. As such, it is best measured in terms of freedom, which places economics in the arena of human rights.[44] Too often economic well-being focuses exclusively on questions of distributive justice (how limited resources ought to be distributed), whereas agency "takes a wider view of the person, including valuing the various things he or she would want to see happen, and the ability to form such objectives and to have them realized . . . the agency aspect pays more complete attention to the person as a *doer*."[45] In his focus on the human person achieving self-realization through acting together with others, Sen sounds similar to John Paul II. While Sen's economic theory is wide ranging, this chapter focuses on two areas: Sen's understanding of poverty and his notion of development as freedom.

Poverty, Capability Deprivation, and Social Exclusion

Sen argues that "ultimately poverty must be seen in terms of poor living, rather than just as lowness of incomes. . . . We must look at impoverished lives, and not just at depleted wallets. . . . [A]n impoverished life is one without the freedom to undertake important activities that a person has reason to choose."[46] From this, Sen derives his "view of poverty as capability deprivation (that is, poverty is seen as the lack of the capability to live a minimally decent life)."[47] Drawing on Adam Smith's claim that certain cultural necessities allow a person "to appear in public without shame" (because even though they are not

---

[43] Ibid., 42.

[44] Ibid., 47.

[45] Ibid., 59. Sen summarizes his approach to ethics and economics as such, "I have tried to argue that the distancing of economics from ethics has impoverished welfare economics, and also weakened the basis of a good deal of descriptive and predictive economics [engineering economics]. . . . Sticking entirely to the narrow and implausible assumption of purely self-interested behavior seems to take us in an alleged 'short-cut' that ends up in a different place from where we wanted to go. The object is to understand, explain and predict human behaviour in a way such that economic relationships can be fruitfully studied and used for description, prognosis and policy. The jettisoning of all motivations and valuations other than the extremely narrow one of self-interest is hard to justify on grounds of predictive usefulness, and it also seems to have rather dubious empirical support" (78–9).

[46] Sen, *Social Exclusion: Concept, Application, and Scrutiny* (Manila: Office of Environment and Social Development, Asian Development Bank, 2000), 3–4, *http://housingforall.org/Social_exclusion.pdf.*

[47] Ibid., 4.

life-sustaining necessities, the lack of them leads to a social exclusion that exacerbates material poverty).[48] Sen concludes:

> The inability to interact freely with others is an important deprivation in itself (like being undernourished or homeless). . . . Second, being excluded from social relations can lead to other deprivations as well, thereby further limiting our living opportunities. For example, being excluded from the opportunity to be employed or receive credit may lead to economic impoverishment that may, in turn, lead to other deprivations. . . . Social exclusion can, thus, be constitutively a part of capability deprivation as well as instrumentally a cause of diverse capability failures.[49]

Thus poverty is not caused by low income alone: low income is instrumental to poverty but not intrinsic to it. For Sen, the capability perspective shifts the primary attention of poverty analysis away from the *means* of poverty "to the *ends* that people have reason to pursue, and correspondingly to the *freedoms* to be able to satisfy these ends," which is not to suggest that income and capability are unrelated.[50] To illustrate his claim that income and capability are related,

---

[48] Sen makes repeated references throughout his writings to Smith's emphasis on the necessity of a person's ability to appear in public without shame. "What counts as 'necessity' in a society is to be determined, in Smithian analysis, by its need to generate some minimally required freedom, such as the ability to appear in public without shame, or to take part in the life of the community"; *Development as Freedom* (New York: Anchor Books, 1999), 73. In other words, the ability to participate in the life of the community is a necessity. Sen goes on to quote the passage from Smith's *The Wealth of Nations* that addresses this necessity. "By necessaries I understand not only the commodities which are indispensably necessary for the support of life, but what ever the customs of the country renders it indecent for creditable people, even the lowest order to be without. A linen shirt, for example, is, strictly speaking, not a necessary of life. The Greeks and Romans lived, I suppose, very comfortably though they had no linen. But in the present times, through the greater part of Europe, a creditable day-labourer would be ashamed to appear in public without a linen shirt, the want of which would be supposed to denote that disgraceful degree of poverty which, it is presumed, nobody can well fall into without extreme bad conduct. Custom, in the same manner, has rendered leather shoes a necessary of life in England. The poorest creditable person of either sex would be ashamed to appear in public without them." (Smith, *The Wealth of Nations*, vol. 2 (Hamburg: Management Library Press, 2007 [1776]), 631).

[49] Sen, *Social Exclusion*, 4–5.

[50] Sen, *Development as Freedom*, 90. "While it is important to distinguish conceptually the notion of poverty as capability inadequacy from that of poverty as lowness of income, the two perspectives cannot but be related, since income is such an important means to capabilities. And since enhanced capabilities in leading a life would tend, typically, to extend a persons' ability to be more productive and to earn a higher income, we would also expect a connection going from capability improvement to greater earning power and not only the other way around" (90). He continues in the following paragraph, "The latter connection [that capability improvement leads to increased income] can be particularly important for the removal of income poverty. It is not only the case that, say, better education and health care improve the quality of life directly; they also increase a person's ability to earn an income and be free of income-poverty, as well. The more inclusive the reach of basic education and health care, the more likely it is that even the potentially poor would have a better chance of overcoming penury" (ibid.).

Sen identifies a number of other categories that should be considered when defining poverty: employment, race, health, and gender.[51]

Building on his thesis that poverty concerns not only income but also capability deprivation, Sen argues that social exclusion magnifies poverty. The excluded often include people who are mentally and physically disabled, elderly, children, minors, addicted, poor, without a regular income, illiterate, social outcasts, uneducated, undocumented, on public assistance, single mothers, immigrants, without the right to vote, racial minorities, and indigenous. The list of socially excluded people includes segments of the population that are often identified as marginalized: the voiceless, the untouchables, and the invisible. Sen cautions against broadening the term *socially excluded* to the point that it becomes a catchall phrase, devoid of any meaning.[52] Not every case of deprivation is a form of social exclusion. The term *social exclusion* is applicable only in cases of deprivation caused by a change in relationships. Social exclusion is only one-way: a relationship change causes a need (e.g., a community begins to discriminate against immigrants or another minority and members of that group are no longer able to find employment). However, a need can also create an instance of social exclusion. For example, hunger caused by a crop failure is not an instance of social exclusion, but hunger caused by crop failure might force people to migrate, thereby making them outcasts. And hunger caused by a drop in wages (because of inflation or increased competition) by itself is not necessarily a form of social exclusion, but can lead to social exclusion. For the category of social exclusion to maintain its potency in poverty analysis, its use must be restricted to instances of poverty that are caused by a change in relationships, and the change in relationships must precede the deprivation.[53]

Development as Freedom

Sen's definition and understanding of development parallels Catholic social teaching's understanding of full or authentic human development.[54] Sen reiterates his distinction between ends/means and intrinsic/instrumental value:

> The ends and means of development require examination and scrutiny for a fuller understanding of the development process; it is simply not adequate to take as our basic objective just the maximization of income

---

[51] Ibid., 94–107.

[52] "There is also a need for caution in not using the term too indiscriminately. . . . Surely enough, the exclusionary perspective can be very useful in some contexts, but it can also be linguistically invoked even when it adds little to what is already well understood without reference to relational features. . . . Since the real merit in using the language of exclusion is to draw attention to the relational features in a deprivation, it is crucial to ask whether a relational deprivation has been responsible for a particular case of starvation or hunger" (*Social Exclusion*, 9–10).

[53] Ibid. 9–12.

[54] See Meghan J. Clark, "Integrating Human Rights: Participation in John Paul II, Catholic Social Thought and Amartya Sen," *Political Theology* 8, no. 3 (2007): 299–317.

or wealth, which is, as Aristotle noted, 'merely useful and for the sake of something else.' For the same reason, economic growth cannot sensibly be treated as an end in itself. Development has to be more concerned with enhancing the lives we lead and the freedoms we enjoy.[55]

Individual agency is essential and instrumental to overcoming the deprivations of poverty and oppression; furthermore, there is a complementary relationship between individual agency and social arrangements. In other words, economic, social, and political freedoms are mutually enriching.

Sen does not reject traditional measures of development; rather, he asserts that growth in the GDP and employment are essential to the ultimate goal of development, namely, the enhancement of human freedom.[56] The error that traditional approaches to development make is that they confuse the end of development (freedom) with the means of development (GDP, industrialization, etc.). The end of development is not the growth of the GDP or even increased wealth per se, but the elimination of impoverishment (i.e., a state of living in deprived conditions), which includes the expansion of freedom.

Freedom, for Sen, "involves both the processes that allow freedom of actions and decisions, and the actual opportunities that people have, given their personal and social circumstances."[57] Freedom has both a constitutive and an instrumental role in development.[58] Development is "a process of expanding the real freedoms that people enjoy [in which] . . . freedom is viewed as both (1) the *primary end* and (2) the *principal means* of development."[59] The constitutive dimensions of development as freedom include basic material necessities (food, clothing, shelter, etc.) and social and political freedoms (political participation, free speech, etc.). When development is viewed from this perspective, the freedom to participate (socially, politically, and economically) becomes the measure of development. Development as freedom, then, sees participation as a constitutive dimension of development, which in turn, requires freedom (i.e., development requires freedom and freedom requires participation). Instrumentally, these freedoms contribute to economic progress and the elimination of poverty. It is to this second aspect of his development-as-freedom formula, namely, the instrumental role of freedom in the elimination of poverty and the enhancement of human development, that Sen devotes particular attention.

---

[55] Sen, *Development as Freedom*, 14.

[56] For Sen, development encompasses the expansion of substantive freedoms, which he asserts are culturally bound. See ibid., 8–9, and "Culture and Development," World Bank Tokyo meeting, December 13, 2000, *http://info.worldbank.org/etools/docs/voddocs/354/688/sen_tokyo.pdf*.

[57] Sen, *Development as Freedom*, 17.

[58] Sen's concept of freedom is quite expansive and functions like a virtue in Catholic social teaching; it is both an end and a means. This is not surprising since both Catholic social teaching and Sen draw heavily from Aristotle.

[59] Ibid., *Development as Freedom*, 36.

Sen identifies five freedoms that are constitutive and causative of full human development. His succinct explications of these freedoms bear repeating:

1. "*Political freedoms*, broadly conceived . . . refer to the opportunities that people have to determine who should govern and on what principles, and also include the possibility to scrutinize and criticize authorities, to have freedom of political expression and an uncensored press, to enjoy the freedom to choose between political parties and so on."[60]

2. "*Economic facilities* refer to the opportunities that individuals respectively enjoy to utilize economic resources for the purpose of consumption, or production, or exchange." He notes that such opportunities are relative to available resources and conditions of exchange.[61]

3. "*Social opportunities* refer to the arrangements that society makes for education, health care and so on, which influence the individual's substantive freedom to live better."[62]

4. "*Transparency guarantees* deal with the need for openness that people can expect: the freedom to deal with one another under guarantees of disclosure and lucidity. . . . These guarantees have a clear instrumental role preventing corruption, financial irresponsibility and underhand dealings." Sen also notes that transparency guarantees serve as the rock bed of trust, which is essential for relationships, interaction, and exchange.[63]

5. "*Protective security* is needed to provide a social safety net for preventing the affected population from being reduced to abject misery [and] . . . includes *fixed* institutional arrangements such as unemployment benefits and statutory income supplements to the indigent as well as ad hoc arrangements such as famine relief or emergency public employment to generate income for destitutes."[64]

These five freedoms serve as the foundation of Sen's assertion that development (including economic development) is achieved by means of human freedom and that human freedom is a necessary condition for authentic human development. These five constitutive and instrumental freedoms advance human capabilities.[65] For Sen, human capability is the exercise of human agency coupled with the opportunity to lead the kind of life one values.

---

[60] Ibid., 38.

[61] Ibid., 38–9.

[62] Ibid., 39.

[63] Ibid., 39–40.

[64] Ibid., 40 (cf. xii).

[65] Sen's understanding of freedom closely parallels Aristotle's notion of virtue, whereby Sen's "general capability of a person" (*Development as Freedom*, 10) is akin to Aristotle's notion of human flourishing, and Sen's understanding of the five freedoms (as both a means and an end) are akin to Aristotle's understanding of the role and function of the virtues (see ibid., 24).

These freedoms can be understood as modes of participation. In other words, participation requires one to exercise these freedoms, that is, to have political freedom, economic and social opportunities, access to information, and physical protection. These freedoms, which he calls "participatory freedoms,"[66] can be recast as forms or arenas of social, economic, and political participation. As such, Sen's *development as freedom* might also be rightly termed *development as participation*. For example:

1. *Political freedoms* are modes of political participation and entitlements (rights) associated with democracies.[67]

2. *Economic facilities* refer to an individual's ability to participate ("to utilize economic resources") in the local economy.

3. *Social opportunities* are "important not only for the conduct of private lives but also for more effective participation in economic and political activities. For example, illiteracy can be a major barrier to participation in economic activities that require production according to specification or demand strict quality control (as globalized trade increasingly does). Similarly, political participation may be hindered by the inability to read newspapers or communicate in writing with others involved in political activities."[68]

4. *Transparency guarantees* are essential means of participation because they guarantee that meaningful interaction and exchange can take place. Without this basic trust, all forms of human exchange would fall into disarray.

5. *Protective securities* safeguard against the exclusion of the destitute and ensure that those who are impoverished are not completely excluded.

Sen's genius is his recognition that freedom and participation are necessary conditions for and means of authentic human development.

Sen's concepts of poverty as capability deprivation and development as freedom (participation) have reoriented and reinvigorated welfare and development economics. In particular, Sen's emphasis on social, political, and economic participation as both the ends and the means of development has significantly influenced the UN Development Programme's (UNDP) analysis of poverty, development, and globalization. In 1990, the UNDP began using a method of development analysis, the Human Development Index (HDI), which draws heavily on Sen's insights. The HDI focuses on three crucial areas of socioeconomic life: income, education, and health/longevity. Recognizing that human existence incorporates much more than these three areas, the HDI is an attempt to provide a broader and more inclusive measure of human development that

---

[66] Ibid., 9.

[67] Sen devotes considerable attention to democracy, which for reasons of space are ignored here. See "Democracy as a Universal Value," *Journal of Democracy* 10, no. 3 (1999): 3–17.

[68] Sen, *Development as Freedom*, 39.

looks beyond GDP. In its measure of these three areas, the HDI uses GDP as an indicator of income levels, adult literacy rates as an indicator of education, and infant mortality rates as an indicator of health/longevity. Since 1990 the UNDP has issued annual Human Development Reports that focus on a host of welfare economics' indicators.[69]

■■ CONCLUSION

Catholic social teaching and Amartya Sen share numerous similarities in their approaches to participation, poverty, and development. For example, both

1. reject strictly econometric definitions of *poverty* and *development* and hold that the purpose of an economy is to meet human needs, not simply to pursue wealth;

2. hold that social justice primarily concerns institutional and structural mechanisms that honor demands of human relationships;

3. recognize that the principal value of human work is not the objective/material dimensions (what is produced) but the subjective/human dimension of labor (that it is done by a human person); that employment is the principal means by which one participates in the economy; and that one's social world is created through work;

4. hold democracy in high esteem and, at least implicitly, assert that it is an effective form of governance in which the end of the state (namely, the common good) is consistent with the means (human freedom and participation);

5. strongly encourage an active civil society and hold that the state has proper administrative, legislative, executive, judicial, and protective roles;

6. uphold human rights as universal values and reject the defense of human rights based on their purely or even primarily legal recognition. Rather, human persons have rights based on their inherent dignity and while legal recognition of rights is important to safeguard those rights, the individual's possession of rights is not based on their legal recognition by any state, government, or constitution. Essentially, human rights are a moral, not a legal, claim.

The category of participation provides a comprehensive, thicker, and embodied understanding of the human person as a social animal embedded in networks of relationships. In using participation as an ethical lens for the moral evaluation of the economy, one frequently moves, quite naturally, in and out of the social, political, and economic arenas. This is the chief strength of a "justice as

---

[69] For a full list and access to the Human Development Reports, see UNHDP, "Human Development Reports," *http://hdr.undp.org/en/reports/*.

participation approach." It emphasizes the symbiotic relationships between the social, political, and economic dimensions of human existence. It recognizes that people inhabit each of these realms simultaneously. It affirms that we are social, economic, and political animals. It asserts that the human person is rightly termed *Homo participans*.

FOCUS QUESTIONS

1. Allman argues that the concept of participation as used in Catholic social teaching and in the work of Amartya Sen is compatible and mutually enriching. Do you agree or disagree? If you agree, provide three examples of how the two approaches to participation are compatible. If you disagree, explain why they are not compatible.

2. Explain Amartya Sen's notions of "poverty as capability deprivation" and "development as freedom" and how they relate to each other. Critique Sen's stand on each of these notions by identifying at least two strengths and two weaknesses to Sen's overall approach.

3. How does using the category of participation affect how an economy is measured? Is this a useful measure of the economy? Why or why not?

PART III

CONTEMPORARY ISSUES
OF ECONOMIC JUSTICE

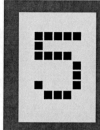

5 Fighting Poverty and Providing Safety Nets

An Agenda for US Catholic Advocacy in Social Policy

Thomas Massaro, SJ

▋▋ INTRODUCTION

We have all heard the mischievous motto "What happens in Las Vegas stays in Las Vegas." Regardless of the moral implications or even the practical accuracy of that phrase, it serves to remind us that there are at least fifty-one cities in the United States that are set apart in a special way. What happens in the fifty state capitals, and above all in our national capital, Washington, DC, by no means stays in these cities. These are locations where lawmakers draft, debate, amend, approve, and promulgate legislation that touches the lives of all Americans. What happens in the halls of Congress and the statehouses does not stay there but branches out to every city and town in our nation. Although the actual texts of most laws remain largely unread and little known by average citizens, state and national legislation nonetheless exert strong effects on all three hundred million Americans and indeed even beyond our nation's borders.

Among the laws arising from these centers of political authority, social legislation is a particularly important and often controversial bundle. The phrase *social legislation* and the related concept *social policy* require explanation. In one sense, every law contains significant social dimensions, because all government actions influence the conditions people face each day, whether as individuals, families, small groups, or larger collectives. Immigration policy, security measures, labor law, tax policy, and safety and health regulations all touch our lives and exert social effects, directly and indirectly. However, most commentators on government issues reserve the terms *social legislation* and *social policy* for matters that more directly pertain to such items as poverty, family life, health care, education, and public health, and the overall physical and emotional well-being of individuals and groups of citizens. By funding essential services and enforcing regulations in these areas, government bodies and public agencies shape the conditions that individuals, families, and larger social groups face.

■ INFLUENCING PUBLIC POLICY: CATHOLIC SOCIAL THOUGHT AND CHURCH LEADERSHIP

For at least a half century now, the Catholic Church has been among the strongest voices in state capitals and in Washington, DC, working for wise and effective social policies. As committed members of a religious community, Catholics naturally favor laws and social arrangements that reflect the core ethical values their Church espouses. For example, Catholic social teaching holds the sanctity of human life in high regard, so Catholics have consistently opposed measures they interpret as threats to life, including abortion, euthanasia, and more recently capital punishment and fetal stem cell research. Beyond this pro-life agenda, Catholics advocate dignified living conditions for all people, whether young or old, employed or unemployed, living in the United States or abroad. These commitments lead Catholic leaders and rank-and-file parishioners to support, for example, legislation to extend educational and job opportunities to groups long excluded from the mainstream. For those who have fallen upon hard times, such as the chronically ill and retirees without adequate income to pay their medical bills, social "safety net" measures such as Medicaid and Medicare have long been part of our nation's social policies that have won broad support among religious people, including the Roman Catholic community.

More than most voices heard in public life, the Catholic Church consistently urges our nation and its citizens to undertake considerable sacrifice for the *common good*, that is, to create conditions that will assist all members of society in their efforts to flourish and reach their full potential.[1] The underlying social philosophy of the Catholic community thus deserves the label *communitarian* (i.e., greatly concerned with the overall health of the larger community) as opposed to *individualistic* (narrowly focused on the liberties of persons in isolation from their wider memberships). Drawing on its rich tradition of thought, its charitable activities, and social justice practices, the Catholic Church has been a staunch advocate of many policy positions, even some rather unpopular ones, that reflect its distinctive values, inspired by the words of Scripture and religious doctrine.

These generalizations require qualification. About a quarter of the US population is Catholic, so tens of millions of Americans identify themselves as Catholic. By no means do all these Catholics fully agree on a given course of action in the public arena. Indeed, millions are barely aware of the social teachings of their Church. Even when they draw upon the same theological sources

---

[1] The clearest definitions of the concept of the common good in recent Church documents come from the 1961 encyclical of Pope John XXIII called *Mater et magistra* (Christianity and Social Progress), no. 65, and from the 1965 Vatican II document *Gaudium et spes* (Pastoral Constitution on the Church in the Modern World), no. 26.

and religious teachings, individual Catholics can and often do reach a wide range of conclusions about which public policies deserve support. There is clearly no cookie-cutter formula for applying Church teachings to political issues. Catholics identify as Republicans and Democrats in nearly equal numbers. Millions more prefer to remain Independent, that is, affiliated with no particular political party. There are politically conservative and politically liberal Catholics. Some Catholics vote according to a single-issue criterion, using issues like abortion or defense policy as a litmus test to determine their support for parties or individual candidates for office, while others consult a broader array of social concerns in shaping their voting and political behavior.

Indeed, the Catholic vote is a highly prized "swing vote" precisely because it has been so closely divided in recent presidential elections. Even when it makes sense to speak of certain patterns and predilections among Catholics as participants in the public arena, as the previous paragraphs do, it is wise to recall that the Catholic community is a diverse lot, whose individual members range across a wide spectrum of political opinions. Perhaps the most succinct summary of Catholic political identity was offered nearly a century ago in a phrase used by the Irish writer James Joyce: "Here comes everybody." There is no monolithic Catholic vote or set of opinions, even though participation in the Catholic community surely shapes the sensibilities of adherents along certain identifiable lines, consistent with the values of community and social responsibility.

Before examining particular matters of American social policy in recent decades, another initial clarification should be considered, this one involving the role of bishops as leaders in the Catholic Church. Without a doubt, by virtue of their important teaching office in the Church, bishops speak authentically for the Catholic Church. This pertains to internal Church matters, such as the regulation of liturgy and the sacraments, and to more external matters, such as making judgments about the implications of faith for public policies and social justice issues. There are nearly two hundred dioceses (or Church geographical jurisdictions) in the United States, and each is administered by a bishop or archbishop, a few of whom also hold the title of cardinal. Within their respective dioceses, bishops (sometimes with the assistance of auxiliary bishops, especially in larger dioceses) exercise rightful teaching authority (the Latin term *magisterium* denotes this concept). There is also a national body of more than three hundred bishops called the United States Conference of Catholic Bishops (USCCB). This organization has changed names and reorganized itself several times since its inception more than one hundred years ago but continues to be the setting where Catholic bishops in the United States join their voices together and jointly exercise their teaching ministry. The bishops themselves meet in plenary sessions once or twice a year and maintain a professional staff with headquarters in Washington, DC. Among the many components of the bishops' conference (as it is commonly called) are the Committee on Domestic Justice and Human Development and the Committee of International Justice and Peace, which together comprise the Office of Justice, Peace, and Human Development.

■■ ADVOCACY EFFORTS OF THE BISHOPS' CONFERENCE

In the area of public policy, the bishops' conference exercises a distinctive brand of activism. On one hand, it is important to remember that bishops are most essentially pastors and teachers, not public policy analysts. On the other hand, through their staff of highly trained and primarily lay professionals, the bishops make great efforts to track issues of import for Catholic principles of social justice, which are crucial to the attainment of Gospel values in contemporary society. Relying on the long-established Catholic social teaching method, *see, judge, and act*, the bishops and their staff study current societal challenges, deliberate on the justice dimensions of various situations, and use the resources at their disposal to act and advocate for better outcomes, in line with their best judgments. Sometimes their response is limited to initiatives within the Church and its institutions, such as changing the policies of Catholic schools to offset racial discrimination, or issuing new directives to Catholic hospitals or charitable agencies to meet the needs of new immigrants or to promote the dignity of human life in various ways.

On other occasions, the bishops exercise religious leadership by reaching out beyond Church boundaries to teach about justice and perhaps influence public policies and their application. Their efforts include issuing many teaching documents on current issues, in policy areas as diverse as labor, education, housing, immigration, gun control, health care, the environment, and the full range of international concerns. Bishops and other representatives of the Church (e.g., officials of Catholic Charities and similar church-based social agencies) sometimes testify before Congress to offer advice and expert opinions on public matters. But more often, the bishops' conference issues public position papers, promulgates pastoral letters, and writes press releases and letters to policymakers in support of official Catholic positions on matters of social justice. In some ways, the efforts of the Catholic Church to influence legislation fit into the category of *lobbying*, the often criticized practice of pressuring lawmakers to support measures favored by particular special interest groups. However, like most lobbying efforts conducted by religious advocacy organizations, bishops' conference interventions tend to focus on advancing ethical principles for public policy, rather than advancing the self-interest of the Church in some crass way. Religious lobbying efforts are really quite different from corporate or industry lobbying efforts.

A few examples of advocacy on the part of the bishops' conference may help illustrate some typical concerns. Annually, the bishop who serves as chair of the Committee on Domestic Justice and Human Development issues a Labor Day Statement that addresses the major concerns of the moment facing workers in the United States and abroad.[2] The statement usually runs between five and ten pages in length and draws from the rich tradition of Catholic teachings on the dignity of work, the rights of workers, and the importance of vibrant labor unions to ensure worker justice. Also on a regular basis, the bishops issue statements regarding priorities that should inform the process by which the annual federal budget is debated and negotiated. Frequently, the bishops' advocacy focuses on the importance of renewing social programs that benefit the most disadvantaged citizens of our land. A good example is the nutrition program for Women, Infants, and Children (WIC), a budget line that requires periodic reauthorization. The bishops, often joined by other Catholic advocacy groups and an array of other religious as well as secular humanitarian organizations, emphasize the priority of funding such programs that serve the neediest. In times of heightened fiscal pressure and growing national debt, anyone who stands up for such measures faces significant opposition from "budget deficit hawks," who favor wielding the budget ax to make ever deeper cuts in social programs like WIC. So it takes considerable courage to stand up for measures that reflect the social teaching priorities of the Catholic Church but do not always match the current conventional wisdom in Washington's corridors of power.

The bishops also find themselves conducting advocacy efforts that are harder to plan, as salient issues sometimes arise unexpectedly on the national policy agenda. For example, no one could have predicted the terrorist attacks of September 11, 2001, but the attacks themselves, as well as the pressure for the United States to respond with force in Afghanistan and eventually in Iraq, prompted a prolonged advocacy effort on the part of the US Catholic bishops, as well as many other religious bodies. Within weeks of the destruction of the World Trade Center in New York, the bishops issued a pastoral statement: "Living with Faith and Hope after September 11."[3] In those months of tumult and emotionally charged calls for vengeance, these Catholic leaders appealed for a carefully calibrated response to Al-Qaeda rather than an indiscriminate and potentially counterproductive "war on terror" that would settle for surrogate enemies and exclusive reliance on military power. The bishops also spoke

---

[2] See, for example, the Labor Day Statement for 2010, "A New 'Social Contract' for Today's 'New Things,'" *http://www.usccb.org/sdwp/national/labor_day_2010.pdf*. It was signed by Bishop William F. Murphy of the Diocese of Rockville Center, NY, who at the time served as chairman of the Committee on Domestic Social Justice and Human Development, and issued by the USCCB on September 6, 2010.

[3] The bishops approved this pastoral letter during their annual November meeting in Washington, DC. It was released November 14, 2001. The full text is available at *http://www.usccb.org/sdwp/sept11.shtml*.

out strongly during the run-up to the March 2003 invasion of Iraq, urging the nation's leaders to exercise restraint and rely on diplomacy rather than on force alone.[4] While these efforts of the bishops were not strictly within the confines of social policy, they illustrate how unforeseeable events can prompt religious advocacy that unfolds on a schedule that no one can predict.

Welfare Reform: A Case Study in Policy Advocacy

Perhaps the best example of a social policy issue that has appeared intermittently on the nation's policy agenda is welfare reform. *Welfare* refers to cash assistance programs for low-income families, usually in households headed by single mothers with young children. During the Great Depression of the 1930s, widowed mothers were one of several demographic groups (in addition to the elderly and the disabled) whose desperate needs were addressed by provisions of the Social Security Act of 1935, part of the New Deal proposed by President Franklin Delano Roosevelt. The national program that recognized the entitlement of qualifying families to a modest income was called Aid to Families with Dependent Children (AFDC), which operated as a matching-grant program between states and the federal government for more than six decades. As time passed and social mores changed, the AFDC program experienced a crisis of legitimacy and found itself criticized on many fronts. A rising percentage of mothers collecting benefits through the program were single not because of widowhood but because of divorce or separation or because they had given birth to children out of wedlock. These conditions raised suspicions that such families might not truly be "deserving poor" but might perhaps knowingly be taking advantage of the welfare system. Further, as large numbers of women entered the workforce in the 1960s and 1970s, rising social expectations that most mothers could manage to work and raise their children robbed the program of much of its original purpose and sent it into a crisis of legitimacy from which it never recovered.

By the late 1970s, many voices called for the reform of AFDC, accusing it of taking away work incentives and encouraging waste, fraud, and intergenerational dependency. Recurring rounds of welfare reform over two decades sought to reduce benefits, restrict eligibility, and institute work requirements (often called workfare) as a condition for single mothers seeking continued public assistance. A number of federal and state initiatives to restructure AFDC, rein in welfare spending, and discourage applicants from collecting benefits to which

---

[4] See the following statements, approved by the entire body of bishops or by Bishop (later Cardinal Archbishop) Wilton D. Gregory, acting in their name as president of the bishops' conference: Bishop Wilton D. Gregory, "Letter to President Bush on the Iraq Situation," *Origins* 32, no. 6 (September 26, 2002): 261–4; USCCB, "Statement on Iraq," *Origins* 32, no. 24 (November 21, 2002): 406–8; Bishop Wilton D. Gregory, "On the Brink of War: A Statement," *Origins* 32, no. 41 (March 27, 2003): 687–8.

they were fully entitled unfolded over these decades, including the bipartisan Family Support Act of 1988. Repeatedly, the difficulty of implementing new program rules stalled welfare reform at every level. The issue came to a head in the mid-1990s, when Democratic President William J. Clinton, who had campaigned on a pledge to "end welfare as we know it," worked with a Republican-dominated House of Representatives (led by Speaker Newt Gingrich and his famous "Contract with America," which included a firm welfare-reform plank) to entirely overhaul the welfare system. After many months of congressional wrangling and two presidential vetoes, in July 1996 Clinton signed into law the "Personal Responsibility and Work Opportunity Reconciliation Act" that formally ended the AFDC program and replaced it with a program called Temporary Assistance for Needy Families. Gone entirely was the entitlement to income for single-parent low-income families. In its place was a system of federal block grants to the states (capped at about $16 billion annually) that turned welfare into a highly conditional benefit governed by a federal time limit of five years of eligibility. States were required to apply work requirements to rising percentages of recipients, and an array of further conditions were imposed upon eligibility for welfare benefits.

During the months when welfare reform was before Congress, the Catholic community was quite active in advocating for a fair and workable resolution of this rhetorically overheated issue or at least for the least harsh outcome for needy families dependent on government assistance. Representatives of the bishops' conference and Catholic Charities testified before congressional committees urging that adequate resources be made available to support the transition from welfare to work for hundreds of thousands of single mothers.[5] These religious voices urged policymakers to provide greater assistance with transportation, job training, and child care for hard-pressed families who would be affected by this momentous change in welfare arrangements. Most noteworthy was a concise but firm document published by the bishops' conference in March 1995 called "Moral Principles and Policy Priorities for Welfare Reform." It called for the following list of priorities to characterize the final legislation, which was moving rapidly through Congress at the very moment it was released:

We will advocate for welfare reform which:

A. Protects human life and dignity;

B. Strengthens family life;

C. Encourages and rewards work;

---

[5] Catholic voices were heard frequently in congressional testimony during the welfare reform debates. One especially well-fashioned document that illustrates these points about Church advocacy appeared January 24, 1994: Catholic Charities USA, *Transforming the Welfare System: A Position Paper of Catholic Charities USA* (Alexandria, VA: Catholic Charities USA, 1994).

    D. Preserves a safety net for the vulnerable;

    E. Builds public/private partnerships to overcome poverty; [and]

    F. Invests in human dignity.[6]

By taking careful note of what this remarkable document accomplishes, even a casual observer of the welfare reform episode can gain much insight into the way the US bishops' conference operates as a force for effective religious advocacy. The mix of faith-based idealism and pragmatic realism in this brief document is clearly evident. The bishops do not imagine they can roll back the full thrust of the "personal responsibility agenda," which had been flowering for decades. Nor do they seek to defend the shortcomings of the AFDC program, such as its tendency to stifle work incentives in cases where paid employment of adult family members is a feasible alternative to reliance on welfare. Yet, the bishops forthrightly declare their continued support for a national commitment to hard-pressed single-parent families and urge political leaders to continue the welfare entitlement in some form. To abandon entirely programs that meet the income needs of the poorest families in our affluent nation would be a violation of many Catholic social teaching principles, including support for human dignity and the preferential option for the poor.[7]

    Further, in the document, the bishops signal their disapproval of a number of myths about welfare dependency, including common but unfair judgments about the motives of recipients of public assistance. No authentic voice of a religion of love and compassion can tolerate the demonization or stigmatization of millions of parents and children, as the ugliest moments of the highly charged welfare debates threatened to do. The genuine well-being of the needy and the search for constructive solutions to the tragedy of grinding poverty in an affluent nation must remain the focus of any national deliberation on public assistance arrangements. Truly successful welfare reform will achieve a careful balance between the imperatives of encouraging the financial independence of most families while recognizing insuperable barriers to employment where they exist.[8]

---

[6] United States Catholic Conference (USCC), "Moral Principles and Policy Priorities for Welfare Reform: A Statement of the Administrative Board of the United States Catholic Conference," *Origins* 24, no. 41 (March 30, 1995): 673–7. It was originally published March 19 as a pamphlet by the USCC (later reorganized and renamed United States Conference of Catholic Bishops).

[7] The Catholic social teaching principles that most immediately apply to social policy in general and welfare reform in particular are discussed in chapters 1 and 4 of Thomas Massaro, *United States Welfare Policy: A Catholic Response* (Washington, DC: Georgetown University Press, 2007).

[8] For a full account of these earlier advocacy efforts and the principles behind them, see Philip S. Land, *Shaping Welfare Consensus: U.S. Catholic Bishops' Contribution* (Washington, DC: Center of Concern Press, 1988).

■ THE CONTRIBUTION OF THE PASTORAL LETTER *ECONOMIC JUSTICE FOR ALL*

The mid-1990s were, of course, not the first time US Catholic bishops weighed in on topics like welfare and poverty. Nearly a decade earlier, the bishops had published their momentous pastoral letter *Economic Justice for All* (*EJA*).[9] Besides offering rich argumentation from Scripture and Christian tradition to support the Church's contemporary concerns about social justice, this ambitious 1986 document contained lengthy sections on topics directly related to social policy. Its third chapter takes up the task of applying the principles of economic justice to selected economic policy issues facing the United States. Among the four topics it treats at greatest length, *EJA* addresses the problem of employment (nos. 136–69) and poverty (nos. 170–215). In each case, the document presents background information (e.g., statistical profiles of the unemployed, demographics of US poverty, and causes of inequality) that supports a subsequent analysis of proposals for improvement and a set of guidelines for action. Once again, a Catholic social teaching document employs the familiar method of *see, judge, and act*, a simple but often fruitful framework for examining, analyzing, and responding to social challenges. Even where the data cited have shifted considerably in subsequent years, the realities uncovered by the bishops and their advisors remain relevant and compelling.

In its section on poverty, for example, *EJA* offers seven proposals for action steps for national policy. These guidelines touch upon the areas of job creation, antidiscrimination measures, tax code reform, education and empowerment programs, family support measures, and (to return to the topic that first brought us to the bishops' letter) welfare reform. Within the latter category, the bishops (in nos. 210–14) offer four priorities for welfare programs, priorities that have provided the framework for all subsequent activism of the bishops' conference on welfare reform. The bishops' call in 1986 for programs that truly support families, discourage unnecessary dependency, and treat fairly eligibility standards and program administration was echoed in Catholic advocacy efforts during subsequent rounds of welfare reform. These include the welfare debates of the late 1980s, mid-1990s (noted above), and fitful attempts after 2002 to reauthorize the landmark welfare reform law of 1996, originally intended as a six-year experiment but repeatedly extended without thorough congressional review. Although the bishops did not really carry the day on welfare reform at any of these junctures, and our nation's welfare system has grown smaller and less readily available to many families in legitimate need, Catholics can be proud of the consistent advocacy efforts of the leaders of their Church during these decades.

---

[9] United States Catholic Bishops, *Economic Justice for All: Pastoral Letter on Catholic Social Teaching and the U.S. Economy* (Washington, DC: USCC, 1986).

Through energetic leadership and a series of eloquent documents, the bishops have offered a coherent position on public and private measures to combat poverty and have communicated the authentic social justice priorities of the Catholic community in impressive ways on the national stage.

■ PROGRESS TOWARD UNIVERSAL HEALTH-CARE COVERAGE

A key social policy area closely related to poverty is affordable health-care coverage. In an era of sharply rising health-care costs, when chronic, catastrophic, or even routine medical needs can quickly bankrupt millions of families, access to affordable health insurance clearly forms an essential part of the social safety net for all but the wealthiest Americans. If one is serious about fighting poverty, a good place to begin is reforming the provision of health care, something that takes a major bite out of most families' budgets and that constitutes a startling and still rising percentage of our nation's productive output every year.

Unlike nearly all Western industrialized nations, the United States entered the twenty-first century without a national policy or coordinated program guaranteeing universal access to quality health care. Most affluent Americans have been well served by private health insurance, often obtained at a considerable discount through their workplace as a benefit of employment, but for decades now tens of millions of middle- and low-income families were left uninsured or seriously underinsured. A frequent lack of portability of health-care coverage from job to job and the inevitability of individuals "falling through the cracks" (with incomes too high to qualify for publicly funded Medicaid benefits but too low to afford adequate private coverage) has doomed tens of millions to the ranks of the uninsured.

Most presidents elected after World War II came into office with a proposal to address the need for affordable health care, but no comprehensive plan ever made it through Congress, until 2010. The most noteworthy near-miss for health-care reform came in President Clinton's first term. Opposition to his rather complex national plan for universal coverage arose from numerous powerful special interest groups, including private health insurers, the pharmaceutical industry, and many doctors and health-care professionals who were wary of change. The passage of President Barack Obama's "Patient Protection and Affordable Care Act of 2010" was complicated by some of the same dynamics that scuttled President Clinton's proposals nearly two decades earlier. It passed by the narrowest of margins, and this was possible only through a series of compromises over many months of congressional negotiations and several "near-death experiences." But in the end it garnered more support than all the previous health-care plans, perhaps for the simple reason that more

Americans than ever before agreed with the Act's three core goals: (1) extend universal coverage, (2) control long-term costs, and (3) improve the quality of health-care delivery.

Whether these three goals can be achieved simultaneously remains, as of this writing, uncertain. It may take decades to gather enough information to fully and adequately assess our nation's new health-care arrangements. It remains entirely possible that key provisions of the law (such as the mandate that individuals buy or otherwise arrange for coverage through state-level insurance exchanges) will be rolled back through legislative action or in the courts. What is certain is that proposals for universal health-care coverage have long been supported by many religious voices in the United States, especially in the Catholic community. The US bishops' long-standing concern about universal and affordable health-care coverage is evident in the broad array of documents they have published in recent decades. Surveying the most significant of these will illuminate the central logic by which the Catholic Church has supported health-care reform and other social policy legislation in recent years.

EJA mentions access to health care only in passing. This may seem surprising, since that document is, to date, the single longest statement the bishops have published on such matters of public policy. However, it is wise to recall that the letter was drafted and promulgated in the mid-1980s, during the middle years of the Reagan administration, a time when no serious health-care proposal was on the table. The prospect of sweeping changes to health-care access had been dealt a blow in the late 1970s, when pro-reform efforts (primarily among Democrats, such as Massachusetts senator Edward M. Kennedy) failed to move the issue forward during the Carter administration, leaving health-care reform efforts to lie fallow for some years. So the relative silence of *EJA* on health-care matters may be interpreted primarily as a result of political timing. Nevertheless, in the document's section on poverty, the bishops voice their distress that lack of health insurance and quality health care plays a disastrous role in the lives of millions of poor Americans, as both a cause and effect of poverty (no. 177). A few pages later, the bishops call attention to the important successes of Medicaid and Medicare in reducing such distressing social indicators as infant mortality and improving access to life-saving medical treatments for low-income Americans (no. 191).

As health-care reform worked its way back onto the national policy agenda in subsequent years, documents published by the bishops' conference reflected this renewal of interest, as well as several distinctive Catholic concerns. The 1992 document *Putting Children and Families First: A Challenge for Our Church, Nation, and World*, published by three major committees of the bishops' conference, contained a prominent and heartfelt paragraph lamenting the persistence of poverty and uneven access to health care among children. The document pulls no punches in blaming a variety of preventable illnesses and even the deaths of many infants and children on "our nation's continuing failure to guarantee access to quality health care for all people."[10]

The US bishops' admonitions on health care became even more pointed the following year, as the new Clinton administration signaled its intention to develop a serious proposal for a comprehensive national health insurance plan. Within five months of Bill Clinton's inauguration, a detailed statement of principles on health-care reform had been drafted by the bishops' Domestic Social Policy Committee and then approved by the administrative board (in March 1993) and then the full body of the bishops' conference at its general meeting (in June 1993). The full title of the document captures its intent: "A Framework for Comprehensive Health Care Reform: Protecting Human Life, Promoting Human Dignity, Pursuing the Common Good." In about twenty-five paragraphs, the statement outlines a series of policy priorities for any responsible health plan, whatever its origin or sponsorship. Among the eight principles highlighted in the document's key list of bullet points are distinctive recurring concerns of the Catholic Church in public policy debates (e.g., pro-life emphasis, priority concern for the poor) and some items with an even broader appeal to many constituencies (e.g., equitable financing through cost-sharing arrangements, cost-containment measures, and maintenance of quality care). The bishops thus joined their voices with a broad coalition of concerned public actors committed to finding a way "to finance universal access to comprehensive health care in an equitable fashion."[11] The motivations of the Catholic community in pursuing this agenda (specific commitments to principles of charity or scripturally based notions of justice) may not have perfectly matched the motivations of other members of the coalition, but nonetheless common grounds were forged supporting advocacy for health-care reform.

Even after the Clinton plan collapsed beneath fierce opposition, the bishops sought to sustain the issue of health-care reform. At every opportunity, documents of the bishops' conference underlined the urgency of addressing the crisis of rising health costs and diminishing access to quality health care for tens of millions of low- and middle-income Americans. For example, the bishops' 1995 pastoral letter marking the tenth anniversary of *EJA* calls attention to the high cost of health care, and especially how the middle class is increasingly "squeezed" and beset by worries about "whether they will keep their jobs and health insurance."[12] A landmark 2002 document addressing the realities of poverty at home and abroad went out of its way to keep health-care reform before the eyes of its

---

[10] USCC, *Putting Children and Families First: A Challenge for Our Church, Nation, and World* (Washington, DC: USCC, 1992), 12.

[11] This phrase appears in the "Criteria for Reform" section of this 1993 bishops' statement, *http://www.usccb.org/sdwp/national/comphealth.shtml*.

[12] National Conference of Catholic Bishops, "A Decade after *Economic Justice for All*: Continuing Principles, Changing Context, New Challenges" (Washington, DC: USCC, 1995), 3.

readers. Called *A Place at the Table: A Catholic Recommitment to Overcome Poverty and to Respect the Dignity of All God's Children*, this was hardly a policy document but rather was labeled a "pastoral reflection of the U.S. Catholic Bishops." Nevertheless, on four occasions in its twenty-four pages, this document cites the struggle to secure health care as among the most pressing challenges facing the poor today, both in the United States and throughout the world.[13]

Each of the documents mentioned above represents bishops' conference efforts to launch new initiatives or to mark moments of particular importance in policy debates. But the issue of guaranteed access to basic health care also found its way into more routine documents regularly issued by Church authorities. The best example is the series of quadrennial statements published by the bishops' conference about a year in advance of each presidential election. Usually referred to as calls to "faithful citizenship" or "political responsibility," these documents represent the Catholic Church's attempt to help potential voters form their consciences on the issues of the day. Strictly nonpartisan and highly principled in tone, these documents contain useful summaries of Catholic social teaching as well as comprehensive lists of current public policy issues that are on the front (or back) burner as the election approaches.

It will come as no surprise that issues relating to health care have been mentioned by the bishops in every such document published since the series began in the 1970s. Since these documents limit themselves to twenty-five or thirty pages in pamphlet format and need to cover much ground on dozens of issues, readers cannot expect extensive coverage of any one policy area. Nevertheless, the bishops' desire to maintain a high profile for the importance of health-care reform has consistently guaranteed a prominent place for the issue in this series of short texts.

Because they recognize the urgency of health-care reform, the bishops do not settle for relegating it to just another slot on a laundry list of social justice items. Rather, the bishops single out health care as a pivotal issue in addressing the needs of low-income people, a constituency far too often overlooked in the corridors of power and national elections. Emblematic of the commitment of the bishops' conference is the following excerpt from the 1995 statement on political responsibility:

> Our national health care system still serves too few and costs too much. Decent health care is an essential safeguard of human life. We believe reform of the health care system must be rooted in values that respect the essential dignity of each person, ensure that human life is protected, and recognize the urgent needs of the poor. . . . Genuine health care reform is a matter of fundamental justice. We urge national leaders to look beyond special interest claims and partisan

---

[13] USCCB, *A Place at the Table* (Washington, DC: USCCB Publishing, 2002).

differences to unite our nation in a new commitment to meeting the health care needs of our people.[14]

One particularly revealing way of framing the bishops' activism on health-care reform in recent decades is to emphasize that health care is one application of a core set of fundamental principles that should guide all Church-based reflection on social policy. Behind the moment-to-moment advocacy concerns corresponding to public policy and political currents is a core of faith-based values that Catholics seek to preserve and advance in the public sphere: fair sharing of burdens and benefits, rights and responsibilities, as well as the imperatives of protecting human dignity and advancing the common good. Advocacy documents from the bishops' conference fall into a genre of literature that cannot afford to dwell for long on the basic principles and values that motivate Catholic activism on specific issues like health care. A full understanding of what is at stake in the task of applying Catholic social thought to public issues requires the consultation of other literature, such as the works of theologians, social ethicists, and Church leaders who turn their attention specifically to the theoretical underpinnings and justifications of policy positions. Fortunately, the US Catholic community has been blessed with a number of such figures in recent decades.

There has been no more eloquent spokesman for these values in the US Catholic Church than the late Joseph Cardinal Bernardin. In the dozen years or so before his untimely death in 1996, this leader among the American bishops delivered a long and impressive series of lectures on the theme he made famous: a consistent ethic of life. Whether he was addressing the specific topic of peacemaking or abortion or social assistance for the poor, Cardinal Bernardin frequently used the phrase "a seamless garment of life" to portray the authentic response of Christians to threats to the dignity and integrity of life. In other words, respect for life is a proper and unifying lens through which to view the full range of social policy issues. Early in this series of influential lectures, Bernardin addressed the topic "The Consistent Ethic of Life and Health Care Systems." The text he read at that May 8, 1985, conference at Loyola University in Chicago included the following signature observation:

> The protection, defense and nurture of human life involve the whole spectrum of life from conception to death, cutting across such issues as genetics, abortion, capital punishment, modern warfare and the care of the terminally ill. . . . The fact that we face new challenges in each of these areas reveals the need for a consistent ethic of life.[15]

---

[14] Administrative Board of the USCC, *Political Responsibility: Proclaiming the Gospel of Life, Protecting the Least among Us, and Pursuing the Common Good* (Washington, DC: USCC, 1995), 22.

[15] Cardinal Joseph Bernardin, "The Consistent Ethic of Life and Health Care Systems," in Alphonse P. Spilly, ed., *Selected Works of Joseph Cardinal Bernardin*, vol. 2, *Church and Society* (Collegeville, MN: Liturgical Press, 2000), 199–207, at 201.

In this address as elsewhere in the corpus of his writings, Cardinal Bernardin clearly articulates the rationale for the Catholic Church's activism on the full array of social policies. To the surprise of some and perhaps the consternation of others, Bernardin portrayed universal access to affordable health care as a pro-life priority. He was eager to demonstrate how the principle of "a consistent ethic of life" extended beyond the Church's strong opposition to abortion, a stance that is commendable but incomplete if it remains isolated from efforts to counter other threats to life. A well-formed Catholic conscience requires a wide variety of actions to protect life and promote human dignity across the lifespan. Whatever obstacles prevent people from obtaining the health care they need to survive and lead secure lives, free from inordinate concern about how they will pay for critical medical treatments they may someday need, are intolerable threats to life that must be addressed.

Universal access to affordable and comprehensive health care emerges, then, as a very precious good. It is among a special set of key goods easily identifiable as necessary for a dignified and secure life. We can live a good life without any number of things we might want at any given moment (luxury cars, expensive vacations); the market mechanisms of supply and demand, price fluctuations, and disposable income suffice to determine access to nonnecessities like these. One may buy what one can afford and survive without coveted but nonessential material goods and services when the budget is exhausted. It is an ethically neutral question whether one has the money to buy a Lexus or fly to Europe this summer for a vacation. But for goods like health care, which has moral value beyond its status as a commodity, a nonmarket mechanism is justified when self-reliance proves impossible. Determining access to health care strictly by one's ability to pay, and thus limiting medical treatments to those with sufficiently deep pockets, constitutes a grave injustice, and, in the long run, dooms untold numbers of people to early deaths. Programs for provision of essential social goods like health care must guarantee access when markets fall short. This is why many voices guided by Catholic social thought have long insisted on universal access to health care, as part of a larger agenda of maintaining a secure social safety net for people whose incomes, for whatever reason, are too low to support a dignified life.

Given the foundations in Catholic social teaching that support the principle of universal access to health care, and given the consistent advocacy record of the bishops' conference on this issue, the greatest of ironies unfolded in the spring of 2010. After decades of delays and upon the wreckage of multiple plans for reform, President Obama's health-care plan (called the Patient Protection and Affordable Care Act) was on the verge of passage. At that moment, to the surprise and dismay of many, the bishops' conference withdrew its support for the president's proposed overhaul. The bishops opposed the bill because of another pro-life issue: abortion. In their study of how the law's proposed funding would work, the bishops feared it would prove impossible to separate taxpayer funds from private insurance funds that cover abortions. Although the Hyde

Amendment had for decades effectively prevented the use of federal funds to pay for abortions, and despite Obama's issuing an executive order prohibiting such an outcome to allay such concerns, the bishops maintained their position. A majority of the bishops showed a particularly strong aversion to the possibility that the operations of some state-level exchanges (or marketplaces for insurance plans) would create loopholes allowing funding sources to mix in ways that facilitated abortion coverage. They also feared even the appearance of government support for abortion due to the way that tax credits apply to health insurance premiums, some of which may wind up supporting abortions, elective sterilizations, and other medical procedures that conflict with the teachings of the Catholic Church.

Other Catholic groups and agencies, however, maintained their support for the legislation. These include the influential Catholic Health Association and the Leadership Conference of Women Religious, which represents many orders of nuns. It must be noted that these groups agreed with the bishops on the importance of opposing abortion but disagreed in their interpretation of the legislation's abortion provisions.[16] When the bill did eventually pass, with the support of most pro-life Democrats in Congress, much media coverage focused on the seeming conflict within the Catholic community. While it is true that prominent Catholics did indeed come to different conclusions about the merits of the legislation, the media often failed to distinguish between basic principles of Catholic social teaching and their prudential application to specific policies.

■■ CONCLUSION

While focusing primarily on welfare reform and the debate over health-care reform, this examination of the advocacy efforts of the US Catholic Church has considered the wider question of how a distinctive set of religious beliefs motivates social concern and activism. Guided by principles like the common good, human dignity, universal solidarity, and sincere concern for the poor, Catholic voices consistently stand up for social policies that provide for many unmet human needs. Other case studies of Catholic advocacy could also have been cited here—instances in recent decades in which the bishops' conference and other Catholic groups weighed in on proposed social legislation.

As critical as their provisions are for the life prospects of the least advantaged members of US society, many proposed expansions of the social safety net

---

[16] A prolonged debate played out in the media between some Catholic bishops and several Catholic researchers and intellectuals; most prominent among the latter was Professor Timothy Stoltzfus Jost, a law professor at Washington and Lee University. See his "Episcopal Oversight: How the Bishops Conference Gets Health-Care Legislation Wrong," *Commonweal*, June 4, 2010, 8–9. See also the series of memoranda and documents posted on the health-care section of the bishops' conference website during spring 2010, analyzing the Obama plan and responding explicitly to Professor Jost's arguments. One such document, a four-page memo dated March 12, 2010, is titled, "What's Wrong with the Senate Health Care Bill on Abortion?" *http://www.usccb.org/healthcare/jost-response.pdf.*

tend to fly under the radar of popular attention. However, no important social policy proposal has gone unnoticed by the US bishops and members of their professional staff at the bishops' conference in Washington, DC. These vigilant advocates for social justice have consistently supported a sustained national commitment to protect the United States' most vulnerable families from the worst effects of deprivation, even when the costs of social policies have come under intense criticism in this era of fiscal pressure and budgetary austerity. Indeed, for at least the past generation, advocates for the poor have mostly been playing defense, fending off proposals for draconian spending cuts and the slashing of programs like food stamps and housing subsidies.

Catholic voices have consistently been among our nation's most prominent advocates for poor people. Both clerical and lay, visible leaders and the rank and file in the pews—Catholics have not been afraid to uphold their national commitment to retain an adequate safety net for citizens in distress. Drawing upon the documents of Catholic social teaching and enacting their social justice principles through a network of schools, hospitals, charitable agencies, and other Church-sponsored institutions, Catholics will continue to make great efforts to lift up the poor among us. Finally, the Catholic Church will no doubt be on the lookout for new partners who also seek to pursue an agenda of responsible social legislation and forward-looking social policy.

FOCUS QUESTIONS

1. Knowing what you do about US politics and about Roman Catholicism, how would you summarize the public policy dimensions of Catholic faith? What key beliefs and commitments within Catholicism lead adherents of this faith community to hold distinctive views on issues of social policy?

2. Are you optimistic that Catholic leaders in the future will frequently be able to join in broad coalitions with other groups to advance common social objectives such as reforms of social policy? Or do you think the Catholic community is destined to stand alone on most of these items of potential social reform?

3. How helpful is the Catholic notion of "the common good"? Do you see other religious and secular traditions as capturing the same basic concept in other terms or phrases? If so, what are some of these phrases?

4. Is there anything objectionable about a religious community (like Christian denominations) drawing upon faith-based values as they advocate for specific social policies? Does this violate any constitutional principles or other values that Americans commonly hold?

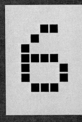

Where Y'at Race, Whiteness, and Economic Justice?

A Map of White Complicity in the Economic Oppression of People of Color

Alex Mikulich

■■ INTRODUCTION

Imagine that you are a member of a racing team set to compete, and you are told you must wait 537 years before you can actually leave the starting line. Imagine further that regular public announcements declare all competitors in the race are equal and have equal opportunity to advance; however, only members of the team with the 537-year head start will set and enforce the rules, and decide who gets training facilities, who will be fined or penalized, and who reaps the benefits of winning.

Members of the first-place team enjoy the advantages of their dominant position while members of losing teams not only suffer the burden of inadequate or nonexistent training facilities, they are constantly penalized—even labeled "criminals" for trying to get ahead by breaking minor rules, and ultimately are marked "losers" by the entire league.

Members of the dominant team deny they have an advantage and sincerely believe the competition is fair. They also object to any protest of league rules, labeling such protests as "whining" from people who should know they are "losers" who need to learn how to play the game fairly and without breaking any rules. "Losers" need to face reality, they are told, and forget the history of how the game was set up and "just get on with life."

Such a game may sound ludicrous and invite laughter or recrimination: no one would ever construct or participate in such a ridiculously unfair game. Yet this is no imaginary construct. This is life in the United States of America. In fact, if the United States proceeds at the current rate of racial income inequality, African Americans will not achieve the same income as white Americans for 537 years.[1]

∷ THE REALITY OF RACE TODAY

Nonetheless, too many whites insist Americans live in a so-called post-racial society in which everyone begins the "race of life"—more or less—on a level playing field. Since the historic passage of the Civil Rights Act in 1964 and Voting Rights Act in 1965, many whites considered the social inequality rooted in slavery as overcome. Although whites disproportionately benefit in all spheres of life in the United States—whether health, education, income, wealth, housing, or the criminal justice system—they tend to remain ignorant or deny the reality of racial inequality. For example, consider the following:

- The Institute of Medicine of the National Academies finds that "Evidence of racial and ethnic disparities in healthcare is, with few exceptions, remarkably consistent across a range of illnesses and healthcare services."[2]

- The median wealth of white households is twenty times that of black households and eighteen times that of Hispanic households, according to analysis of government data available through 2009. These are the largest wealth ratios found since the government began publishing this data a quarter century ago.[3]

- Although whites make up 70 percent of all drug users nationally, blacks are eleven times more likely to be arrested for drug possession than whites. Blacks constitute only 14 percent of drug users nationally but they account for 35 percent of all drug arrests, 55 percent of all drug convictions, and 75 percent of all prison admissions for drug offenses.[4] One—certainly not the only—dimension of this inequality concerns how law enforcement overlooks affluent white college student drug users and dealers.[5]

---

[1] Dedrick Muhammad, *40 Years Later: The Unrealized American Dream* (Washington, DC: Institute for Policy Studies, April 2008), 5.

[2] Brian D. Smedley, Adrienne Y. Stith, and Alan R. Nelson, eds., *Unequal Treatment: Confronting Racial and Ethnic Disparities in Health Care* (Washington, DC: National Academies Press, 2003), 5 and 77–9.

[3] Rakesh Kochhar, Richard Fry, and Paul Taylor, "Wealth Gaps Rise to Record Highs between Whites, Blacks, Hispanics," Pew Research Center, July 26, 2011, 1, *http://www.pewsocialtrends. org/2011/07/26/wealth-gaps-rise-to-record-highs-between-whites-blacks-hispanics/*.

[4] Human Rights Watch, *Targeting Blacks: Law Enforcement and Race in the United States* (Washington, DC: May 2008), 2, *http://www.hrw.org/sites/default/files/reports/us0508webwcover.pdf*.

[5] Rafik Muhamed and Erik D. Fritsvold, *Dorm Room Dealers: Drugs and the Privileges of Race and Class* (Boulder, CO: Lynne Rienner Publishers, 2009).

- A 2006 Center for Responsible Lending study found that when income and credit risks were equal, black and Latino borrowers were more than 30 percent more likely to receive a higher-rate loan than whites.[6]
- An extensive study of hiring outcomes in Milwaukee, Boston, and Chicago reveals that white applicants with a criminal record were just as likely to receive a callback as a black applicant *without* any criminal history. Despite the fact that white applicants revealed evidence of felony drug conviction and reported having returned from one and a half years in prison, employers viewed them as no more risky than a young black male with *no* criminal record.[7]
- Fifty years after the US Supreme Court decided that school segregation was unconstitutional and "inherently unequal," a national study of the resegregation of the nation's schools finds that "white students are by far the most segregated from all other races in their schools. Whites on average attend schools where less than a fifth of the students are from all other groups combined. Blacks and Latinos are next in terms of isolation, but far behind, attending schools with 53 to 55 percent students of their own group." Gary Orfield concludes, "research consistently shows that segregated schools . . . offer vastly unequal educational opportunities."[8]

These examples illumine only the proverbial "tip of the iceberg" of racial inequality. "My white wherewithal," explains the white Protestant theologian James Perkinson,

> is *constituted in* Afro (as indeed Latino- and Filipino- and aboriginal-, etc.) American impoverishment. Their loss is my gain. The relationship is utterly asymmetrical and the asymmetry is utterly relational.[9] (italics in the original)

In other words, the consequences of race in America are thoroughly unequal and the inequality thoroughly interconnects whites and people of color.

Nevertheless, whites tend to be ignorant of, or to justify, the disproportionate burdens borne by blacks, Latinos, and Native Americans enduring substandard health care, inadequate education, declining income and wealth, and the

---

[6] Debbie Gruenstein Bocian, Keith S. Ernst, and Wei Li, *Unfair Lending: The Effect of Race and Ethnicity on the Price of Subprime Mortgages*, Center for Responsible Lending, 2006, 3, *http://www.responsiblelending.org/mortgage-lending/research-analysis/rr011-Unfair_Lending-0506.pdf.*

[7] Devah Pager, *Marked: Race, Crime, and Finding Work in an Era of Mass Incarceration* (Chicago: University of Chicago Press, 2007), 89–91.

[8] Gary Orfield, "Schools More Separate: Consequences of a Decade of Resegregation," The Civil Rights Project, 2001, *http://civilrightsproject.ucla.edu/research/k-12-education/integration-and-diversity/schools-more-separate-consequences-of-a-decade-of-resegregation/orfield-schools-more-separate-2001.pdf, 34.*

[9] James W. Perkinson, *White Theology: Outing Supremacy in Modernity* (New York: Palgrave MacMillan, 2004), 15.

indignities of a system of incarceration that imprisons black men at a rate "much higher" than that during apartheid South Africa.[10]

In their 1986 pastoral letter *Economic Justice for All* (*EJA*), the US Catholic bishops contend the best way to honor the dream of "liberty and justice for all" would be by "working for the day when all our sisters and brothers share adequately in the American dream" (no. 9).[11] The bishops note that far too many Americans—some 40 to 60 million people—live in poverty or struggle to make ends meet. For these Americans, the so-called American dream is at best a myth, at worst a nightmare.

The bishops wrote with two key purposes in mind: first, to provide guidance for members of the Catholic faith to form their consciences about economic matters, and, second, for the bishops to add their voices to the public debate on the direction of the US economy. Although *EJA* was written from the perspective of Catholic social teaching and primarily directed toward Catholic Christians in the United States, the bishops address their pastoral letter to all people of faith and citizens of goodwill who seek to build a truly common good.

As a Roman Catholic social ethicist, my work demands that I converse with key texts of my tradition. The wide variety of documents that constitute the Roman Catholic Church's teaching on social, political, economic, and cultural matters is called Catholic social teaching. While this chapter presents an analysis of one pastoral letter of the US Catholic bishops, *EJA* (1986), it also draws widely upon Catholic social teaching to develop its line of reasoning. This chapter, like Catholic social teaching and the US Catholic bishops, addresses people of faith and citizens from all traditions who seek to end social injustice and create a truly shared and good society for all.

In the spirit of the bishops' effort, a word of warning. As the Dalai Lama explains, the social conditioning that gives rise to racial bias can only be undone by "actively disputing the distorted ideas and false beliefs, [and] presenting a case for revising these beliefs, by pointing out where there are false premises upon which they base those beliefs, false projections and so on. It is a matter of discovering the reality."[12] In an earlier book, I reflected on how I am continually learning how ignorant I am of my complicity in white racism, and how I need to learn from the wisdom and experience of people of color.[13]

---

[10] Holly Sklar, "Imagine a Country—2006," in Paula S. Rothenberg, ed., *Race, Class, and Gender in the United States: An Integrated Study* (New York: MacMillan, 2006), 334.

[11] Generally, papal, magisterial, and local episcopal documents of the Roman Catholic Church are enumerated by paragraph. These paragraphs are cited in the text when possible.

[12] Howard Cutler and Dalai Lama, *The Art of Happiness in a Troubled World* (New York: Harmony Books, 2009), 69.

[13] Alex Mikulich, "(Un)Learning White Male Ignorance," in Laurie Cassidy and Alex Mikulich, eds., *Interrupting White Privilege: Catholic Theologians Break the Silence* (Maryknoll, NY: Orbis Books, 2007), ch. 9.

Having taken nearly twenty-five years to "discover the reality" of how I and other good white people contribute to racial inequality, readers are humbly invited into a shared work of self-critique, reflecting upon your own physical, social, economic, and spiritual setting in life, both as individuals and collectively, within the communities where you live, work, study, and play. It is only through this shared work of critical self-reflection, explains the great black American writer James Baldwin, "that one begins to achieve a level of personal maturity and freedom which robs history of its tyrannical power, and also changes history."[14]

In my home of New Orleans, people stop and begin to talk with each other by asking "Where y'at?" The question may elicit only a passing comment about the weather, or someone might share his or her life story. This chapter invites readers to reflect deeply about "where y'at" as a way to probe critically what scholars call social location. The "where y'at" question invites a shift away from abstract notions of race as something out there, disconnected from personal life, and toward the concrete places where race shapes all of us individually and collectively.

The reality of racial inequality first hit home for me when I survived a bone marrow transplant in 1984 for life-threatening leukemia. Had I been a black American male, I learned, I most likely would have died due to lack of access to health insurance and the best health care. While readers need not face death to understand how racial inequality can produce death in America, the work of racial justice requires that all of us recognize the myriad ways racism "malforms, conforms, and deforms us into an alien identity radically at odds with Christian belief"[15] and an authentic humanity.

In the spirit of the universal appeal of Catholic social teaching and the US Catholic bishops, this chapter examines the need for a new vision advocating economic justice for all. I believe the bishops' prophetic and realistic vision of economic justice should be celebrated by applying the fullness of this vision to the reality of racial and economic injustice in the United States today.

The title "Where Y'at Race, Whiteness, and Economic Justice?" suggests the basic point of this essay: *EJA* misplaces "race" by overemphasizing the role of individual racism while failing to address the much larger role of historical, cultural, systemic, and structured white advantage, which creates an enduring exclusion and oppression for people of color. *EJA* lacks analysis of the historical and material conditions—social, political, and economic—that have created persistent advantage for whites to the detriment of people of color in every sphere of US life. I use the term *white complicity* with other scholars to indicate the

---

[14] James Baldwin, "White Man's Guilt," in *The Price of the Ticket: Collected Nonfiction, 1948–1985* (New York: St. Martin's Press, 1985), 410.

[15] Bryan N. Massingale, *Racial Justice and the Catholic Church* (Maryknoll, NY: Orbis Books, 2010), 25–6.

complex ways that good white people both benefit from and contribute to persistent racial inequality.[16]

The argument here proceeds in four sections: First, the biblical, theological, and moral perspective of *EJA* is introduced, and the document's approach to race is discussed. Second, the way that disproportionate white income and wealth evolved historically to enforce severe black economic disadvantage is explored. Third, the relationship between white housing segregation and how whites learn to view US racial inequality as normal and natural is considered. Fourth, the question of how citizens and people of faith can confront white complicity in racial and economic oppression, a challenge that goes to the heart of *EJA*'s call to practice Eucharistic memory and hope, is posed.

■ CHRISTIAN VS. AMERICAN VALUES

The US Catholic bishops begin their reflection on economic justice with the biblical understanding that each person is sacred and social, created in God's image, and thus to share in the goods of the earth as part of a community of justice and love. The biblical story of creation, in which God creates human beings in God's image, is the basis of the theological and moral principle of the universal dignity of every person. A second critical insight from the Bible that the bishops draw upon is God's call to love and do justice to the most vulnerable members of society. This is the basis of the principle that the moral measure of economic justice is how the poor and vulnerable are faring.

These insights are found in the heart of Hebrew and Christian Scripture and inform the Catholic understanding of the unity of the commandments to love God and love neighbor. God's call to welcome and care for those who are vulnerable reveals the radically universal love of God: God's love overflows for the whole of creation, and humans are called to share that love with all others. However, practicing love—or what the bishops call solidarity—is no easy task for white, economically advantaged North American Christians whose relative power may block them from hearing, much less practicing, the biblical call to treat the vulnerable as members of one's own family.

I say "the radically universal love of God" because in the Torah (the first five books of Jewish Scripture), God's call to the people of Israel to extend love to the stranger in their midst would have sounded absurd to a tribal people.[17] Indeed,

---

[16] Barbara Applebaum, *Being White, Being Good: White Complicity, White Moral Responsibility, and Social Justice Pedagogy* (Lanham, MD: Lexington Books, 2010), 8–21.

[17] Victor H. Matthews and Don C. Benjamin, *The Social World of Ancient Israel: 1250–587 BCE* (Peabody, MA: Hendrickson Publishers, 1993), xviii. See also Jerome H. Neyrey and Bruce J. Malina, "First Century Personality: Dyadic, Not Individualistic," in *The Social World of Luke-Acts: Models for Interpretation* (Peabody, MA: Hendrickson Publishers, 1991), ch. 3.

it may sound too abstract to North Americans as well, unless they attend to its historical context. In the ancient Middle East, the gods of most groups were narrowly tribal or nationalistic. Also, there was no notion of the individual as it has developed in Western modernity.[18] Identity was wrapped up with the tribe and in the demands of the tribal gods. Identity—and physical survival—was impossible if one was separated from the clan.

The book of Exodus recounts Israel's experience of a God radically different from those of other tribes or groups. The God of Exodus is intimate—this God has "witnessed the affliction of my people in Egypt and have heard their cry of complaint against their slave drivers, so I know well that they are suffering. Therefore I have come down to rescue them from the hands of the Egyptians and lead them out of that land into a good and spacious land, a land flowing with milk and honey" (Ex 3:7–8).

God's radically universal love erases any tribal or nationalistic boundaries. The Lord God calls the people to practice love in a radically different way: "When an alien resides with you in your land, do not molest him. You shall treat the alien who resides with you no differently than the natives born among you; have the same love for him as for yourself; for you too were once aliens in the land of Egypt. I, the Lord, am your God" (Lv 19:33–34). This call is unequivocal and radical.

God's call to Israel to practice love is radical because in the ancient context, if a person was separated from the tribe, one of two things would likely happen: they would either be enslaved or killed.[19] Not only does God call the people not to kill, God clearly calls the people to treat the widow, orphan, alien, or stranger—anyone disconnected from their tribe and vulnerable—as a member of one's own family and community.

Welcoming the vulnerable, the excluded, and the stranger is the radical mark of the universal love of God. God calls the people to recognize their commonality with, and moral responsibility for, vulnerable strangers in the land. This story is integral to Jewish memory as a covenantal people who recognize themselves and their shared humanity in others who are oppressed in any way.

Jesus fulfills this Jewish tradition of justice and love in his teaching and action. The US bishops celebrate Jesus' three great parables centered on preferential love for the oppressed: the Good Samaritan in Luke 10, the rich man and Lazarus in Luke 16, and the dramatic judgment of Matthew 25. Through these stories, and by the people with whom he associates, Jesus dramatically identifies himself with the poor and measures individuals and nations by deeds of justice and love.

---

[18] Jerome Neyrey and Bruce J. Malina, "Comparing U.S. Values with the Mediterranean View," in *Calling Jesus Names: The Social Value of Labels in Matthew* (Sonoma, CA: Polebridge Press, 1988), 145–51.

[19] Matthews, *Social World of Ancient Israel*, xviii.

Moreover, Jesus' identification with the poor stands in contrast to the popular myth of the American dream. Indeed, Jesus' statement that "the last will be first, and the first will be last" (Mt 20:16) violates the United States' most cherished cultural assumptions, including the so-called American dream. At its core, this cultural myth assumes that any person can become whoever she or he dreams of becoming, regardless of race, class, gender, or geographical location.

Consider how Americans react to waiting in lines. Many cry foul if anyone cuts in front of them at the grocery store, gas station, ticket counter, or in a traffic jam. Jesus' statement conflicts with American's common sense: if anyone cuts in front of them, they are angry and protest, and yet if they gain advantage through no merit of their own, they tend to remain silent. That Jesus flips the entire order of the line—and society—upside down is even more difficult and unimaginable for them. This conflict between the Scriptures and America's most cherished myth of equal opportunity becomes most apparent in the racial inequality in income, wealth, housing, and schools.

The universal dignity of the human person and God's preferential love for the oppressed provide two solid biblical and theological foundations for the US Catholic bishops' argument for economic justice. These foundational principles support the bishops' view that the economy must serve people, not the reverse.[20] Under the principle of God's preferential love for the poor, the moral measure of how the economy is working is how the poor and vulnerable are faring. If the poor and vulnerable lack the resources to attain minimal needs for human dignity and basic justice, society cannot claim a common good for all its members.

These biblical, theological, and moral insights are the foundation for the US bishops' argument for economic justice. At its core, *EJA* integrates a realistic understanding of social sin with a prophetic vision for personal and social transformation as part of its theological and moral wisdom. *Social sin* concerns "patterns of exclusion" in which people or groups are actively or passively treated as "nonmembers of the human race. To treat people this way is effectively to say that they simply do not count as human beings" (no. 77). This understanding of social sin is rooted deeply in the Catholic understanding of the social nature of human beings and so the bishops cite documents from Vatican II, Pope Paul VI, and Pope John Paul II to emphasize this important point.[21] The bishops are clearly

---

[20] Any economic or social theory that reduces human beings to economics, an instrument of economics, or that subordinates human beings to the economy is called "the error of economism" by Pope John Paul II. See Pope John Paul II, *Laborem Excercens* (On Human Work), The Vatican, 1981, no. 13, *http://www.vatican.va/holy_father/john_paul_ii/encyclicals/documents/hf_jp-ii_enc_14091981_laborem-exercens_en.html*.

[21] In their footnote to the term *social sin*, in no. 77, the bishops cite *Gaudium et spes* (The Pastoral Constitution on the Church in the Modern World), 1965, no. 25; the Synod of Bishops, *Justice in the World*, 1971, no. 51; Pope John Paul II, *The Gift of Redemption: Apostolic Exhortation on Reconciliation and Penance*, (1984), no. 16; and Congregation for Doctrine of the Faith, *Instruction on Christian Freedom and Liberation*, 1986, nos. 42, 74.

concerned with the ways that a culture of individualism excludes and divides people against one another and God, as well as the ways that unjust economic structures make vulnerable people into instruments of economic gain for a privileged few. Failure to work to end these patterns of exclusion constitutes "a sinful dereliction of Christian duty" (no. 77).

"The quest for economic and social justice," the bishops state, "will always combine hope and realism, and must be renewed by every generation" (no. 55). By realism, the bishops mean understanding how the global economy works. Most important, from a Gospel and Catholic moral perspective, the bishops call attention to how the economy helps or hinders the full human flourishing of all members of society, especially the most vulnerable. The bishops call people of faith to embody the values of a new creation in Christ Jesus, of the Covenant, and of a community that welcomes, loves, and does justice to every person who is in any way oppressed, excluded, or abandoned by society. Hope means living by, and realizing, the universal dignity of the human person through preferential love for the most vulnerable.

■■ HOW *EJA* ADDRESSES THE INTERSECTION OF RACE AND POVERTY

In three key paragraphs addressing race and poverty, numbers 147, 181, and 182, *EJA* names blacks, Hispanics, and Native Americans as people who bear disproportionate burdens of discrimination, lack of jobs, poor education, and poverty. The document cites racial discrimination in labor markets, educational systems, and electoral politics. Acknowledging that blacks, Latinos and Hispanics, and Native American peoples are not treated fairly in three major social institutions necessary for human flourishing is a concrete way the bishops recognize the reality of institutionalized racism. The bishops see redressing these racial inequalities as integral to the achievement of economic justice.

EJA invites readers to recall the history of racial oppression with "sober humility" (no. 7). The bishops recognize how the nation was born in the "face of injustice to native Americans," and that "[s]lavery stained the commercial life of the land through its first 250 years and was ended only by a violent civil war" (no. 7). The bishops further cite movements for women's suffrage, protection of industrial workers, elimination of child labor, and the 1960s civil rights legislation as successful struggles that transformed the political and economic institutions of the nation. However, the bishops fail to cite the legacy of white resistance to the Emancipation Proclamation or the establishment of Jim Crow segregation laws that persisted for over a century after the Civil War.

To their credit, the bishops' 1979 pastoral letter, *Brothers and Sisters to Us*, offers prophetic criticism of US racism. *Brothers and Sisters to Us* states that the "structures of society are subtly racist" and "geared to the success of the majority and the failure of the minority." They concluded their 1979 pastoral by acknowledging their own complicity: "We must seek to resist and undo injustices we have not ceased, lest we become bystanders who tacitly endorse evil and so share guilt in it."[22]

Unfortunately, in *EJA* the bishops did not continue this analysis of white moral complicity and leave too much unsaid. The document does not define discrimination, nor does it differentiate between individual and institutional forms of racism. It never addresses the role of whites in creating these social conditions nor how a predominantly white culture creates the conditions of racial inequality. When considered in terms of Catholic social teaching, in which we are all interconnected and interdependent, created in God's image, in the Covenant, and through community—the failure to address the relationship between privilege and oppression is at best puzzling. The document misjudges how white Catholics understand the role of race in economic injustice.

Through this omission, the document assumes that everyone knows the meaning of different forms of individual, institutional, and systemic racism. In so doing, it ignores that part of the problem is that racial inequality persists because of white "common sense knowledge." By white "common sense," I draw upon the great twentieth-century philosopher-theologian and Jesuit priest Bernard Lonergan's notion of common sense knowledge in which individuals take things for granted as the way things are. In Lonergan's words:

> Common sense commonly feels itself omnicompetent in practical affairs, commonly is blind to long-term consequences of policies and courses of action, commonly is unaware of the admixture of common nonsense in its more cherished convictions and slogans.[23]

Common sense knowledge is a good thing. Common sense is a practical, concrete knowledge that facilitates human functioning. However, common sense knowledge is oriented to self-interest rather than to a scientific understanding of how things actually relate to each other.

The problem with US American white "common sense" theory is that it holds three key erroneous assumptions: (1) the notion of race is biologically valid, (2) racism is entirely a matter of individual belief, and (3) racial prejudice is part of the human condition.

The first assumption, that the concept of race is biologically valid, persists even though physical anthropologists and geneticists long ago demonstrated there is but one race, the human race. An example of how this nonscientific, white common sense assumption persists is found in the argument that racial

---

[22] United States Conference of Catholic Bishops, *Brothers and Sisters to Us: U.S. Catholic Bishops Pastoral Letter on Racism*, 1979, *http://www.usccb.org/saac/bishopspastoral.shtml*.

[23] Bernard Lonergan, *Method in Theology* (Minneapolis, MN: Seabury Press, 1979, [1972]), 53.

intermarriage will erase racial difference and conflict. In other words, the common sense assumption advances a genetic solution to a nongenetic, social construction.

This erroneous biological view also persists in the "one drop rule," which dates back to seventeenth-century colonial America and held that any trace of African ancestry made a person black.[24] Whites enforced the "one drop rule" during the Jim Crow century (1865–1965) to prevent interracial marriage and segregate whites from blacks legally, politically, educationally, and culturally. This "one drop rule" assumption can be seen in the way Barack Obama was described as the "only black in the U.S. Senate" and the "first African American" president even though he describes himself as the son a white, Kansas mother and a Kenyan father.[25]

A second assumption of white common sense theory holds that racism is entirely a matter of individual belief and that the ignorance of this belief can be corrected by education. This assumption is commonly communicated in blog or newspaper opinion pieces that rightfully desire an end to racism and decry the use of racial epithets. While the antiracist intention is good, the commonly proposed solution for educating "ignorant" individuals is completely inadequate to the task of addressing institutional and systemic racist practices. Moreover, this individualist assumption fails to attend to the way that US culture cultivates the white common sense theory of race.

An editorial in the New Orleans *Times-Picayune*, November 20, 2009, by a Louisiana State University senior is an example of the individualist assumption. The piece, entitled "Tackling Bigotry at Ole Miss, LSU, and Other SEC Schools," rightly criticizes common racist talk, attitudes, and practices at South Eastern Conference (SEC) football games. However, like white common sense theory, the major assumption of the editorial is that "it's unfortunate for the individuals ignorant enough to believe such behavior is OK." After all, "hopefully," white racism is not "in the majority." Although the behavior widely persists in the institutional and cultural context of SEC football games, the proposed solution is to educate individuals to overcome "intolerance," ignoring how these beliefs and practices are rooted in US culture.

A third key assumption of white common sense theory is that prejudice is part of the human condition, a view that is commonly described in the statement that "all people prefer to be with their own kind." Instead of listening to the experience and wisdom of people of color, or interrogating the magnitude of white power, whites use this third assumption to shift the onus of their own responsibility to the victims of racism. For example, whites commonly point out that nonwhites "prefer to be with each other." A stereotypical example used to

---

[24] F. James Davis, *Who Is Black? One Nation's Definition* (University Park: Pennsylvania State University Press, 1991), 33.

[25] Barack Obama, "Acceptance Speech," 2008 Democratic Convention, *New York Times*, August 28, 2008, *http://www.nytimes.com/2008/08/28/us/politics/28text-obama.html?pagewanted=all*.

make this point is the way that self-segregating seating occurs in school cafeterias. White common sense theory blames segregation on students of color and treats white self-segregation on the same moral plane as students of color without analysis of the power issues at stake in schools and society.

Lonergan also explains how the inability of common sense knowledge to accurately understand reality offers an opportunity to think critically and question how human relationships can create dehumanizing social conditions. Lonergan argues that the key to an intellectual and moral conversion away from the bias of common sense theory is that "one has to listen to criticism and protest. One has to remain ready to learn from others."[26]

That most white Americans tend to remain ignorant of the criticism articulated throughout US history by such diverse black Americans as Phillis Wheatley, Frederick Douglas, Ida B. Wells, W.E.B. Du Bois, Stokely Carmichael, Audre Lorde, Malcolm X, Margaret Walker Alexander, and many others, underscores Lonergan's point. Yet Lonergan's insight is easily missed by white Americans if whites continue to live in self-segregated localities separate from the experience and perspectives of people of color, a point that is developed below.

Both Lonergan and the bishops, through their economic analysis, invite people to intellectual conversion and to see how things in the world actually relate to one another, rather than through the narrow lens of common sense. While the bishops generally broaden their audience's intellectual horizon with their economic analysis, they miss a similar depth of analysis of race and white American culture.

By failing to dispel these erroneous common sense assumptions, and by focusing exclusively on people of color, it is more likely that *EJA* reinforces white cultural assumptions that people of color are to blame for their plight. In other words, the document identifies symptoms in a way that focuses exclusively on people of color without examining the conditions that create disproportionate benefits for whites and burdens for people of color in the first place. The document does not help white Americans to look at the economy from the perspective of those who are most negatively impacted by economic injustice and thus misses a critical opportunity to educate white Americans about the roles privileged groups play in society. The bishops also miss the opportunity to demonstrate how people of color are not merely victims; rather, they are people with whom people of privilege need to be in relationship and from whom people of privilege need to learn.

This has been a persistent problem of white responses to America's systemic racism, to a society that has been structured to benefit whites to the detriment of blacks and other people of color throughout its history. Whites tend to focus on the consequences of racism without addressing the culture and relationships of power that create these inequalities in the first place.

---

[26] Lonergan, *Method*, 240.

At best the document leaves undone the work of critiquing the relationship between white advantage and racial oppression; at worst, *EJA* reinscribes the dominant white cultural perception that people of color are the problem and that white advantage is "normal" and "natural." The failure to critique white privilege is not only a problem of analysis and understanding, the silence of *EJA* on this topic contradicts the Church's most fundamental theological and moral claims for universal human dignity as well as its call for conversion to authentic practices of preferential solidarity that can build a truly common good.

Science and Catholic social teaching agree that there is but one race—the human race—and all humans trace their roots to Africa.[27] Race has no genetic basis—no one gene distinguishes members of one so-called race from another. In fact, all human beings are far more alike genetically than different. Every individual shares 99.99 percent of the same genetic material as everyone else. In fact, there is greater genetic variation within the same "race" than between people in different "races."[28] For example, the human genome sequence "reveals that many people of black African descent are closer genetically to whites than they are to other black Africans."[29]

Thus, the International Convention on the Elimination of Racism concludes,

> any doctrine of superiority based on racial differentiation is scientifically false, morally condemnable, socially unjust and dangerous, and . . . there is no justification for racial discrimination in theory or practice.[30]

In 1995, the American Association for the Advancement of Science also concluded that race has no genetic basis.[31] The United Nations Educational, Scientific and Cultural Organization declared in 1951 and 1978 that there is no scientific basis for race.[32] The Institute of Medicine of the National Academies, in an exhaustive 2003 study of racial inequality in health care finds that because affluent whites tend to "over-utilize some services" and racial minorities tend to receive a lower level of care than whites, "disparities in care are not simply a function of disproportionate use by whites or greater disease severity among minorities."[33]

---

[27] Catholic social teaching cites a 1951 United Nations Educational, Scientific, and Cultural Organization (UNESCO) statement: "Experts generally recognize that all human persons living today belong to the same species, homo sapiens, and that they descended from the same stock." See Pontifical Council for Justice and Peace, *The Church and Racism: Toward a More Fraternal Society*, The Vatican, 1988, no. 18.

[28] Nell Irvin Painter, *The History of White People* (New York: W.W. Norton, 2010), 391.

[29] "Slicing Soup," *Nature Biotechnology* 20, no. 7, (July 2001): 637.

[30] Office of the United Nations High Commissioner for Human Rights, General Assembly Resolution 2106, International Convention on the Elimination of All Forms of Racism, December 21, 1965, *http://www2.ohchr.org/english/law/cerd.htm*.

[31] Painter, *History of White People*, 391.

[32] UNESCO, *Declaration on Race and Racial Prejudice*, adopted November 27, 1978, and published in 1982, *http://www.unesco.org/education/information/nfsunesco/pdf/RACE_E.PDF*.

[33] Smedley, *Unequal Treatment*, 78.

Nevertheless, some doctors and pharmaceutical companies advocate for the idea of a genetically based racial medicine and thereby perpetuate "the race myth."[34] Yet, any effort to define "race" by genetics, explains an editorial in the prestigious scientific journal *Nature Biotechnology*, "is like slicing soup. You can cut whatever you want, but the soup stays mixed."[35]

ARE ALL AMERICANS AFRICAN AMERICANS?

An African proverb states, "I am because we are." Drawing upon this insight, the rock star Bono asks, "Could it be that all Americans are, in that sense, African-Americans?"[36] Bono invites us to notice the innumerable ways in which "I am because we are."

©Helga Esteb/Shutterstock.com

Bono

---

[34] Joseph L. Graves, Jr., "How Biology Refutes Our Racial Myths," in *The Race Myth: Why We Pretend Race Exists in America* (New York: Dutton, 2004), 1–19. See also Joseph L. Graves, *The Emperor's New Clothes: Biological Theories of Race at the Millennium* (New Brunswick, NJ: Rutgers University Press, 2001).

[35] "Slicing Soup," *Nature Biotechnology*, 637.

[36] Bono, "Rebranding Africa," *New York Times*, July 10, 2009, editorial.

Although "race" lacks a scientific basis, the US social construction of race delivers deadly consequences. Race is not about biology or color; rather, it is a set of power relations that grant whites "unearned advantage and conferred dominance"[37] while severely impairing the social, political, educational, and economic opportunities for people of color. Although various attempts have been made throughout US history to correct this oppression, the enduring reality of systemically imposed racial inequality and injustice stands in contradiction to the Gospel and the democratic vision the bishops advocate.

All people—people of faith and citizens of goodwill alike—need to examine how white privilege and complicity work to tear apart the human relationships that bind us to one another as members of one race, as brothers and sisters, and as children of God.

▪▪ WHITE ECONOMIC PRIVILEGE AND RACIAL OPPRESSION

In the United States, many people assume that "the playing field is level" and that everyone starts at the same starting line in economic matters, much like the imaginary race described earlier. Economists at the Harvard Business School and Duke University recently asked a nationally representative panel of "regular" Americans to estimate the current level of wealth inequality.[38] Respondents dramatically underestimated the existing wealth gap. Cultural assumptions of wealth distribution do not stand up against the facts.

Since the day Dr. Martin Luther King, Jr., was assassinated in 1968, the income gap between blacks and whites has narrowed by just three cents on the dollar. In 2005, the median per-capita income stood at $16,629 for blacks and $28,946 for whites. Scholars note that at this rate of progress, income equality will not be achieved for another 537 years.[39]

In Mississippi, whites live an average of four years longer than blacks, and whites' average personal earnings exceed that of blacks by more than $10,000.[40] In Florida, "when compared to white workers, black workers in 2008 made only 79.9 cents for each dollar earned by whites, and Hispanics made 82 cents for

---

[37] Peggy McIntosh, "White Privilege and Male Privilege: A Personal Account of Coming to Understand Correspondences through Work in Women's Studies," Working Paper No. 189, Wellesley Center for Research on Women, 1988.

[38] Michael Norton and Dan Ariely, "Building a Better America—One Quintile at a Time," *http://www.people.hbs.edu/mnorton/norton%20ariely%20in%20press.pdf*.

[39] See note 1 in this chapter.

[40] Sarah Burd-Sharps, Kristen Lewis, and Eduard Borges Martins, *A Portrait of Mississippi: Mississippi Human Development Report 2009*, American Human Development Project of the Social Sciences Research Council, 18, *http://measureofamerica.org/wp-content/uploads/2009/01/a_portrait_of_mississippi.pdf*.

each dollar earned by whites."[41] In Louisiana, 7 percent of white families have incomes below $15,000 and 25 percent have incomes above $100,000. The exact opposite is the case for blacks: fewer than 7 percent of blacks have incomes above $100,000, and fully 25 percent earn less than $15,000.[42]

Wealth—what you own minus what you owe—is vital to economic, health, educational, and overall well-being. The gap in wealth is perhaps more significant than the earnings gap because wealthier families are able to afford the best education, access to capital to start or expand a business, health coverage and expensive medical procedures, and homes in safer neighborhoods. They are also able to procure better legal representation, transfer wealth to subsequent generations, and withstand financial hardship caused by emergencies or economic downturns. As one of the most significant indicators of racial inequality, the wealth gap exposes the myth that Americans live in a "post-racial" society.

The latest evidence indicates that the wealth gap between white and black families quadrupled over a generation. From 1984 to 2007, the racial wealth gap increased by $75,000, from $20,000 to $95,000. No evidence demonstrates that this was due to whites' hard work, patience, and dogged determination to save. Some concede that there is a racial wealth gap but still hold that Americans live in a post-racial society. They argue, first, that blacks are less frugal; and second, that blacks do not manage financial assets as well as whites. This argument was expressed by Federal Reserve Chairman Ben Bernanke in an April 2009 lecture. Neither argument holds up to the facts.[43]

Economists on the political right and left find that blacks save at a rate moderately higher than whites. Many higher-income blacks offer more support to lower-income relatives than do whites, suggesting even greater black frugality with less to save. Recent research finds no racial differences in asset appreciation rates for families with positive net worth.

It is commonly, but incorrectly, assumed that Americans gain wealth through savings and portfolio management. The combination of inheritances, bequests, and intra-familial transfers account for the racial wealth gap more than any other demographic factor, including education, income, and household structure. These intra-familial transfers—the primary source of wealth for most Americans with positive net worth—are transfers from blatantly nonmerit resources. That means that the beneficiaries of these transfers did not earn them.

[41] Fred Kammer, "Poverty and the Gulf South States," *JustSouth* (Winter 2009), 3, *http://www. loyno.edu/jsri/sites/loyno.edu.jsri/files/justsouth-quarterly-winter-2009.pdf*.

[42] Sarah Burd-Sharps, Kristen Lewis, and Eduardo Borges Martins, *A Portrait of Louisiana: Louisiana Human Development Report*, American Human Development Project of the Social Science Research Council, 2009, 21, *http://www.measureofamerica.org/wp-content/uploads/A_Portrait_of_Louisiana.pdf*, 27.

[43] Darrick Hamilton and William Darity, Jr., "Race, Wealth, and Intergenerational Poverty: There Will Never Be a Post-Racial America If the Wealth Gap Persists," *American Prospect*, September 16, 2009.

These nonmerit transfers account for 50 to 80 percent of the wealth advantage conferred to subsequent generations.[44]

Contrary to a common white refrain—the past is over, so get over it—history is critical for understanding the racial wealth gap. Simply put, wealth begets more wealth and lack of wealth begets lack of wealth. Economist T. Kirk White developed an economic model to demonstrate that the conditions of wealth inequality at black emancipation (1863) could dictate current disparity even if "there had been no further bumps in the road."[45] At emancipation, nearly 100 percent of black households had zero net worth, having been forced to build wealth for whites for generations.

Yet the historical record is clear that blacks have faced multiple bumps on the road after emancipation. Not only did the nation fail to endow ex-slaves with the promised "40 acres and a mule" after the Civil War, blacks were systemically deprived of property—especially land accumulated between 1880 and 1910—by government complicity, fraud, and seizures by white terrorists.[46]

While some may cringe at the term *terrorists*, it is curious that white Americans forget that in 1921, white citizens of Tulsa, Oklahoma, commandeered planes from the local army base to firebomb the city's black neighborhood and destroy it. That white Americans presume 9/11 is the nation's first terrorist air attack on American soil, observes scholar Jennie Lightweis Goff, "indicates how deeply the term *terrorist* is raced, since white communities are so often protected from the stigma of its application."[47] In an article entitled "The Terrorists" in the March 1912 edition of *The Crisis* (the journal founded by W.E.B. Du Bois for the National Association for the Advancement of Colored People [NAACP]), the terrorists described were not members of Al-Qaeda but white people from all walks of life and parts of the United States. Black theologian Anthony Pinn explains that terror has always been a basic category of experience and theology for peoples stripped from their African families and cultures through the Atlantic Slave Trade.[48]

Black Americans hit more economic "road bumps" during the 1930s. The original Social Security legislation of 1935, created during the height of the Great Depression to establish a basic level of economic security for workers, effectively denied benefits to 75 percent of blacks by excluding domestic and agricultural workers from this historic policy. The Federal Housing

---

[44] Hamilton, "Race, Wealth, and Intergenerational Poverty."

[45] T. Kirk White, "Initial Conditions at Emancipation: The Long-Run Effect on Black-White Wealth and Earnings Inequality," *Journal of Economic Dynamics and Control* 31 (2007): 3370–95.

[46] William Darity, "Forty Acres and a Mule in the 21st Century," *Social Science Quarterly* 89, no. 3 (September 2008): 656–65.

[47] Jennie Lightweis Goff, *Blood at the Root: Lynching as American Cultural Nucleus* (Albany: State University of New York Press, 2011), 12–13.

[48] Anthony Pinn, *Terror and Triumph: The Nature of Black Religion* (Minneapolis, MN: Fortress Press, 2003).

Administration's (FHA) selectively administered mortgage program financed development of white suburbs while it disinvested in and denied housing and small business loans to urban black neighborhoods.

Suburbanization of the white middle class from the 1950s through the 1970s was further facilitated by federal highway and transportation policies that included eviscerating formerly healthy urban neighborhoods by building highways through them, and provided mortgages for white veterans, mortgage-tax exemptions, and massive tract housing that fueled white suburbanization after World War II.

While FHA financing structures spurred white suburbanization in the 1940s through 1970s, the FHA and banks also used "redlining," the practice of denying mortgage assistance for homes and financing for new businesses, based upon the racial composition of the neighborhood.[49] Blacks bore the greatest burden of such lending discrimination. Restrictive covenants (which exclude people of color from white developments), as well as housing and lending discrimination, inhibited blacks from accumulating wealth. All of these practices and public policies exacerbated historic racial inequalities.[50]

How do whites protest these enduring inequalities today? As many people of color throughout US history have said, the silence is deafening. Too often and in too many ways, whites tacitly accept, if not outright support, this social and economic inequality. The predominant silence of white Americans on this issue bespeaks complicity in privilege and racial inequality. As Dr. Martin Luther King, Jr., put it in his famous "Letter from Birmingham Jail":

> We will have to repent in this generation not merely for the vitriolic words and actions of the bad people, but for the appalling silence of the good people. We must come to see that the wheels of progress never rolls in on the wheels of inevitability. It comes only through tireless efforts and persistent work of men [and women] willing to be co-workers with God.[51]

■■ PLACING WHITENESS: A HISTORY AND ENDURING LEGACY

In *The Cross and the Lynching Tree*, black theologian James Cone draws upon the twentieth-century Protestant theologian Reinhold Niebuhr's *The Irony of*

---

[49] Douglas S. Massey and Nancy A. Denton, *American Apartheid: Segregation and the Making of the Underclass* (Cambridge, MA: Harvard University Press, 1993), 52–5.

[50] See Catholic Charities USA, *Poverty and Racism: Overlapping Threats to the Common Good: A Catholic Charities USA Poverty in America Issue Brief* (Chicago: Catholic Charities, 2008), 11–14. *http://www.catholiccharitiesusa.org/Document.Doc?id=614.*

[51] Martin Luther King, Jr., "Letter from Birmingham Jail," in James M. Washington, ed., *A Testament of Hope: The Essential Writings of Martin Luther King, Jr.* (San Francisco: Harper and Row, 1986), 296.

American History.[52] Niebuhr confronted America with its myth of innocence and the need for Americans to see themselves through the eyes of those at the bottom. One of the central ironies of American history is that unless America confronts its myth of innocence, especially its white myth of racial innocence, whites will not work to create an authentic democracy or embrace the Gospel call to loving and just conversion. In other words, until whites address the enduring legacy and consequences of racism and until they learn from people of color, whites will repeat past patterns of oppression.

Confronting the myth of white racial innocence is no easy task because it involves developing critical insight into where and how whites reproduce this myth to create systemic and structured inequality. The national resegregation of schools and housing likely constitutes one of the most critical means of reproducing systemic, structured white advantage, wealth, and power. Significant gains have been won for people of color in the last fifty years. For example, due largely to the success of Civil Rights Fair Housing legislation, black homeownership increased from one in three in 1950 to nearly one in two by 2000. These gains should be celebrated.

However, sociologists call hyper-segregation the "structural linchpin" of American racial inequality.[53] Housing location is critical to predicting access to quality public education, development of personal wealth, employment, health and safety, democratic participation, transportation, and child care. The national extent of white hyper-segregation cannot happen without the participation of the majority of white people and institutions, including whites who claim good intentions toward people of color.

The link between home ownership and wealth in America is well established.[54] Nationally, whites are more likely to gain home ownership, own a home earlier in life, and acquire more home equity over a lifetime than people of color.[55] Studies indicate that the greater amount of whites' initial wealth derives from inheritances and gifts.[56] At age 25, nearly 40 percent of whites and fewer than 20 percent of nonwhites are homeowners. By age 35, nearly 80 percent of whites own their home, compared with less than half of nonwhites. More important, whites are 2.65 times more likely than nonwhites to achieve $50,000 in home

---

[52] James Cone, *The Cross and the Lynching Tree* (Maryknoll, NY: Orbis Books, 2011), 51–2. See also Bill Moyers' interview with James Cone on November 23, 2007, *http://www.pbs.org/moyers/journal/11232007/watch.html.*

[53] John A. Powell, "Reflections on the Past, Looking to the Future: The Fair Housing Act at 40," *Journal of Affordable Housing and Community Development Law* 18, no. 2 (Winter 2009): 145–68.

[54] Melvin Oliver and Thomas Shapiro, *Black Wealth/White Wealth: A New Perspective on Racial Inequality,* 2nd ed. (New York: Routledge, 2006), 8–10.

[55] Mark R. Rank, "Measuring the Economic Racial Divide across the Course of American Lives," *Race and Social Problems* 1, no. 2 (June 2009): 57–66.

[56] Edward N. Wolff, "Racial Wealth Disparities: What Are the Causes?" *Indicators* 1, no. 2, (Spring 2002): 63–76, at 68.

equity, 3.9 times more likely to achieve $100,000, and 6.15 times more likely to achieve $200,000 in home equity. The real-estate mantra "location, location, location" is also about the ways that home valuation is color-coded.[57]

Even the wealthiest black suburban communities lack access to the opportunities available in predominantly white neighborhoods. People of color find it increasingly difficult to translate economic gains, including home ownership, into neighborhood quality. Real-estate steering and discrimination, exclusionary zoning and localism,[58] and discriminatory lending compound and exacerbate the geography of racial wealth disparity.

A study by the Center for Responsible Lending finds that black and Latino borrowers are more likely to receive higher-rate subprime loans than white borrowers, even when studies are controlled for legitimate risk factors.[59] Institutional discrimination in housing and lending markets is a significant way that racial wealth inequality extends into the future.

Racial inequality and segregation are not only evident between cities and suburbs; increasingly, in the South "within-city segregation and within-suburb segregation contribute equally to overall metropolitan segregation levels."[60] Segregation may be even greater in suburbs and more difficult to change.

For example, in Louisiana, the white section of Baton Rouge has the highest median income ($32,631), the lowest percentage of adults without a high school diploma (8.8 percent), and the second highest life expectancy (77.3 years) in the state. This part of Baton Rouge is nearly 70 percent white, 23 percent black, and 5 percent Latino. Yet the neighboring and predominantly black part of Baton Rouge has the lowest median income ($16, 398), the third-lowest life expectancy (72.7 years), and a population that is 88 percent black, 9 percent white, and 1 percent Latino.[61]

Housing resegregation also contributes to resegregation of the nation's schools, another locus where US racial inequality is reproduced. Fifty years after the US Supreme Court ruled that school segregation is unconstitutional and "inherently unequal," the resegregation of schools shows that

> white students remain the most segregated from all other races in their schools. Whites on average attend schools where less than 20 percent of the students are from all other racial and ethnic groups combined. On average, blacks and Latinos attend schools with 53% to 55% students of their own group.[62]

---

[57] Oliver, *Black Wealth/White Wealth*, 8–10.

[58] James W. Loewen, *Sundown Towns: A Hidden Dimension of American Racism* (New York: Touchstone, 2005). Loewen describes only one dimension of white localism in US history.

[59] Bocian, *Unfair Lending*, 2006, *http://www.responsiblelending.org/mortgage-lending/research-analysis/rr011-Unfair_Lending-0506.pdf*.

[60] Powell, "Fair Housing Act at 40," 149.

[61] Burd-Sharps, *A Portrait of Louisiana*.

[62] Orfield, "Schools More Separate."

Gary Orfield concludes that "research consistently shows that segregated schools are usually isolated by both race and poverty, and offer vastly unequal educational opportunities."[63] Southern Gulf states, which made tremendous gains in school integration in the 1980s, becoming the nation's most integrated schools, are now losing their leadership in this sphere.[64]

■ THE WHERE AND HOW OF WHITENESS

Francis Cardinal George, archbishop of the Archdiocese of Chicago, in his pastoral letter *Dwell in My Love*, uses the term *spatial racism* to describe residential hyper-segregation. Cardinal George notices how spatial racism creates a "visible chasm between rich and poor, and between whites and people of color."[65] Yet whites tend not to be aware of this chasm, or view it as normal and natural. More important, white physical, social, and moral separation from people of color is tied up with whites' inability to understand or feel empathy for people of color, much less practice the solidarity called for by the US Catholic bishops in *EJA*.[66]

Lack of cross-racial empathy becomes apparent in the everyday assumptions by which whites live.[67] In other words, the assumptions of white common sense knowledge described earlier do not develop in a vacuum. It is critical to understand where whites live, how they live, and how whites educate whites into a racialized society, to understand how white common sense theory develops. Sociologists call this process *socialization,* whereby groups shape individuals through primary education and socialization (broadly understood) into society.[68]

Sociologist Eduardo Bonilla-Silva explains how white socialization or "white habitus" creates intra-group identity and cohesion. He defines *white habitus* as "a racialized, uninterrupted socialization process that conditions and

---

[63] Ibid.

[64] Gary Orfield and Chungmei Lee, "Historic Reversals, Accelerating Resegregation, and the Need for New Integration Strategies," Civil Rights Project, University of California at Los Angeles, August 2007, *http://civilrightsproject.ucla.edu/research/k-12-education/integration-and-diversity/historic-reversals-accelerating-resegregation-and-the-need-for-new-integration-strategies-1/orfield-historic-reversals-accelerating.pdf*.

[65] Francis Cardinal George, OMI, "Dwell in My Love: A Pastoral Letter on Racism," April 2001, *http://www.archchicago.org/cardinal/dwellinmylove/dwellinmylove_2.shtm*.

[66] This inability is termed *social alexithymia* by social scientists. This "white frame of mind" has difficulty understanding where people of color are coming from and what the racialized experiences of people of color are like. Most simply put, social alexithymia is the "significant lack of cross-racial empathy." Joe Feagin, *Racist America: Roots, Current Realities and Future Reparations*, 2nd ed. (New York: Routledge, 2010), 89.

[67] Jane H. Hill, *The Everyday Language of White Racism* (Malden, MA: Wiley-Blackwell, 2008).

[68] Peter L. Berger and Thomas Luckmann, *The Social Construction of Reality: A Treatise in the Sociology of Knowledge* (Garden City, NY: Anchor Books, 1966), 51–61.

creates whites' tastes, perceptions, feelings, and emotions and their views on racial matters."[69] White habitus occurs within a separate residential and cultural life that fosters a white culture of solidarity and negative views about nonwhites. Perhaps too simply put, white habitus entails both *position*—the social geography, location, and power of whiteness—and *practice*—the ways whites are socialized to perceive and act within the world.

Described in more complex terms, white culture both shapes the social geography of residential and educational segregation and is shaped by the moral landscape of white segregation.[70] White self-segregation physically, socially, and morally structures the societal relationship between privilege and oppression. As theologian M. Shawn Copeland explains, "ordinarily, [nonwhite] bodies are 'invisible' in the process of historical, cultural, and social creativity and representation, but should these non-white bodies step 'out of place,' they are subordinated literally to surveillance, inspection, discrimination, assessment, and containment."[71]

Ethnographic studies of how whites describe their own experience demonstrate that within white gated communities, white self-perceptions of "niceness" and fear of others is initially used as a rhetorical way to justify living in a residential development that excludes racial others. More important, when whites describe themselves as "nice" and nurture fear of others, they inscribe racist assumptions into the landscape. Although the physical landscape and the perceptions that whites use to describe the landscape are socially constructed, this reality is seen as normal by whites and is outside whites' everyday awareness. Thus, for example, within the white habitus, a white neighborhood is normal, while a black neighborhood is "racially segregated." In other words, white habitus constitutes a racially biased intellectual and moral horizon that defines, controls, and segregates different, other, nonwhite bodies.

As demonstrated by Bonilla-Silva and other social scientists, whites are not likely to engage in interracial friendships that include a high degree of interaction, interdependence, and closeness, despite their self-professed support for racial equality. Regardless of the level of assimilation of black Americans, white geographical isolation from blacks does not "provide fertile soil upon which primary interracial associations can flourish."[72]

The problem of white habitus and white hyper-segregation is that it is a dynamic locus for the reproduction of white dominance in the power dynamics of neighborhood, state, and nation. The mechanisms of white habitus include

---

[69] Eduardo Bonilla-Silva, *Racism without Racists: Color-Blind Racism and the Persistence of Racial Inequality in the United States*, 2nd ed. (Lanham, MD: Rowman and Littlefield, 2006), 103.

[70] Bryan N. Massingale, *Racial Justice and the Catholic Church* (Maryknoll, NY: Orbis Books, 2010). See Massingale's description and analysis of white culture, 13–42.

[71] M. Shawn Copeland, *Enfleshing Freedom: Body, Race, and Being* (Minneapolis, MN: Fortress Press, 2010), 15.

[72] Bonilla-Silva, *Racism without Racists*, 124.

physical, social, and moral distancing from people of color, as well as denial of whites' sense of racial superiority, fear of racialized others, and intra-white solidarity. Perhaps most significantly, profound evil derives from whites' lack of empathy for people of color and inability to see how whites need people of color to become fully human and open to transformation in God's love.

■■ CONCLUSION: CONTENDING WITH WHITENESS IN THE STRUGGLE FOR ECONOMIC JUSTICE

A contemporary Christian ethic of ecomomic justice demands confrontation with the white American myth of innocence and how it is reproduced within the geography of US racial and economic inequality. Confronting white complicity presents a bind for US Catholics, especially bishops, theologians, and pastoral leaders, as for all Christians. On the one hand, if the Catholic Church and white Christians generally, continue past patterns of silence regarding white privilege and racial oppression, they will most likely prove again James Baldwin's insight that whites are "still trapped in a history they don't understand; and until they understand it, they cannot be released from it."[73] On the other hand, confronting white dominance in church and society will be no easy task for it involves whites contending with their own biases, fears, and contradictions.

Baldwin's insight and the long-standing wisdom of black, Latino, and Native American Catholics ought to give pause and make one wonder: How does the operation of white habitus impair the ability of bishops, theologians, and pastoral leaders to see their church's participation in social reality? How does white habitus thwart churches' ability to perceive the sacred in all of their members? How does white habitus, and ultimately dominance, distort churches' mission, self-understanding, and ability to witness to a living God?

In Bernard Lonergan's description of authentic teaching authority, teachers must practice the Christian message in order to know and communicate it.[74] Teaching presupposes that teachers enlarge their own horizons to include an accurate and intimate understanding of all the cultures and languages of the people they address. Too often, Christian reflections on economic justice, like *EJA*, do not reveal an intimate understanding of the role of white privilege or of the wisdom of people of color. What would be necessary to create the conditions for US white Catholics, Christians, and citizens to authentically interrogate and interrupt their participation in white dominance in church and society? Confronting this question is essential, not only for contending with the scandal of white supremacy but also for the possibility of white people's redemption.

---

[73] James Baldwin, *The Fire Next Time* (New York: Vintage Books, 1993 [1962]), 8.
[74] Lonergan, *Method*, 362.

On the other hand, if churches at the institutional level as well as individual whites would take up the arduous task of "working through whiteness,"[75] such work would demand that whites confront the contradiction between professed claims to equality and how whites actually live.

Official Roman Catholic social teaching on race is perhaps one of the best kept secrets in US Catholicism. Given the understanding of human participation in social sin, as well as the particular global history of racism, the Pontifical Justice and Peace Commission has unequivocally called for racial conversion in three major statements since 1988.[76] The conversion called for, states the commission's *Church and Racism*, will not occur without "strengthening spiritual convictions regarding respect for other races and ethnic groups. The Catholic Church asks pastors, preachers, teachers, and catechists to explain the true teaching of Scripture and Tradition about the origin of all people in God, their final common destiny in the Kingdom of God, and the value of the precept of fraternal love" (no. 25).

Not only does the Roman Catholic Church call for dialogue, sharing, mutual aid, and collaboration among all ethnic groups, it clearly calls Catholics and people of goodwill to repair the injury and harm done to others through the duties of restitution and reparation. In *Contribution to World Conference against Racism* (2001), the Catholic Church recognizes that reparation may take multiple forms, including monetary compensation or formal apologies, and it is clear that such reparation is a duty that must be made in an appropriate way (no. 12).

If white US Catholics intend to witness to the redeeming memory of Jesus, then our spirituality and theology must practice the kind of memory that remembers the hopes, dreams, aspirations for life, love, anger, and suffering of all those forgotten, broken bodies that are strewn across the Atlantic Ocean through the slave trade, buried on stolen lands of Native American peoples, lynched, and imprisoned in US detention centers, jails, prisons, and city streets.[77]

Eucharistic hope and memory does not forget or turn its back on these injustices. "Do this in memory of me" (Lk 22:19) means living in a way that makes life and authentic hope for all possible, by giving priority to listening, and hearing, the stories of those who have borne the deadly brunt of US white racism.

Remembering will not be easy, because whites will need to learn to listen in ways they have not in the past and to learn from the depth and breadth of

---

[75] Cynthia Levine-Rasky, ed., *Working through Whiteness: International Perspectives* (Albany: State University of New York Press, 2002).

[76] Documents by the Pontifical Commission on Justice and Peace, the highest teaching authority of the Roman Catholic Church on these matters, include *The Church and Racism: Toward a More Fraternal Society* (1988); *Contribution to World Conference against Racism: Racial Discrimination, Xenophobia, and Related Intolerance* (2001); and *The Compendium of the Social Doctrine of the Church* (2005).

[77] For a history of lynching, see Phillip Dray, *At the Hands of Persons Unknown: The Lynching of Black America* (New York: Modern Library, 2002). For an interpretation of the ritual of lynching, see Orlando Patterson, *Rituals of Blood: Consequences of Slavery in Two American Centuries* (New York: Basic Civitas, 1998), especially ch. 2, "Feast of Blood: 'Race,' Religion and Human Sacrifice in the Postbellum South," 169–232.

wisdom of people of color throughout our history and today. Re-membering will be difficult, because whites need to hear the cries of the oppressed of their past, including those who carry the persisting memories of the trauma of lynching, among many forms of terror. Should whites not engage the impasse and unfinished business of these dangerous memories in the multiple communities where lynching and racial violence have never been fully confronted, where the complicity of ordinary citizens and community institutions in condoning racial terror continue to impede hope for new life? The conversion to which whites are called will not be easy because white people—in all their diversity[78]—tend to cling to the need to be in control, to their advantage, to their fears, and to their desire to blame victims, and because of a strong tendency to deny how they inherit historical advantages of unearned privilege.

If whites take up the prophetic call of *EJA* to risk Gospel memory and hope, and re-member all those who have suffered and survived US racism, perhaps whites may yet open themselves to mourning the loss of life, the loss of their own humanity, and find new ways to walk with Jesus in their brothers' and sisters' shoes. Perhaps whites will yet recognize that forgetfulness of black, red, yellow, and brown bodies constitutes forgetfulness of themselves, as fundamentally interdependent and interconnected with all others. Then, perhaps, white people may yet experience transformation into the audacity of Jesus' hope to "Do this in memory of me" (Lk 22:19) and glimpse who they are called to be at the full communion of God's table of love and life.

FOCUS QUESTIONS

1. What data demonstrates that racial inequality permeates and endures in US society?

2. How does the chapter affirm the argument of the US Catholic bishops in *EJA*? How and why is the chapter critical of the US Catholic bishops' argument regarding race in *EJA*?

3. Why should the US Catholic bishops contend with white complicity in economic justice?

4. Develop an analysis of white complicity in racial oppression in your local community. Where would you begin your analysis? What questions emerge through your inquiry?

5. Using insights from this chapter, how would you begin to resist "white habitus" and dominance in your life? What is at stake theologically, morally, spiritually?

---

[78] For an analysis of the complexity of the social construction of whiteness, see John Hartigan, Jr., *Odd Tribes: Toward a Cultural Analysis of White People* (Durham, NC: Duke University Press, 2005).

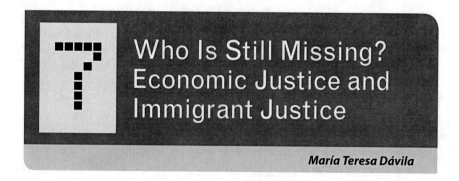

Who Is Still Missing?
Economic Justice and
Immigrant Justice

María Teresa Dávila

■ INTRODUCTION

Christians in the United States face a particularly difficult and often intensely emotional discussion on migration, in all its manifestations.[1] These emotions, which stem from political affiliations, economic circumstances, and cultural and even racial presuppositions, make an informed and just discussion on the life of migrants quite difficult—indeed, almost impossible—especially for people of faith who understand the migrant holds a special place in God's love for creation as evidenced in the Bible.[2] Therefore, it is extremely important that Christian churches provide theologically sound expositions of Christian perspectives on hospitality to the stranger and the preferential option for the poor *and* spaces where safe conversations on immigration can take place in which such teachings are engaged. In facing this extremely difficult social challenge, Christian churches must be a source of imagination and hope—providing perspectives that counter fear of the other and of a scarcity of resources with a vision that is liberating and inclusive for all.

---

[1] Often the public discussion regarding migration distinguishes between documented and undocumented migrants. However, the distinctions of "legal/illegal" or "documented/undocumented" contribute to the dehumanization of those other-documented migrants as well as perpetuate the political and almost theological importance of citizenship as an existential category. The terminology available is problematic, at best, and damaging in most instances. While this essay attempts to address issues of migration across the spectrum regardless of citizenship status, it privileges the perspective of those whose legal status places them at a particular disadvantage and vulnerability.

[2] Prominent among the biblical stories about migration, hospitality to the stranger, and God's special love for the displaced are the Exodus story and the story of Mary and Joseph encountering no room at the inn. For a full exposition on the theme of migration in the Bible, please refer to "The Bible as the Ultimate Immigration Handbook: Written by, for, and about Migrants, Immigrants, Refugees and Asylum Seekers," by Joan M. Maruskin, Church World Service Immigration and Refugee Program, 2003, *http://www.umc-gbcs.org/atf/cf/%7B325AB72F-313E-4CC3-BB1A-EF0A52968A8D%7D/850Bible_as_Immigration_Handbook__Maruskin_.pdf.*

The Roman Catholic Church's position on immigration has been boldly and clearly stated in numerous documents, both at the level of the Roman Curia[3] and from the bishops in the United States.[4] These documents serve as the foundation for diverse ministries to immigrants, especially in locations with a high immigrant population. However, they are often unknown to the faithful facing ongoing choices in their communities and in their political lives.

■■ THE PLACE OF THE IMMIGRANT IN *ECONOMIC JUSTICE FOR ALL*

This reflection seeks to consider the place of the immigrant in the 1986 pastoral letter *Economic Justice for All (EJA)*. When I first read the document many years ago, I was deeply impressed with its commitment to human dignity, shaped by the lens of the preferential option for the poor. I remember thinking that these two pillars, human dignity and the option for the poor, focus the document on people affected by the injustices, abuses, and imbalances in the US economy, and that these principles ought to serve as guides in the reform of the economic system. Farm owners and families, working parents, and laborers in foreign lands figure prominently in the document, but immigrants, a significant element of the US labor force (then and much more so now) are relatively absent.

Although *EJA* concerns the US Catholic Church's teaching on the US economy, the two topics of the economy and immigrant populations remain disconnected. In the letter, the words *immigrant* and *migrant* show up only seven times, and most of these in reference to the heritage of immigrants in US history. The reflection "A Decade after *Economic Justice for All:* Continuing Principles, Changing Context, New Challenges,"[5] does not mention immigrants at all. Considering the vibrant tradition of social teaching on immigration and on racism by the US Conference of Catholic Bishops (USCCB), this split between the teaching on justice in the economy, on the one hand, and justice for immigrants, on the other, should be examined. While this peculiar split between economic

---

[3] Pope John XXIII's groundbreaking document *Pacem in Terris* (Peace on Earth), nos. 25 and 105, specifically speaks to the right to migrate in search of political and economic safety. In 1988 Pope John Paul II instituted the Pontifical Council for the Pastoral Care of Migrants and Itinerants. Various speeches by John Paul II in honor of World Migration Day also bring to light Catholic teaching on migration. See, for example, "The Church and Illegal Immigration" (1996) and "Show Concern for Plight of Migrants" (1997), *http://www.justpeace.org/docu.htm*.

[4] See *Strangers No Longer* (2003), *Welcoming the Stranger among Us* (2000), and *From Newcomers to Citizens: All Come Bearing Gifts* (1999). The full texts of these documents are accessible at *http://www.usccb.org/mrs/pastoralstatements.shtml*.

[5] United States Catholic Bishops, "A Decade after *Economic Justice for All:* Continuing Principles, Changing Context, New Challenges," 1995, *http://www.usccb.org/jphd/economiclife/pdf/a_decade_after_ejfa.pdf*.

and immigrant justice could be considered a matter of nuancing these as distinct conversations, it may prevent us from a more critical assessment of the US economic system. In particular, the insights from liberation theology ask that we consider whether any system demands the sacrifice of a human underclass to fuel production and the provision of cheap goods, sustaining the presence of an invisible service workforce on which to fuel economic progress. Liberation theology contends that the political economy of a nation has the potential to create an underside, to make parts of a population disappear or appear invisible.[6] Often those who perform the most menial and unwanted jobs, the jobs that support an economy, are anonymous, without name, face, or representation.

LIBERATION THEOLOGY

In the seminal volume that defined liberation theology, Peruvian theologian Gustavo Gutiérrez describes the preferential option for the poor. Gathering the wisdom collected throughout the Christian tradition and Scripture, this insight seeks to take the perspective of the poor as theologically important, not because of any special merit of the poor, but because God exhibits divine love in history on the side of the poor and oppressed (e.g., in the Exodus story, in Jesus' Sermon on the Mount [Mt 5–7], and in the narrative of the Rich Man and Lazarus [Lk 16:19–31]).

The option for the poor, as an integral element of Christian discipleship, delineates three key aspects of poverty: poverty as material—the lack of the material goods necessary for human life, identified as a result of sin by the prophets of Hebrew Scripture; poverty as spiritual—radical openness to and dependence on God's will in one's life rather than idolatrous dependence on material possessions; and poverty as solidarity—taking on some of the suffering of the poor as people of goodwill join in the struggle against the injustices that sustain poverty and oppression. See Gustavo Gutiérrez, *A Theology of Liberation: History, Politics, and Salvation*, fifteenth anniversary edition (Maryknoll, NY: Orbis Books, 1988).

As an ethicist grounded on liberation theology and the preferential option for the poor, I take my middle-class US context as my particular location for theological and ethical reflection. I am committed to understanding how the US

---

[6] Jon Sobrino, in particular, discusses in depth the nature of the "invisible" poor in most economies, especially in the globalized economy. See his *The Principle of Mercy: Taking the Crucified People off the Cross* (Maryknoll, NY: Orbis Books, 1994).

bishops' conference suggests that the faithful approach economic activity and reform based on human dignity and the option for the poor. Based on this, I believe that the split between immigrant and economic justice in the teaching of the US Catholic bishops is the result of three distinct elements: (1) a deep commitment to the American experiment and civil society, in particular the role of the state, in shaping the content and form of the common good, (2) a privileging of the rights and responsibilities of citizenship over other forms of being in community, and (3) an emphasis on conversion in order to transform existing social structures into more just and equitable institutions. These "commitments" are hallmarks of the Catholic social teaching (CST) tradition. They are also part of the tension between liberationist thought and CST, for much of liberation theology demands these commitments be radically reformed or completely reconsidered if people of goodwill are to seek a just society grounded in the option for the poor. However, it is my hope that new visions for economic justice can address the dangers inherent in these three elements such that a more coherent and integrated vision for economic *and* immigrant justice in the United States can be offered to the faithful.

These goals require clarification of how the commitment to the state, the privileging of citizenship as a virtue, and the limited view of the role of conversion—focused mainly on personal and social transformation rather than radical questioning of economic and cultural assumptions about the economy on behalf of the poor—prevent available teachings on the economy from considering the plight of immigrants as part of a full vision of economic justice. At the same time, possibilities for overcoming these challenges from within the tradition need to be explored. The main contribution of documents such as *EJA* to the new American experiment is the epistemology of suffering embedded in the option for the poor and its commitment to radical solidarity, linking the destinies of those who benefit from, with those who are victimized by, the economy in which both participate.

■ IMMIGRANTS AND ECONOMIC JUSTICE

The question of immigrant justice simply cannot be separated from the question of economic justice. There is wide agreement among progressive labor and economic justice groups that including humane and comprehensive immigration reform is integral to economic reform and jobs recovery in the current economy. Commentator Kathryn Baer, for example, cites that in 2008, undocumented immigrants comprised more than 5 percent of the US workforce.[7] This figure underrepresents the actual number. Undocumented immigrants are a significant

---

[7] Kathryn Baer, "Where Immigration Reform and Economic Justice Overlap," *Change.org*, March 28, 2010, *http://news.change.org/stories/where-immigration-reform-and-economic-justice-overlap*.

part of our labor force and the engine of our economy.[8] Describing a March 2008 demonstration for jobs with justice, Baer states:

> "Our vision," say the organizers, "includes immigrants and native-born U.S. citizens working shoulder to shoulder to achieve better wages, working conditions and labor protections, and of an America that's back to work, with a fair balance between Main Street and Wall Street." Americans can be put back to work without immigration reform, but an overhaul of our immigration system is key to the rest of the vision.[9]

The main argument uniting labor reformers and immigration advocates is that an immigration reform that includes some form of resident labor program and worker permits will improve working conditions and wages for everyone.

Immigrant laborers in the United States suffer from particular injustices for which they have few avenues of redress. Poor working conditions lead to a high incidence of workplace accidents (which often go untreated and unreported due to their citizenship status); wages are underpaid or stolen; access to education and advancement is blocked; and there is little or no possibility for participation in the political and economic systems that control their destiny. These hardships make this a particularly vulnerable segment of our population. In addition, immigrant women are subject to particular abuses that further demean their humanity.[10] The USCCB has spoken clearly about the cultural, religious, and social implications of welcoming the stranger and practicing hospitality toward the immigrant, but it has systematically failed to include the economic plight of the immigrant and the particular vulnerabilities of illegal immigrants in the United States.

---

[8] See, for example, Gordon H. Hanson, *The Economic Logic of Illegal Immigration*, Council on Foreign Relations, Council Special Report no. 26 (April 2007), *http://www.cfr.org/immigration/economic-logic-illegal-immigration/p12969*. In this report, Hanson argues that the benefits of illegal immigration for the US economy outweigh the costs because illegal immigration more easily responds or adapts to the labor demands of the economy. Legal immigration, on the other hand, often follows family relations, not labor demand, and therefore brings into the country a labor force that may or may not fit the demands of the US economy at the time. An alternative perspective can be found in a National Public Radio report highlighting the negative impact of illegal immigration on wages for low-skilled labor. For US born African Americans and Hispanics in particular, illegal immigration has a more negative influence in labor and wage markets. See Adam Davidson, "Illegal Immigrants and U.S. Economy," March 30, 2006, *http://www.npr.org/templates/story/story.php?storyId=5312900*. However, most perspectives agree that of the 12 to 20 million illegal immigrants currently in the United States, more than half (more than the 5 million officially reported) are in the workforce, mainly in low-skilled, low-wage jobs.

[9] Baer, "Where Immigration Reform and Economic Justice Overlap," *Change.org*.

[10] See, for example, "Housekeepers Across America Speak Out against Abuses at Work," *http://unitehere.org/housekeepers/*. Interfaith Worker Justice (*http://www.iwj.org/template/index.cfm*) offers many resources that detail the particular stresses and grievances of the undocumented labor force in the United States.

While *EJA* directly addresses the effects of US global economic policy on other parts of the world, labor conditions abroad, and particularly the question of foreign aid, it fails to recognize how these policies fuel the global movement of peoples. Even ten years after *EJA*, the damaging effects of North American Free Trade Agreement—acknowledged as a key force affecting Mexican and Latin American agricultural economies and leading to the movement of farm workers to urban centers and the United States in search of work[11]—remain unacknowledged. The ways US economic policies affect the international movement of peoples and migration into the United States are complex. However, these should be carefully studied and analyzed by those responsible for presenting ethical and Christian ways of ministering to the most vulnerable and marginalized groups and assessing the impact of the US economy on these groups.

Ethicist Miguel de la Torre warns of the type of bifurcation that leads one to speak of one kind of injustice while neglecting the fullness of systemic oppression and violence on the most vulnerable.[12] When this happens, de la Torre suggests, one continues to promote critiques of the system that merely call for reform, when what is required for true justice is a comprehensive restructuring of the economy in ways that address such oppression and violence and empower those whom our economy silences and prefers to keep invisible. Reform simply shifts the damage from one population to another, all the while continuing to protect the interest of those who benefit the most from the status quo: the capitalist order and state authority supported by corporate interest.

A Christian call for justice grounded in the preferential option for the poor cannot simply advocate for reform of a system that depends on a large number of underpaid, politically voiceless, and legally invisible human capital. Justice in this context demands their needs be the first and central principle for change, demanding from the Church concrete discussions on the sin of US economic structures, and pointing the faithful to a form of Christian discipleship that is more in solidarity and sacrificial in nature than what is currently promoted. This cannot be achieved with a bifurcated social teaching that presents social and cultural issues as distinct from economic and political issues, even if its goal is an integrated understanding of these issues.

---

[11] Miguel de la Torre, *Latina/o Social Ethics: Moving Beyond Eurocentric Moral Thinking* (Waco, TX: Baylor University Press, 2010), 30, 50; Unitarian Universalist Service Committee, "Economic Justice and Migration," *http://www.uusc.org/files/ej_immigration.pdf.* The economic dynamics produced by the North American Free Trade Agreement (1993) are complex. However, the evidence points to it negatively influencing traditional economies in Mexico, especially its agricultural economies, through the influx of subsidized grain from the United States. This in turn caused agricultural workers to begin to move to find employment and sustain their families. The mobilization of Mexican farmers followed the pattern of movement from rural to urban centers at first, then toward diverse factories and industries that took advantage of incentives to relocate in border towns, then finally northward to find employment in the United States.

[12] De la Torre, *Latina/o Social Ethics.*

■ WHAT'S WRONG WITH THIS PICTURE? THREE POSSIBLE CAUSES FOR THIS DANGEROUS SPLIT

The vision of human dignity and its relationship to economic activity presented in *EJA* is nothing short of inspiring. Drawing from almost one hundred years of CST, the document begins with the following:

> Our faith calls us to measure this economy not by what it produces, but also by how it touches human life and whether it protects or undermines the dignity of the human person. Economic decisions have human consequences and moral content; they help or hurt people, strengthen or weaken family life, advance or diminish the quality of justice in our land. (*EJA*, no. 1)

Further, the document states:

> Every economic decision and institution must be judged in light of whether it protects or undermines the dignity of the human person. *The pastoral letter begins with the human person. We believe the person is sacred—the clearest reflection of God among us.* Human dignity comes from God, not from nationality, race, sex, economic status, or any human accomplishment. We judge any economic system by what it does *for* and *to* people and by how it permits all to *participate* in it. The economy should serve people, not the other way around. (*EJA*, no. 13, italics added)

Clearly the letter is grounded in a Christian understanding of the human person, which includes notions of God-given human dignity and the vision in Genesis that humanity is a reflection of the very being of Divine life. But the document moves from this all-inclusive vision of human dignity and worth to a more restricted sense of the person as citizen. This transition is somewhat justified by the document's focus on the US economy. However, I believe that it too quickly presents a direct identification of citizenship as a particular expression of Christian character and virtue, effectively silencing dimensions of the collective population that fall outside of that political, cultural, and social category. Readers then get statements such as these:

> The pursuit of economic justice takes believers into *the public arena, testing the policies of government* by the principles of our teaching. *We ask you to become more informed and active citizens,* using your voices and votes to speak for the voiceless, to defend the poor and the vulnerable, and to advance the common good. *We are called to shape a constituency*

of conscience, measuring every policy by how it touches the least, the lost, and the left-out among us. This letter calls us to conversion and common action, *to new forms of stewardship, service, and citizenship.* (*EJA*, no. 27, italics added)

Because the letter seeks to bring the conversation of a Christian vision of economic justice into the public arena, its language speaks of citizens, citizenship, and votes, governments, and civil society. The US bishops have a tradition of calling citizens who are Catholic to exercise the particular responsibilities this entails with clarity as to the demands of the Christian faith.[13] Immigration has been one of the issues lifted by the Church as a moral concern relevant to the political life of the faithful in the United States.[14] While the words *immigrant* or *migrant* appear only seven times in *EJA*, the word *citizen* appears twenty times and *citizenship* appears ten. To be clear, there are no references to the noncitizen or to the economic responsibilities of the citizen to the noncitizen or the undocumented. This, when the document is shaped at the height of the First Sanctuary Movement in the mid-1980s in which the Roman Catholic Church in the United States and other Christian churches played a significant role. Instead, the pastoral letter presents the identification of the rights and responsibilities of citizenship for a just society aligned with a life of Christian virtue:

> *The virtues of citizenship are an expression of Christian love* more crucial in today's interdependent world than ever before. These virtues grow out of a lively sense of one's dependence on the commonweal and obligations to it. This *civic commitment* must also guide the economic institutions of society. In the absence of a vital sense of citizenship among the businesses, corporations, labor unions, and other groups that shape economic life, society as a whole is endangered. *Solidarity is another name for this social friendship and civic commitment* that make human moral and economic life possible. (*EJA*, no. 66, italics added)

Civic commitment, the virtues of citizenship, social friendship, solidarity, and Christian love are put on the same plane. The pastoral reflects deep commitments to the American experiment as US society has inherited it and as the

---

[13] The *Faithful Citizenship* program of the Catholic Church tries to orient the faithful as to key electoral and civic questions each election cycle. While the documents and study guides provided do not attempt to dictate the "Catholic vote," they do ask that Catholics keep in mind doctrinal teaching on specific issues relevant in a given election period, *http://www.faithfulcitizenship.org/*.

[14] United States Conference of Catholic Bishops, *Forming Consciences for Faithful Citizenship: A Call to Political Responsibility for the Catholic Bishops of the United States with Introductory Note*, rev. ed., October 2011, *http://www.usccb.org/issues-and-action/faithful-citizenship/upload/forming-consciences-for-faithful-citizenship.pdf*. References to the current challenge of immigration are numerous throughout this document.

bearer of potential prosperity for the disenfranchised and the unemployed/
underemployed, and a stronger corporate commitment to ecology. Stepping off
the successes and prosperity generated thus far by the American experiment, the
pastoral letter proposes that a renewed commitment to the common good by
civil society and the private and public spheres that contribute to its development will bring about a more economically just society.

There is no failure of critique in the pastoral letter. During its survey of the
history of economic progress in the United States the pastoral suggests:

> [W]e should recall this history with sober humility. The American
> experiment in social, political, and economic life has involved serious
> conflict and suffering. Our nation was born in the face of injustice to
> native Americans, and its independence was paid for with the blood
> of revolution. Slavery stained the commercial life of the land through
> its first 250 years and was ended only by a violent civil war. The estab-
> lishment of women's suffrage, the protection of industrial workers, the
> elimination of child labor, the response to the Great Depression of the
> 1930s, and the civil rights movement of the 1960s all involved a sus-
> tained struggle to transform the political and economic institutions of
> the nation. (*EJA*, no. 7)

The American experiment bears within it not only the marks of violence and
oppression perpetrated on particular groups but also the potential for transformation toward justice. It recalls the labor struggles and how the right to
unionization and labor representation was hard won, and it presents the particular plight of women, African Americans, and farming families in the economic climate at the time.[15] But this vision of the American experiment seems
self-contained; it does not seem to acknowledge that lack of citizenship is a key
source of exclusion and oppression in the United States.

Next, the pastoral letter privileges life in community organized around
government as the place where the common good is defined and developed.
Life in community requires the practice of love and solidarity in special
ways enabled by the structures of society and government. This sometimes
demands that new structures and new systems be designed, as with the passage of Social Security and other social safety nets (e.g., Medicare, Medicaid,
and unemployment assistance), essential elements of a community that values
the human dignity of all. But is the pastoral's construct of life in community
sufficient to address the places where our economy sacrifices human dignity

---

[15] *EJA*, ch. III. This chapter details the plight of those most affected by economic policies that place
profit above integral development. It specifically analyzes unemployment (part A), poverty (part B),
and food and agriculture (part C). These sections specifically describe the ways African Americans,
women, and farmers suffer the economic consequences of discrimination and offers policy suggestions to address each one.

and flourishing for the sake of profit and efficiency? In other words, does the pastoral letter offer sufficient critique of the basic elements of our economic system, or does it settle for a compromise between US civil society as described above and the Christian call for solidarity with the invisible and suffering nonmembers of our community?

The bishops' robust understanding of civil society's and ·government's responsibility to protect the vulnerable leads them to an untenable position regarding the Christian disciple's concern with economic justice beyond the limits of civil society:

> More specifically, it is the responsibility of all citizens, acting through their government, to assist and empower the poor, the disadvantaged, the handicapped, and the unemployed. Government should assume a positive role in generating employment and establishing fair labor practices, in guaranteeing the provision and maintenance of the economy's infrastructure, such as roads, bridges, harbors, public means of communication, and transport. It should regulate trade and commerce in the interest of fairness. (*EJA*, no. 123)

The pastoral letter is clear that "a new American experiment" that can guarantee the economic rights of all is in order. But this suggestion of a new American experiment is complicated by the concept of *person* that is dominant in the letter. While very clearly *all* are included in the notion of person in the social teachings of the Catholic Church, often many are considered nonpersons in the dominant culture. This is a concept that liberation theology emphasizes in its discussion of the option for the poor. The nonperson needs to have a name, to be recognized as human first, and therefore, as having claims, both economic and civil. Where does the noncitizen belong in the categories of personhood within the new American experiment? While this question might seem moot in the parlance of CST, it is truly a question that US policymakers and those in so many other segments of US society—including Catholic faithful—struggle with. We are sold a particular message by the economy and all the cultural production of our economy—that illegal immigrants are not part of civil society and their lives therefore don't count—even in our considerations of those who are poor and marginalized, who should be the meter of just economic policies as stated in this pastoral letter. In other words, it is quite possible that many faithful, agreeing with most of the content of this pastoral letter, would actually not consider its recommendations applicable to illegal immigrants or even immigrants in the United States with proper documentation, even though they are a significant part of an economy that depends on depressed prices for produce, meats, construction, and other products and services.

■■ INTEGRATING JUSTICE: A HOLISTIC VISION FOR JUSTICE AND SOLIDARITY

The bishops suggest the direction that the new American experiment ought to take:

> Completing the unfinished business of the American experiment will call for new forms of cooperation and partnership among those whose daily work is the source of the prosperity and justice of the nation. The United States prides itself on both its competitive sense of initiative and its spirit of teamwork. Today a greater spirit of partnership and teamwork is needed; competition alone will not do the job. It has too many negative consequences for family life, the economically vulnerable, and the environment. Only a renewed commitment by all to the common good can deal creatively with the realities of international interdependence and economic dislocations in the domestic economy. The virtues of good citizenship require a lively sense of participation in the commonwealth and of having obligations as well as rights within it. (*EJA*, no. 296)

Indeed, a new American experiment demands that the notion of who is part of US economic life and activity be expanded to include the noncitizen, their families in their nations of origin, the economies they participate in by crossing borders, and the economic relations governments establish that lead many to seek the basic necessities for human flourishing beyond their own borders. To a very great extent, the noncitizens are "those whose daily work is the source of the prosperity and justice of the nation."

However, if the new American experiment is to be guided and shaped by the preferential option for the poor, then the best that CST can offer the US economy is a visionary shift to an epistemology of suffering, approaching reality from the perspective of those for whom every day is a struggle to attain the basic necessities for human life and flourishing. To see the US economy from the perspective of its underclass is to see those whom the economy requires to stay silent and invisible in jobs that, really, no one else will take. The bishops clearly declare "the fundamental duties" of life in community:

> *Basic justice demands the establishment of minimum levels of participation in the life of the human community for all persons.* The ultimate injustice is for a person or group to be treated actively or abandoned passively as if they were nonmembers of the human race. To treat people this way is effectively to say that they simply do not count as human beings. This can take many forms, all of which can be described as varieties of marginalization, or exclusion from social life. (*EJA*, no. 77, italics in the original)

EJA counts those commonly held as nonpersons in the global or local economy as central to a criterion for a just economy premised on Christian principles of human dignity and the option for the poor. "To treat people this way is effectively to say they simply do not count as human beings." This is also one of the central arguments of liberation theology: the crucified people, those who suffer victimization in the accepted political and economic systems, are the measure of each person's own humanity, each person's ability to treat the children of God as sisters and brothers. This perspective must trump the commitment to civil society, the virtues of citizenship, and the American experiment also propounded in the pastoral letter. That the "good" or ordered society the United States has thus far, has come at great costs to countless marginalized groups must be acknowledged. This perspective should be the clarion call for a radical critique of the status quo, the lens through which Christian discipleship in the United States is shaped and put into practice.

The notion of conversion promoted in *EJA* as a primary conduit for transformation needs to be mentioned here. Every act of social transformation begins with conversion. It is the witness of Oscar Romero and countless others, who, through an epistemology of honesty with the real and deep solidarity with the poor, understand that a new and more just society will require great sacrifice and true friendship with the poor. A conversion capable of producing a new American experiment, as the bishops suggest, needs to be a conversion grounded in the hard truths elicited by an epistemology of suffering, a conversion that opens Americans' personal and collective social lens in ways that critically question their economic choices.

EJA seems to suggest that the preferential option for the poor and the American experiment (the construction of a democratic capitalist civil society) are not mutually exclusive; however, for those who experience the negative effects of the US project that crosses the political with the economic with the military[16]—they very well could be. An epistemology of suffering would suggest there must be a radical interruption to current notions of "virtuous citizenship" or civil society because these happen to be the very tools with which the human dignity of the migrant is threatened every day. *EJA* and subsequent efforts to describe economic or immigrant justice do not offer any logical resolution to this dichotomy between civil society and the option for the poor. How would the bishops react if, as a result of applying the epistemology of suffering and seeing

---

[16] Sociologist Juliett Schor, for example, carefully describes how the US military intervened abroad on a number of occasions to protect US middle-class interests such as low produce prices. See, for example, her "Prices and Quantities: Unsustainable Consumption and the Global Economy," in *Ecological Economics* 55 (2005): 309–20. Government documentation of the 1954 CIA intervention in Guatemala to protect the interest of US-based United Fruit Company (bananas) is also available through the Freedom of Information Act, available through the US Department of State, *http://history. state.gov/historicaldocuments/frus1952-54Guat/comp1*.

the US economic and political system from the perspective of its victims, a study group or task force recommended a radical dismantling of structures of oppression and dehumanization? How far would a new document go in demanding the interruption of a system that inflicts the ultimate injustice on persons or groups "treated actively or abandoned passively as if they were nonmembers of the human race"?

■ CONCLUSION

I am often amazed at how committed Christians, even those committed to the moral vision and practical application of the social teaching of the churches, hesitate to apply the option for the poor to the noncitizen. For many, there seems to be something about "breaking the law," having crossed a border illegally, that makes the immigrant stand outside the purview of human dignity with respect to the economic teaching of the Church. *EJA*'s emphasis on citizenship as a Christian virtue, the common good as defined by civil society, and the commitment to the American experiment can seem to provide support for those who feel compelled to leave the immigrant outside of the purview of economic justice. However, the bishops' letter also includes elements of the Christian tradition that recall the all-inclusive understanding of human dignity and its demands for economic justice for *all*.

What the pastoral letter loses in its troublesome commitments to US civil society and its embrace of the rights and duties of citizens to construct the common good within the existing social and political arrangements of the American experiment—it recovers in its commitment to the option for the poor as a lens through which to determine whether the US economic system is upholding the life and dignity of all, at home and abroad, and in-between, including the migrant. Commitment to the option for the poor should promote the epistemological shift to look beyond those accepted as members of civil society to an expanded view of the American experiment that includes all who contribute to its economy and who suffer from its abuses, excesses, and unending need for an underside of invisible noncitizen workers.

EJA's acknowledgment of sin as a trait of human life in community and of how sin seeps into economic life to produce real human damage can motivate people to shift their lens. This acknowledgment demands that people refocus from an overly optimistic appreciation of US economic progress to grapple with how they are inevitably participating in an economic system that does violence to others and to the environment. Perhaps this epistemic change, present in the pastoral but not engaged to its fullest, can help us address the liberationist challenge to social teaching that demands concrete transformation above and beyond reform.

FOCUS QUESTIONS

1. In what ways does *EJA* define the American experiment?
2. In what ways does *EJA* address the condition of migrants, legal or undocumented, in the US economy?
3. How would you define the preferential option for the poor?
4. What elements of the American experiment and the US economy do you find helpful for fighting poverty and upholding human dignity?
5. What elements of the American experiment and the US economy do you find challenging or destructive to the common good of all?

8

Becoming *Synergoi*
Food, Justice, and Economic Cooperation

Margaret R. Pfeil

■■ INTRODUCTION

In their pastoral letter *Economic Justice for All* (*EJA*), the US bishops emphasized the concept of justice understood as participation of all members of society in service of the common good. Cooperative economic practices, they suggested, exemplify justice as participation. Since their letter, the imperiled state of the world's ecosystems has generated increasing concern about local food systems, representing an urgent issue of justice at the present time and sparking new questions about the structures of participation that would fulfill the demands of justice. In a globalized industrial economy, food production and consumption practices have become dependent upon the capacity of large agricultural and food corporations to manufacture and ship goods around the world at the cheapest price, burning up scarce energy supplies and further threatening Earth's ecological integrity. At the same time, disparities of power have rendered healthy food relatively inaccessible to certain populations, resulting in disproportionate health risks for poor people of color in urban US communities.

The bishops' pastoral letter, together with Scripture, liturgy, and other resources of the Christian tradition, offers a way of addressing these global food, energy, and ecological signs of the times in light of the demands of justice as participation. By understanding creation first and foremost as belonging to God, the Creator, humans may see themselves as God's co-workers. This basic theological concept serves to ground cooperative economic practices in support of more localized food systems. Local food cooperatives bring together urban residents and regional growers as co-workers with one another and with God. As they forge relationships among themselves and with the land about them, they bear witness to the radical interdependence of God's creation, manifested so clearly in the interconnection among all living members of a particular ecosystem. Supporting the integrity, or wholeness, of God's creation through cooperative local food practices represents the work of justice as participation in service of the common good.

■■ COOPERATION

In the introduction to their pastoral letter, the bishops state, "*All people have a right to participate in the economic life of society.* Basic justice demands that people be assured a minimum level of participation in the economy" (no. 15, italics in the original). Building on this foundational point, chapter 4 (nos. 295–325) emphasizes the value of cooperation in effecting justice as participation with a view toward serving the common good. In highlighting cooperative practices, the bishops draw from a deep wellspring in the Christian social tradition, beginning with Scripture.

In 1 Cor 3:7–9, Paul addresses discord within the Corinthian church: "Therefore, neither the one who plants nor the one who waters is anything, but only God, who causes the growth. The one who plants and the one who waters are equal, and each will receive wages in proportion to his labor. For we are God's co-workers; you are God's field, God's building." The original Greek word for the phrase "God's co-workers" is *synergoi.* So, by emphasizing the value of cooperation, *EJA* invites readers, particularly US Catholics, to discern how all might become *synergoi*, people who work cooperatively toward fuller economic participation, particularly of the poorest and most vulnerable, a very countercultural vision then and now.[1]

The bishops write:

> The biblical vision of creation has provided one of the most enduring legacies of Church teaching. To stand before God as the Creator is to respect God's creation, both the world of nature and of human history. *From the patristic period to the present, the Church has affirmed that misuse of the world's resources or appropriation of them by a minority of the world's population betrays the gift of creation since 'whatever belongs to God belongs to all.'* (*EJA*, no. 34)[2]

The concept that God's creation belongs to all is known in Catholic social thought as the principle of the universal destination of created goods. It serves

---

[1] See, for example, ch. 4, no. 24. *Catholic Social Thought*, expanded ed., ed. David J. O'Brien and Thomas A. Shannon (Maryknoll, NY: Orbis Books, 2010). Unless otherwise noted, all subsequent references to Catholic social teaching documents will be taken from this source and identified by paragraph number.

[2] Italics are in the original. The quotation is from St. Cyprian, "On Works and Almsgiving," no. 25, trans. R.J. Deferrari, "St. Cyprian: Treatises," no. 36 (New York: Fathers of the Church, 1958), 251.

as a means to adjudicate questions of material possessions and advocate practices of economic sharing. In his 2009 encyclical letter, *Caritas in veritate* (Charity in Truth), Pope Benedict XVI used the principle of the universal destination of created goods to frame his appeal for a "people-centered" economic ethic, suggesting cooperatives as a promising practice.[3] In doing so, he appealed to *Populorum progressio* (On the Development of Peoples), Pope Paul VI's 1967 encyclical letter on the development of peoples and Vatican II's *Gaudium et spes* (Pastoral Constitution on the Church in the Modern World), which reads:

> "God intended the earth and all that it contains for the use of every human being and people. Thus, as all men follow justice and unite in charity, created goods should abound for them on a reasonable basis." All other rights whatsoever, including those of property and of free commerce, are to be subordinated to this principle. They should not hinder but on the contrary favor its application. It is a grave and urgent social duty to redirect them to their primary finality.[4]

Populorum progressio, number 23, continues this theme, recalling St. Ambrose's injunction dating from the fourth century:

> "You are not making a gift of your possessions to the poor person. You are handing over to him what is his. For what has been given in common for the use of all, you have arrogated to yourself." That is, private property does not constitute for anyone an absolute and unconditioned right. No one is justified in keeping for his exclusive use what he does not need, when others lack necessities.[5]

Though the principle of the universal destination of created goods represents an important ethical criterion in Catholic social thought, the signs of the present time speak to its disregard. According to the Congressional Budget Office, the top 1 percent of the US population receives 17.1 percent of the nation's after-tax income, while the bottom fifth receives 4.9 percent.[6] The chief executive officers of the top fifteen US companies received wages 520 times greater than that of the average worker in 2007.[7] Globally, it is estimated that "women perform 66

---

[3] *Caritas in veritate*, nos. 45 and 66–7.

[4] Paul VI, *Populorum progressio*, no. 22, quoting *Gaudium et spes*, no. 69. *Caritas in veritate*, in turn, cites this passage in no. 6. For further treatment of the universal destination of created goods in recent Catholic social teaching, see also *Compendium of the Social Doctrine of the Church*, nos. 446, 481–5.

[5] The citation from Ambrose is *De Nabuthe* (On Nabuth) c. 12, n. 53 (P.L. 14, 747). In his 2010 World Day of Peace message, Benedict XVI also cites *Gaudium et spes*, no. 69, to emphasize the principle of the universal destination of created goods in addressing environmental degradation.

[6] Arloc Sherman and Chad Stone, "Income Gaps between Very Rich and Everyone Else More than Tripled in Last Three Decades, New Data Show," Center on Budget and Policy Priorities, June 25, 2010, *http://www.cbpp.org/cms/?fa=view&id=3220*.

[7] International Labor Organization, "World of Work Report 2008: Income Inequalities in the Age of Financial Globalization," *http://www.ilo.org/public/english/bureau/inst/download/world08.pdf*.

percent of the world's work, produce 50 percent of the food, but earn 10 percent of the income and own 1 percent of the property."[8] Since the 2008 recession, black households have experienced the largest decline in median income of any racial or ethnic group, at 4.4 percent. Women across racial and ethnic groups continue to earn less than men, but the gap in median income is greatest for black and Hispanic women.[9]

These data demonstrate the value of systemic analysis in discerning the requirements of justice, focusing attention on the dynamics of class, gender, and race to highlight economic power disparities. They also reveal the need for more vigorous cultivation of cooperative economic practices in light of the Catholic social tradition's emphasis on the universal destination of created goods. Among these goods, the accessibility of food, as a fruit of God's creation, has become a central point of ethical concern.

■■ FOOD JUSTICE: CULTIVATING RELATIONSHIPS BETWEEN URBAN AND RURAL LOCAL COMMUNITIES

In chapter 3, numbers 216–50, *EJA* devotes considerable attention to food and agriculture as one of the most pressing issues of economic policy. Reading this from a contemporary standpoint, the bishops' sobering assessment of the trend toward industrialization of agriculture proved all too accurate. Indian physicist Vandana Shiva sharply summarizes the current dilemma:

> We are now facing a triple convergence of crises, each of which threatens our survival.
>
> **Climate:** Global warming threatens our very survival as a species.
>
> **Energy:** Peak oil spells the end of the cheap oil that has fueled the industrialization of production and the globalization of consumerism.
>
> **Food:** A food crisis is emerging as a result of the convergence of climate change, peak oil, and the impact of globalization on the rights of the poor to food and livelihood.
>
> Of the three crises, the emerging food crisis poses the most immediate threat to the survival of the poor.[10]

---

[8] UNICEF, "Gender Equality—The Big Picture," summarizing findings of *State of the World's Children 2007: The Double Dividend of Gender Equality*, http://www.unicef.org/gender/index_big-picture.html.

[9] Women of Color Policy Network, "Income and Poverty in Communities of Color: A Reflection on the 2009 U.S. Census Bureau Data," September 2010, 2–3, http://wagner.nyu.edu/wocpn/publications/files/IncomeAndPovertyInCommunitiesofColor.pdf.

[10] Vandana Shiva, *Soil Not Oil* (Boston: South End Press, 2008), 2–3.

The food crisis stems directly, she argues, from the long-term process of industrialization of agriculture and the more recent dynamics of globalization, including liberalization of agricultural trade policies.

> One billion people are without food because industrial monocultures robbed them of their livelihoods in agriculture and their food entitlements. Another 1.7 billion are suffering from obesity and food-related diseases. Monocultures lead to malnutrition—for those who are underfed as well as those who are overfed. . . . Farmers are being destroyed because prices of farm products are driven down through a combination of monopolistic buying by global corporations and dumping of subsidized products.[11]

These dynamics of climate, energy, and globalization of food production span the globe but have profound effects upon local communities precisely in their particularity. Moving toward localization of food economies, Shiva concludes, is an ethical imperative.

The bishops may have anticipated her insight when they advocated "cooperation of rural and urban interests in resolving the challenges and problems facing agriculture" (*EJA*, no. 250). Surprisingly, though, they did not draw any explicit connection between the industrialization of agriculture and the reality of malnutrition as a mark of urban poverty, especially among the one in four children, and one of every two black children, under the age of 6 who were growing up in poverty in the United States at that time (*EJA*, no. 172 and 176ff).[12] The pastoral letter makes reference to food security only in global terms as a matter of agricultural trade policy (*EJA*, no. 239).

Though the bishops addressed the perduring problem of racism in US society and in the farming economy specifically (*EJA*, nos. 229–30), they did not make a direct connection to food security in the manner that the current language of "food justice" connotes, that is, locating "the need for food security—access to healthy, affordable, culturally appropriate food—in the contexts of institutional racism, racial formation, and racialized geographies."[13] The West Oakland Food Collaborative, for example, is located in an area of northern California with one grocery store serving forty thousand residents, primarily low-income and black. It seeks to foster relationships specifically between the urban black community and the region's black farmers. Based upon their ethnographic research, Alison Alkon

---

[11] Ibid., 122–3.

[12] In 2009, the number of black (35.3 percent) and Hispanic children (32.5 percent) under age 18 living in poverty in the United States reached an all-time high, three times greater than that of white and Asian children. See Women of Color Policy Network, "Income and Poverty," September 2010, 2.

[13] Alison Hope Alkon and Kari Marie Norgaard, "Breaking the Food Chains: An Investigation of Food Justice Activism," *Sociological Inquiry* 79, no. 3 (August 2009): 289–305, at 289.

and Kari Norgaard report that members of the collaborative "attribute the historic decline of black farmers nationwide to the United States Department of Agriculture (USDA)'s denial of loans, subsidies, and other support that enabled white farmers to transition to mechanized agriculture."[14]

Even the sustainable agriculture movement that has blossomed since the bishops' pastoral letter, which ostensibly holds as one of its main goals the promotion of justice for those engaged in agriculture, has not considered the race-based systemic injustice visited upon black farmers and low-income urban residents. Instead, Mark Winne reports, it has focused on "the farmer's place; his or her use of sustainable, if not organic, production methods; and the size of his or her farm," but the criterion of social justice is notably absent in the movement's efforts.[15] One of its proponents acknowledged, "As a mostly white movement, we were largely blind to hunger, race, and class issues."[16]

By contrast, in conscious response to precisely these issues, the West Oakland Food Collaborative offers an important urban market venue for black farmers, while also addressing the systemic roots of the dearth of healthy, affordable food options in their local community. As Alkon and Norgaard note, "With nearly 1.5 times as many corner liquor stores as the city average as well as an abundance of fast food establishments, West Oakland is typical of low-income, African American food deserts in other cities."[17] Creating an alternative, local food system that affords urban black residents access to healthy, locally grown food and provides black farmers with market space serves the end of food justice by transforming the structures of institutionalized racism and white supremacy.

To the extent that the poorest and most vulnerable members of society, like the residents of West Oakland, find ready access to the basic goods required for human flourishing, it serves the common good of the entire society. As the bishops stated in their pastoral letter, "From the Scriptures and church teaching we learn that the justice of a society is tested by the treatment of the poor" (no. 16).[18] When some members of society experience deprivation of that

---

[14] Ibid., 294. On this point, they cite Jess Gilbert, Gwen Sharp, and Sindy M. Felin, "The Loss and Persistence of Black-Owned Farms and Farmland: A Review of the Research Literature and Its Implications," *Southern Rural Sociology* 18 (2002): 1–30. They note that all the black farmers involved in the West Oakland Food Cooperative have roots among Southern sharecroppers.

[15] Mark Winne, *Closing the Food Gap: Resetting the Table in the Land of Plenty* (Boston: Beacon Press, 2008), 132.

[16] Ibid., 133. See also Alkon and Norgaard, "Breaking the Food Chains," 291.

[17] Alkon and Norgaard, "Breaking the food Chains," 295, citing California Alcoholic Beverage Control, "Fact Sheet: Oakland Alcohol Retailers," *http://Z;\Community Safety and Justice/Alcohol outlets\Website\Factsheet_1.24.6.doc*, and Jason P. Block, Richard A. Scribner, and Karen B. DeSalvo, "Fast Food, Race/Ethnicity, and Income: A Geographic Analysis," *American Journal of Preventative Medicine* 27 (2004): 211–7.

[18] See also no. 8 and ch. 2, nos. 28 and 38.

which is necessary for their integral well-being, the common good of all suffers. Attending to right relationship as part of the adjudication of justice contributes to the restoration of the integrity, or wholeness, of God's creation.

■ LINKING COOPERATION, FOOD, LITURGY, AND THE INTEGRITY OF CREATION: JUSTICE AS RIGHT RELATIONSHIP

Since EJA in 1986, Catholic social teaching texts have given greater attention to the integrity of creation, reflecting a more holistic understanding of its radical interdependence.[19] These treatments have typically come in response to evidence of significant degradation and abuse of ecosystems. Benedict XVI offered perhaps the most compelling account of the current ecological signs of the times and their ethical implications in his 2010 message for the World Day of Peace:

> Can we remain indifferent before the problems associated with such realities as climate change, desertification, the deterioration and loss of productivity in vast agricultural areas, the pollution of rivers and aquifers, the loss of biodiversity, the increase of natural catastrophes and the deforestation of equatorial and tropical regions? Can we disregard the growing phenomenon of "environmental refugees," people who are forced by the degradation of their natural habitat to forsake it—and often their possessions as well—in order to face the dangers and uncertainties of forced displacement? Can we remain impassive in the face of actual and potential conflicts involving access to natural resources? All these are issues with a profound impact on the exercise of human rights, such as the right to life, food, health and development.[20]

For Benedict XVI, indifference, lack of regard, and passivity do not represent appropriate ethical responses to these limit situations because they would not serve the end of justice. If all aspects of creation stand in mutual relationship, as the intricate balance of ecosystems reveals, then violation of any one part disrupts the integrity of the whole. The emphasis on justice as participation in *EJA* represents a promising starting point for generating ethical actions of solidarity and restoration in the face of environmental degradation.

---

[19] See *EJA*, nos. 12 and 216, and Pontifical Academy of Sciences Working Group, "Fate of the Mountain Glaciers in the Anthropocene" May 11, 2011, *http://www.vatican.va/roman_curia/ pontifical_academies/acdscien/2011/PAS_Glacier_110511_final.pdf.*

[20] Benedict XVI, "If You Want to Cultivate Peace, Protect Creation," World Day of Peace, January 1, 2010, no. 4, *http://www.vatican.va/holy_father/benedict_xvi/messages/peace/documents/ hf_ben-xvi_mes_20091208_xliii-world-day-peace_en.html.*

But, looking back on the 1986 pastoral letter, deeper connections among the themes of cooperation, food justice, and the radical interdependence of creation emerge. I suggest that a synthesis and further development of these concepts leads to reconsideration of the bishops' concept of justice as participation. A restorative model of justice rooted in right relationship, one that includes the value of participation but also requires interrogation of the existing economic systems, would better ensure that participation does not inadvertently lead to perpetuation of injustice. To test this point, the example of the supermarket industry in the United States proves illuminating.

Today, food security is not only a global concern but also a US problem, particularly in *food deserts*, defined by the 2008 US Farm Bill as "an area in the U.S. with limited access to affordable and nutritious food, particularly such an area composed of predominantly lower-income neighborhoods and communities."[21] One research study notes, "Both median income and population density have a close relationship to the amount of supermarket capacity that can be found in a given community, with the former bearing a somewhat stronger correlation to the pattern of store locations than the latter."[22] This finding is corroborated by the USDA Economic Research Service data showing that "low-income households in rural areas and poor central cities have less access to reasonably priced, high-quality food than other households."[23]

Furthermore, there is a direct correlation between lack of healthy, affordable food choices and the incidence of diet-related diseases, including obesity, diabetes, cancer, and heart disease, which disproportionately affect low-income blacks and Latinos.[24] These data have prompted one group of researchers to suggest that the term *food swamp* may be more appropriate than *food desert*, since the most pressing issue in US urban settings is not insufficient access to food calories but rather the inundation of low-income communities of color with unhealthy, energy-dense snack foods through corner "quick marts."[25]

Even if low-income communities were successful in wooing supermarkets to their backyards, would that necessarily support a healthier diet or a more just economy? One could argue that by organizing effectively to bring about this outcome, a particular community would have enacted justice as participation. But, viewed systemically, such an outcome might actually undermine the goal

---

[21] Donald Rose et al., "Deserts in New Orleans? Illustrations of Urban Food Access and Implications for Policy," a paper prepared for University of Michigan National Poverty Center/USDA Economic Research Service Research Conference, "Understanding the Economic Concepts and Characteristics of Food Access," February 2009, 10, citing the 2008 US Farm Bill, *http://www.npc.umich.edu/news/events/food-access/rose_et_al.pdf*.

[22] Winne, *Closing the Food Gap*, 87, quoting the 2006 Hartford Food System report, "Connecticut Supermarkets: Can New Strategies Address the Geographic Gaps?"

[23] Ibid., 92.

[24] Ibid., 92, 124. See also Alkon and Norgaard, "Breaking the Food Chains," 295–6.

[25] D. Rose et al., "Deserts in New Orleans?" 15.

of food justice in that community due to the structure of the food economy. As a vendor in the West Oakland Food Collaborative bluntly put it, "I don't want Safeway or Albertsons. They abandoned the inner city. They sell poison. They pay crap wages.'"[26] A recent longitudinal study, in fact, has found that greater access to supermarkets generally does not lead to improved quality of diet.[27] In the context of a holistic understanding of justice as right relationship, the pastoral letter's emphasis on justice as participation may be too narrow to address the systemic aspect of food security facing local communities around the world. Equity of participation alone does not satisfy the demands of justice when the economic system that structures participation has been fundamentally corrupted by gross disparities in power.

Where food is concerned, the supermarket industry exemplifies what Wendell Berry calls "the total economy," in which everything "has a price and is for sale. In a total economy significant and sometimes critical choices that once belonged to individuals or communities become the property of corporations."[28] Two of the marks of a total economy are ignorance and vulnerability, he notices:

> [O]ne does not know the history of the products that one uses. Where, exactly, did they come from? Who produced them? What toxins were used in their production? What were the human and ecological costs of producing them and then of disposing of them? . . . Though one is shopping amid an astonishing variety of products, one is denied certain significant choices. In such a state of economic ignorance it is not possible to choose products that were produced locally or with reasonable kindness toward people or toward nature. . . . To be a consumer in a total economy, one must agree to be totally ignorant, totally passive, and totally dependent on distant supplies and self-interested suppliers.[29]

Ignorant, passive, and dependent—these are just the sort of responses that Benedict XVI's World Day of Peace message excluded as unethical in the face of the current ecological crisis and its implications. But Berry poignantly illustrates the pervasive systemic forces at work to ensure the future of industrial food production and consumption, prompting the question: What course of action would be ethically appropriate and possible?

To elude the anesthetizing tentacles of the total economy, local initiatives like the West Oakland Food Collaborative seek to create an alternative food

---

[26] Quoted in Alkon and Norgaard, "Breaking the Food Chains," 296.

[27] Janne Boone-Heinonen et al., "Fast Food Restaurants and Food Stores: Longitudinal Associations with Diet in Young to Middle-Aged Adults: The CARDIA Study," *Archives of Internal Medicine* 171, no. 13 (July 11, 2011): 1162–70.

[28] Wendell Berry, "The Idea of a Local Economy," in *In the Presence of Fear: Three Essays for a Changed World* (Great Barrington, MA: The Orion Society, 2001), 11–31, at 25.

[29] Ibid., 28.

system that affords full participation directed toward the end of food justice. One person interviewed by Alkon and Norgaard reflected, "[It's about] building a community that takes care of each other's needs. And we can self sustain outside of the dominant system. . . . We want to buy and sell from each other . . . in a way that helps us sustain our neighborhoods or our communities. That's different than consuming in a way that sustains a mega business that's separate and distinct from us."[30]

Active participation in the cultivation of an alternative food system directed toward food justice not only fosters relationships between local urban residents and regional farmers but also serves to re-member the web of relationships connecting humans with the rest of God's creation. As humans have greater opportunity to practice conscious eating, remembering the farmer who grew that particularly luscious tomato, having perhaps helped her to till the land and bring the crop to the local urban farmer's market, we may become more attuned to the sounds of distress in our local ecosystems.[31] No longer is it just another video image on the nightly news of a collapsing ice shelf in the Antarctic or an apocalyptic statistic racing across the bottom of a muted screen in an airport. Now we become aware that the soil suffering erosion is right beneath our feet and under our fingernails, and the river being polluted courses like a vein through our city, sustaining—or contaminating—all life forms in and around it. No longer are we *industrial eaters*, Berry's term for "one who does not know that eating is an agricultural act, who no longer knows or imagines the connections between eating and the land."[32] Through cooperative work to bring about an alternative food system, we know we are inextricably related to the land and the humans who cultivated it, bound together with the other fruits of God's creation that sustain our lives.

For the bishops' audience of US Catholics, these connections between eating and the land carry further significance because eating is a sacramental act and the land is the gift of God's creative abundance. In their letter, the bishops readily connected liturgy and justice through food: "From the Lord's command to feed the hungry, to the Eucharist we celebrate as the Bread of Life, the fabric of our faith demands that we be creatively engaged in sharing the food that sustains life. There is no more basic human need" (no. 282). Jesus demonstrated the essential relationship among food, liturgy, and justice by eating and drinking his way through ministry—dining, forgiving, and healing, right up until his final meal with his disciples. They, in turn, followed his directive to remember him by commemorating the Last Supper in a liturgy of thanksgiving, the Eucharist.

---

[30] Quoted in Alkon and Norgaard, "Breaking the Food Chains," 296.

[31] For a fine meditation on conscious eating, see Elizabeth Groppe, *Eating and Drinking* (Minneapolis, MN: Fortress Press, 2011).

[32] Wendell Berry, "The Pleasures of Eating," in *Bringing It to the Table: On Farming and Food* (Berkeley, CA: Counterpoint, 2009), 228.

As Benedictine scholar Virgil Michel indicates, the act of offering as part of the Eucharistic liturgy is radically social.[33] In ancient practice, each person would bring a gift as part of the communal offering of all for all, including those present and absent, living and dead, to be shared with the poor in solidarity. These gifts represented the fruits of the worshippers' physical labor exercised with intentionality: as *synergoi,* God's co-workers, they produced bread and wine from grain and grapes, the fruits of God's creation.

Participants in the Christian liturgy of Eucharist (Mass or the Lord's Supper) recognize all of material creation as a sacrament of communion with God, the Creator—receiving all creation as gift and offering it back to God, through the dynamic, creative exercise of each person's vocation as one made in the image of God.[34] In giving thanks, the human person becomes more fully himself or herself before God. In Eucharistic communion, God responds by giving God's own son, Jesus Christ, as food to sustain God's people. By taking, eating, and drinking as Jesus invited his disciples to do, Christians become Christ's body in the world, united with him and with one another, and ready to participate in the restoration of the integrity of God's creation.[35]

Alexander Schmemann has observed that the original meaning of the Greek word *leitourgia* referred to "an action by which a group of people become something corporately which they had not been as a mere collection of individuals—a whole greater than the sum of its parts."[36] In the Eucharistic liturgy, the ecclesial community eats and drinks God's love, enabling them by God's grace to offer that love in return to God, neighbor, and all of creation, the basis for justice as right relationship. Practicing Eucharistic liturgy shapes participants to become *synergoi,* people ever more attuned to injustice as a violation of love, people who work together with God toward restoration and healing.[37]

Desiring to trace the connections among liturgy, food, and justice further, in Spring 2011, I taught a community-based research course at the University of Notre Dame called "*Synergoi*: The Theological Ethics of Food Cooperatives." Students directed their research efforts toward collaboration with neighbors of

---

[33] Virgil Michel, "The Social Nature of the Offertory," in *The Social Problem, Book Four: The Mystical Body and Social Justice,* compiled by St. John's Abbey (Collegeville, MN: Order of St. Benedict, 1938), 5–10.

[34] See Kallistos Ware, "The Value of Material Creation," *Sobornost* 6, no. 3 (1971): 154–65, and Elizabeth Theokritoff, "From Sacramental Life to Sacramental Living: Heeding the Message of the Environmental Crisis," *Greek Orthodox Theological Review* 44, nos. 1–4 (1999): 505–24.

[35] See Alexander Schmemann, *For the Life of the World: Sacraments and Orthodoxy* (Crestwood, NY: St. Vladimir's Seminary, 1973), 23–46, at 39–40, and Virgil Michel, "The Social Nature of Communion," in *The Social Problem, Book Four: The Mystical Body and Social Justice,* compiled by St. John's Abbey (Collegeville, MN: Order of St. Benedict, 1938), 11–6, at 13–5.

[36] Schmemann, *For the Life,* 25.

[37] Walter J. Burghardt, "Just Word and Just Worship: Biblical Justice and Christian Liturgy," *Worship* 73 (1999): 386–98, at 392.

Used with permission Monroe Park Grocery Cooperative

Monroe Park Grocery Cooperative

Monroe Park in South Bend, Indiana, to start a cooperative grocery store. Monroe Park, a majority black, low-income area, meets the technical definition of a food desert, being located more than a mile from any full-scale grocery store. It also qualifies as a food swamp, with the local gas station providing the fast food of choice for children in the neighborhood.

Local farmers are cooperating with neighbors to bring fresh, locally grown produce to the co-op at affordable prices, and members may purchase these goods with food stamps. The farmers, including members of the Amish community, value access to a much-needed market venue for their goods, while the neighbor members are able to purchase enough produce to feed their families.

Neighbor members of the co-op invest three hours of work per month, and one of the areas of labor involves tending the community gardens in the neighborhood.[38] The produce from these gardens is available to everyone free of charge. In this way, the co-op hopes to extend the availability of fresh produce as much as possible while also building neighborhood cohesion.

The Monroe Park Grocery Cooperative values participation as part of justice, as the bishops' pastoral letter advocated. But, like the West Oakland Food Collaborative, it seeks to cultivate a local food economy as an alternative to the global system of industrial food production and trade. If the dominant food

---

[38] For more information on South Bend's Unity Gardens, two of which are in Monroe Park, see *http://www.theunitygardens.blogspot.com/*.

system reifies and magnifies the very ethical concerns raised by the US bishops in 1986 and decried more recently by Benedict XVI and Vandana Shiva, among others, then justice as participation ought not to reinforce that system; rather, justice will require new practices of right relationship and exploration of creative economic alternatives, like local food cooperatives.

Over the longer term, the co-op membership hopes to collaborate with other grassroots efforts in the region to give shape to South Bend as a "transition community," part of a movement among local communities that began in Ireland and England about a decade ago. Faced with the urgent need to scale down their level of energy consumption and to develop renewable sources of energy, "transition communities" around the world are exploring ways to retool, re-skill, and reconnect with one another in order to build "the capability to produce locally those things that we can produce locally."[39]

The transition movement seeks to foster communities of resilience in solidarity with other local communities, reflecting the necessary connection in Catholic social thought between the principles of subsidiarity and solidarity. Subsidiarity encourages satisfaction of social needs at the most local level possible, while solidarity urges attention to the well-being of each and every member of the community, because, as Pope John Paul II put it in his 1987 encyclical letter, "we are all really responsible for all."[40]

The movement also emphasizes the value of distributive justice considered in terms of systemic right relationship, situating socioeconomic structures within the larger framework of ecological systems.[41] Taking seriously the warnings of Shiva and other experts, its theoretical departure point is the radical interdependence of living systems, which gives shape to the ethical imperative of human cooperation toward holistic restoration.

■ CONCLUSION

For Christian communities, the interdependence of God's creation provides the defining context that informs humans' socioeconomic practices. The rightness of relationships emerges from the need for each part of creation to flourish as part of realizing the common good. Local, cooperative practices directed toward food justice represent an urgent creative response to the ecological, social, and economic degradation wrought by a globalized industrial food system. These initiatives afford the opportunity for greater participation, as the bishops urged twenty-five years ago, but they also address the matrix of gender, race, and class issues as required by an understanding of justice as right relationship.

---

[39] Rob Hopkins, *The Transition Handbook: From Oil Dependency to Local Resilience* (White River Junction, VT: Chelsea Green, 2008), 68.

[40] John Paul II, *Sollicitudo rei socialis* (On Social Concern), no. 38.

[41] On distributive justice, see *EJA*, no. 70.

Ultimately, as each part of creation thrives, it will be better able to contribute to the integrity of creation as a whole. As in Eucharistic liturgy, and for Christians, *through* that liturgy, members of creation collaborating together as *synergoi* have the opportunity to notice that by living ever more deeply into the reality of interdependence, we live more fully in God's love, the ground of justice as right relationship.

FOCUS QUESTIONS

1. What is the difference between a *food desert* and a *food swamp*?
2. What does the term *food justice* connote? How might it be useful in the analysis of a local food system?
3. How do you understand the relationship between liturgy, particularly the celebration of Eucharist (the Lord's Supper), and justice? What role might food play in this relationship?
4. Christian social teaching emphasizes the concept of the universal destination of created goods in adjudicating questions of ownership in light of the common good. How might this idea shape a particular society's approach to their food system?
5. The interdependence of creation is a key value in Christian ecological ethics. What implications might this value have for human beings as they consider the question, "Who is my neighbor?" Does the notion of right relationship extend beyond the human community to the rest of creation, and if so, what are the ethical implications of this broader understanding of interconnection?

9 Liturgy, Discipleship, and Economic Justice

Christopher P. Vogt

■ INTRODUCTION

If you were brainstorming ideas about where to start a movement to transform the American economy, "at Mass" or "in church" probably would not be at the top of your list. For many people today, the realms of economics and religion could not seem further apart. Even Christians who are deeply committed to working for economic justice might not easily see the connection between their activism and their acts of worship. However, there are many good reasons why liturgy—that is, the church's official, public rites of prayer and worship—should be a primary source of insight for Christians as they figure out what constitutes a just economy and how that vision of social justice might be realized.[1]

■ CONNECTING LITURGY AND JUSTICE: A MISSED OPPORTUNITY IN *ECONOMIC JUSTICE FOR ALL*

As mentioned elsewhere in this book, the US Conference of Catholic Bishops (USCCB) launched a major initiative in the 1980s promoting a Christian vision of economic life. At the center of this effort was a pastoral letter entitled *Economic Justice for All* (*EJA*). In it the bishops said their aim was twofold: "to provide guidance for members of our own Church as they seek to form their consciences about economic matters" and "to add our voice to the public debate about the directions in which the U.S. economy should be moving" (no. 27). The bishops were quite successful in their attempt to accomplish these two tasks simultaneously, but the

---

[1] "Liturgy," *HarperCollins Encyclopedia of Catholicism*, ed. Richard P. McBrien (San Francisco: HarperSanFrancisco, 1994), 787.

voice of reason and matters of public policy ultimately received stronger emphasis. The section of the letter on "selected economic policy issues" (nos. 127–325) is more than four times as long as the section offering concrete recommendations regarding the life of the Catholic Church (nos. 326–65).

The bishops' decision to emphasize public policy was not without merit. The specificity of their policy proposals attracted the attention of mainstream media and led to considerable public discussion. However, this move was not without cost. Critics of the letter noted that it failed to articulate adequately a spirituality that could undergird a political commitment to the promotion of justice.[2] The bishops' goal may have been to change hearts and minds, but it was the mind that got most of the attention. Their key strategy for making the economy more just was to provide a careful description of a "The Christian Vision of Economic Life" (the title of chapter 2 of the letter) and then to discuss the practical implications of that vision, especially as it pertained to public policy. In other words, they sought to achieve their goals through the force of argument and persuasion. They engaged citizens, public servants, and their own Church in the same manner—intellectually.

By no means was it a mistake for the bishops to offer an intellectually rigorous account of the demands of social justice. On the contrary, the bishops' effort in this regard is to be commended. However, simply detailing a vision of economic life is not in itself sufficient to realize either of the bishops' said goals in writing the letter. It is neither adequate for shaping the direction of US policy nor for the formation of anyone's conscience. Articulating a vision of economic justice is essential, but the moral life is about far more than achieving an intellectual understanding of justice, or, in this case, grasping a "vision of economic life." Achieving these goals also entails a proper cultivation of emotions or formation of affections.[3]

The American Catholic bishops seem to have recognized this point themselves when they acknowledged that *personal conversion* and societal transformation are intimately linked (*EJA*, no. 328). However, the bishops did not devote the same level of analysis or resources to considering how to bring about such a conversion of heart, or to how the faithful could grasp the link between a deepened life of faith and a deeper dedication to promote economic justice.

Sadly the bishops clearly did not succeed in bringing about a fundamental shift in the direction and shape of the American economy in the quarter-century following the release of their landmark document. Indeed, 1986 did not even mark the beginning of a dramatic shift in the way Roman Catholics think

---

[2] Charles E. Curran, "The Reception of Catholic Social and Economic Teaching in the United States," in *Modern Catholic Social Teaching: Commentaries and Interpretations*, ed. Kenneth R. Himes et al. (Washington, DC: Georgetown, 2005), 483.

[3] Stanley Hauerwas, "Worship, Evangelism, Ethics: On Eliminating the 'And'," in *Liturgy and the Moral Self: Humanity at Full Stretch before God*, ed. E. Byron Anderson and Bruce T. Morrill (Collegeville, MN: Liturgical Press, 1998), 95–106, at 99.

about economic justice. If the Catholic bishops or any other Christians hope to bring about justice and social change, they must do more than distribute a plan for reform or teach right doctrine about how we should live. To promote social justice faithfully and effectively, there must be a much stronger focus on how to create a widespread conversion or change or heart. If the Church is to bring people to pursue and uphold justice, it must join the promotion of social justice with the liturgy and with concrete practices that foster the formation of people in virtues such as compassion, hospitality, and solidarity.[4] In short, the bishops' effort to promote social justice should be reconceived as primarily a matter of calling their own flock to live out the Gospel more faithfully and of developing effective models of moral formation.[5]

The liturgy is crucial for such a Christian movement for social justice, because it is in worship that the heart is moved. It is in prayer that Christians are drawn toward deeper conversion. In worship, Christians contemplate and understand more fully what it means to be Christian in the public, social sphere, and they are moved to act upon that understanding. Writing on why Virgil Michel understood liturgy as vital in the pursuit of social justice, Kenneth Himes, a Catholic theologian who teaches at Boston College, observed:

> [T]he Eucharist enables the individual to act upon moral commitments. The cause of justice, as with any moral ideal, requires a visceral as well as a cerebral commitment. . . . More than a recitation of facts was needed if people were to be moved to take up the arduous task of social reform. Required was an object of desire. This need was addressed by the community's worship.[6]

Learning what is right and being moved to act upon that knowledge are two significantly different things. Participating in the liturgy deepens a person's understanding of what is right and, perhaps more important, ought to inspire a person to act upon that understanding. For most Christians, their faith and their very identities are bound up with prayer and worship. Unfortunately, few Christians read theological texts or pastoral letters from the bishops. The place where Christians meet the church—its people and its teaching—is at worship.[7]

---

[4] Christopher P. Vogt, "Fostering a Catholic Commitment to the Common Good: An Approach Rooted in Virtue Ethics," *Theological Studies* 68, no. 2 (2007): 394–417.

[5] J. Brian Benestad has offered a similar suggestion. He criticized the bishops' approach to justice, claiming they ignored the vital importance of character formation as a dimension of political teaching. J. Brian Benestad, *The Pursuit of a Just Social Order: Policy Statements of the U.S. Catholic Bishops* (Washington, DC: Ethics and Public Policy Center, 1982), cited in Scott Hebden, "Liturgy and Social Justice: Recovering the Prophetic Vision of Virgil Michel," *Chicago Studies* 46, no. 2 (Summer 2007): 247.

[6] Kenneth Himes, "Eucharist and Justice: Assessing the Legacy of Virgil Michel," *Worship* 62, no. 3 (1998): 223.

[7] John Coleman, "How the Eucharist Proclaims Social Justice, Part II," *Church*, Spring 2001, 12.

Virgil Michel, a Catholic, Benedictine theologian and a leading figure in the American liturgical movement of the early twentieth century, was one of the foremost advocates of linking liturgy and the pursuit of social justice.[8] Michel was convinced that social harmony and economic justice could not be achieved without God's help and believed that for social reform to be authentic and truly just, it must ultimately be rooted in God and Jesus Christ. He wrote, "The lesson of history is that any movement toward Christian ideals, when fostered apart from all relation to Christ, will soon decline; it will, in spite of its manifest idealism, be of the earth . . . and will go the way of all flesh."[9] Michel believed efforts at social reform that ignore the need for Divine assistance and inspiration can never definitively succeed. As a Catholic priest, he experienced the Eucharistic liturgy (Mass) to be where he and the whole community of the Church were most profoundly connected to Jesus Christ. He reasoned that an approach to social justice grounded in the liturgy would remain connected to Christ, thereby improving its prospects for success and safeguarding its authenticity. Thus for practical and theological reasons, he said, a Christian movement for social justice should have deep roots in the liturgy.

What Are the Connections between Liturgy and Ethics?

Liturgy is not an ethics class. It is for the glorification of God and to be celebrated as a good in and of itself.[10] Liturgy should not be thought of in a utilitarian sense; it is not a tool to be used for the purpose of promoting even lofty goals such as social justice and solidarity. However, as the Second Vatican Council's *Sacrosanctum concilium* (Constitution on the Sacred Liturgy) notes, the liturgy is not exclusively for giving glory to God; it is also for the sanctification of the assembly.[11] It helps people become more holy. One way the liturgy fulfills this role is by forming the Church as a people of God. In other words, it is the liturgy that gives members of the Church their sense of being united to one another in a common purpose and in a shared identity.

---

[8] Patrick Malloy, "Virgil Michel: Founder of the American Liturgical Movement," in *How Firm a Foundation: Leaders of the Liturgical Movement*, ed. Robert L. Tuzik (Chicago: Liturgy Training Publications, 1990): 151–9.

[9] Virgil Michel, "The Cooperative Movement and the Liturgical Movement," in *Catholic Rural Life Objectives* (St. Paul, MN: National Catholic Rural Life Conference, n.d.). Cited in Michael J. Baxter, CSC, "Reintroducing Virgil Michel: Towards a Counter-Tradition of Catholic Social Ethics in the United States," *Communio* 24 (1997): 509.

[10] As Don Saliers has written, "Liturgy is the non-utilitarian enactment of the drama of the divine-human encounter." See Don E. Saliers, "Liturgy and Ethics: Some New Beginnings," in *Liturgy and the Moral Self: Humanity at Full Stretch before God*, ed. E. Byron Anderson and Bruce T. Morrill (Collegeville, MN: Liturgical Press, 1998), 34.

[11] Keith F. Pecklers, *Worship: A Primer in Christian Ritual* (Collegeville, MN: Liturgical Press, 2003), 15.

As Daniel Groody, a moral theologian who teaches at the University of Notre Dame, has written:

> The Eucharist is a grace that invites people to partake actively in and be transformed by the very life-giving relationship they are celebrating. Celebrating the Eucharist means not only witnessing bread and wine change into the body and blood of Christ, but also it means becoming what one receives: a sacrament of love for the world. In summary, the transubstantiation of the bread and wine into the body and blood of Christ, as Benedict XVI notes, is the beginning of the transformation of believers, which should lead to the transformation of the world until Christ becomes all in all.[12]

Let us take a moment to unpack what Groody is saying here. The Eucharist is a ritual meal that is both a remembrance and a reenactment of the saving sacrifice of Jesus Christ.[13] In hearing the Gospel and in the prayers and ritual of the Eucharist, those gathered remember what Jesus preached and what he did (e.g., forgave sins, healed the sick, reconciled outcasts and society) and are reminded that they as Christians are called to align their lives with what Jesus began. Near the close of the Eucharist, the congregation eats bread and sips wine that Catholics believe have been transformed (transubstantiated) into the body and the blood of Christ (not physically, but in essence). In this ritual Christians are intimately united with Christ and his mission and ministry of transforming the world.

It is not so much that the liturgy should be used as a tool to encourage people to act morally or ethically; that would be to misconstrue the nature of liturgy. The point is that when the faithful are deeply engaged in a liturgy done well, it moves them toward a particular way of understanding themselves and the world, which then leads them to think about right and wrong in specifically Christian ways.

Liturgy communicates understandings about the human condition—for example, it suggests that human beings are social by nature, that all people share an inalienable, fundamental dignity, and so on. These are moral claims that together undergird a Christian vision of justice, including economic justice. Indeed one of the building blocks of the bishops' ethical norms for economic life is the view that human beings are "social animal[s]" who are "made for friendship, community, and public life" (*EJA*, no. 65). By immersing themselves in the language and logic of liturgy, everyday Christians can develop a lived understanding of what it means to be a member of a living community that can help them overcome today's radical individualism.[14]

---

[12] Daniel G. Groody, *Globalization, Spirituality, and Justice: Navigating the Path to Peace* (Maryknoll, NY: Orbis Books, 2007), 220. Groody is referencing Benedict XVI, "Eucharist: Setting Transformations in Motion" (XX World Youth Day, Cologne, Germany, August 21, 2005), *Origins* 35, no. 12 (September 1, 2005): 202.

[13] John Coleman, "How the Eucharist Proclaims Social Justice, Part I" *Church*, Winter 2000, 6.

[14] Himes, "Eucharist and Justice," 222.

Don Saliers, a Methodist theologian, describes liturgy as a "characterizing" event that gives participants a sense of their fundamental location and orientation in the world.[15] Thus liturgy offers a fundamental moral formation that serves to place a participant within a universe of meaning.[16] Liturgy tells participants they are not alone in the world. Their very being comes from God and is sustained by God. They are part of a people; this membership in community comes with responsibilities, and so on. As Protestant theologian Stanley Hauerwas puts it, the Eucharist shapes participants so that they may properly hear, understand, and enact the Gospel story; it is through liturgy that one learns the skills to know what the "Good News" of the Gospel is really about.[17] In other words, active and conscious participation in good liturgy trains a person's imagination and affections to recognize and respond to the omnipresence of God.[18] It helps one learn to see the world as God sees it.[19]

Put differently, liturgy plays a crucial role in calling Christians to a deeper conversion and commitment to Christ. As we read in *EJA*:

> The transformation of social structures begins with and is always accompanied by a conversion of the heart. As disciples of Christ each of us is called to a deep personal conversion and to "action on behalf of justice and participation in the transformation of the world." . . . But personal conversion is not gained once and for all. It is a process that goes on through our entire life. Conversion, moreover, takes place in the context of a larger faith community: through baptism into the Church, through common prayer, and through our activity with others on behalf of justice. (no. 328)

Liturgy is perhaps the most important form of "common prayer" that sustains the spiritual life of Christians and leads them to deeper conversion.

Let me offer one example of how a person's self-understanding and beliefs about justice and equality can be shaped by their participation in worship. The Roman Catholic liturgy of the Eucharist is meant to be an occasion in which the divisions of sex, age, race, and class are erased and the profound value of each and every human person is acknowledged;[20] sometimes Christians are reminded of this fact very directly when the Scriptures are proclaimed. For example, Saint Paul's

---

[15] Saliers, "Liturgy and Ethics," 17.

[16] Paul Ramsey, "Liturgy and Ethics," *Journal of Religious Ethics* 7, no. 2 (1979): 146.

[17] Stanley Hauerwas, "The Gesture of a Truthful Story: The Church and 'Religious Education,'" *Encounter* 43, no. 4 (1982): 325.

[18] Peter E. Fink, "Life as Prayer: Contemplation and Action," in *Liturgy and the Moral Self: Humanity at Full Stretch before God*, ed. E. Byron Anderson and Bruce T. Morrill (Collegeville, MN: Liturgical Press, 1998), 134.

[19] Keith F. Pecklers, *Worship: A Primer in Christian Ritual* (Collegeville, MN: Liturgical Press, 2003), 17.

[20] Ibid., 174.

First Letter to the Corinthians proclaims that the celebration of the Eucharist is unsound if it fails to break down barriers and welcome all to the table on an equal footing (11:17–22).[21] The importance of unity and equality are communicated in more subtle ways as well. At the Eucharistic table, the community shares in one loaf of bread broken and shared (also a symbol of how the entire community is joined to Christ; see the section on the "Mystical Body of Christ" on page 255).[22] Robert Hovda describes quite powerfully the ways the ritual of the Eucharist communicates a belief in fundamental equality: at liturgy, everyone is

> addressed and sprinkled and bowed to and incensed and touched and kissed and treated like somebody—all in the very same way. Where else do czars and beggars get the same treatment? Where else are food and drink blessed in a common prayer of thanksgiving, broken and poured out, so that everybody, everybody shares and shares alike?[23]

By participating in the ritual of the liturgy, these fundamental truth-claims about equality and the importance of solidarity shape those present consciously and unconsciously. In this way, liturgy helps lay the foundation for social concern. As *EJA* makes plain, recognizing the equal dignity of all persons is crucial to a Catholic worldview and a Christian vision of economic life (no. 69). Social inequality is a serious moral issue.[24] Regular participation in the Eucharistic liturgy should help make Christians more aware of the truth of the universal dignity of all, and more sensitive to inequality in the world.

Liturgy not only helps participants understand what is happening in the world in a particular way but also communicates what an appropriate response might look like. It helps Christians answer two essential moral questions: What sort of person should I become? and What should I do? A recurring image in the literature on liturgy and ethics is that of a "rehearsal room." This image helps us understand what sort of gathering a liturgy really is. A liturgy is not a political rally or a classroom but rather a rehearsal room in which actions are repeated over and over again until participants have identified with the part assigned to them as actors in the church and the world.[25] "Learning one's part" includes

---

[21] Coleman, "How the Eucharist . . . Part I," 6.

[22] Ibid., 6.

[23] Quoted by Walter Burghardt, "Worship and Justice Reunited," in *Liturgy and Justice: To Worship God in Spirit and Truth*, ed. Anne Y. Koester (Collegeville, MN: Liturgical Press: 2002), 40.

[24] For a helpful discussion of economic inequality within a framework of Catholic social ethics, see Dennis McCann, "Inequality and Wealth: When Does It Become Immoral, and Why?" in *Rediscovering Abundance: Interdisciplinary Essays on Wealth, Income, and Their Distribution in the Catholic Social Tradition*, ed. Helen Alford (Notre Dame, IN: University of Notre Dame Press, 2006), 189–208.

[25] Mark Searle, "Serving the Lord with Justice," in *Vision: The Scholarly Contributions of Mark Searle to Liturgical Renewal*, ed. Anne Y. Koester and Barbara Searle (Collegeville, MN: Liturgical Press, 2004), 19. Similarly, Don Saliers, in "Liturgy and Ethics," writes that good liturgy is a kind of "deliberate rehearsal" of bringing all aspects of our character into harmony with God's will for us.

learning to be a certain kind of person or allowing one's affections to be shaped by the story of which one seeks to be a part.

Liturgy of the Word: Scripture and Social Justice

The Liturgy of the Word (the part of the Mass when passages from the Bible are proclaimed) is decisive in forming the identity of Christians and shaping their understanding of justice. The Bible is about many things, but one of the most prominent, recurring themes in Scripture is justice.[26] As the US bishops observe, "The Scriptures contain many passages that speak directly of economic life" (*EJA*, no. 29). Indeed the bishops begin their discussion of "The Christian Vision of Economic Life" by attending to Scripture, mining the narratives of creation, covenant, and so on to describe an understanding of "economic life worthy of the divine revelation" (*EJA*, no. 29).

The complex understandings of justice in the Bible should not be underestimated. In fact, the issue of justice comes up so often in the Bible, it is impossible to describe *the* biblical understanding of justice. There is no one word in the languages of the original texts (Hebrew and Greek) that corresponds directly to the English word *justice*.[27] Although the theme of Scripture and justice cannot be explored adequately here, the topic cannot be ignored.[28] Bruce Morrill writes that liturgy is both indicative (i.e., makes a statement of fact) and imperative (i.e., says something that should be done).[29] Liturgy proclaims what God has done in Jesus Christ and commands Christians to respond appropriately. It is primarily from Scripture that Christians learn who God is as well as what sort of people they are called to become in response to God's activity in the world. Therefore it is essential to pause and consider at least a few of the most basic lessons or meanings of justice one learns from hearing Scripture proclaimed at liturgy.

Although justice embodies many forms, the main idea of justice in the Bible can be described as "fidelity to the demands of a relationship."[30] A person acts

---

[26] Burghardt, "Worship and Justice," 35.

[27] John R. Donahue, "The Bible and Catholic Social Teaching: Will This Engagement Lead to Marriage?" in *Modern Catholic Social Teaching: Commentaries and Interpretations*, ed. Kenneth R. Himes et al. (Washington, DC: Georgetown, 2005), 13.

[28] In addition to Donahue, "The Bible and Catholic Social Teaching" (see n. 27), anyone seeking an introduction to the theme of justice in Scripture might consult Mary Katherine Birge, "Biblical Justice," in *The Heart of Catholic Social Teaching: Its Origins and Contemporary Significance*, ed. David Matzko McCarthy (Grand Rapids, MI: Brazos, 2009), 19–30. A helpful bibliography can be found in John R. Donahue, *What Does the Lord Require? A Bibliographical Essay on the Bible and Social Justice* (St. Louis, MO: Institute of Jesuit Sources, 2000).

[29] Bruce Morrill, "The Struggle for Tradition," in *Liturgy and the Moral Self: Humanity at Full Stretch before God*, ed. E. Byron Anderson and Bruce T. Morrill (Collegeville, MN: Liturgical Press, 1998), 69.

[30] Donahue, "The Bible and Catholic Social Teaching," 14.

in accordance with biblical justice when he or she lives in right relationship with God and with all members of the community. The bishops draw from this biblical idea and build upon it in *EJA* when they discuss what they call "The Responsibilities of Social Living" and "The Minimum Conditions for Life in Community" (nos. 63–84). Biblically grounded notions of the shape of right relationship between God and God's people as well as among all members of the community can be traced back to God's covenant with Israel, established at Sinai.

Law and Covenant

One of the most memorable and important stories in the Hebrew Bible is that of the liberation of the Israelites from their enslavement in Egypt and their establishment as a nation in the Holy Land. This long narrative is found in the book of Exodus. At the beginning of the story, the Israelites are living under conditions of "cruel slavery" in Egypt (Ex 1:13). Suffering, the Israelites call out to God, who hears their cries. The story tells of God speaking the following words to Moses, a man that Jews, Christians, and Muslims believe was called by God to lead the Israelites out of Egypt:

> I have witnessed the affliction of my people in Egypt and have heard their cry of complaint against their slave drivers, so I know well what they are suffering. Therefore I have come down to rescue them from the hands of the Egyptians and lead them out of that land into a good and spacious land, a land flowing with milk and honey. (Ex 3:7–8)

Here already a theme of justice is emerging. God hears the cries of those who are oppressed and suffer injustice, and God acts to relieve that suffering. This is significant, if Christians are truly called to live in response to how they believe God has acted in history. Although it is true that this story tells of God's liberating power, the story is actually much more complex.[31] It is a story about not only liberation from injustice but also the establishment of a community based on a new model of relationship. It is not only a freedom from oppression; it is a calling to live in the new way described in a covenant that Yahweh establishes with Israel (i.e., the Law, or Torah). Israel is to live as God's chosen people—worshipping God alone and living in a manner consistent with God's ways. The Law of ancient Israel was understood by that community (and by Jews today) as a gift because it makes known how to live if one wishes to be in right relationship with God and one's fellows. Thus, "Far from being an arbitrary restriction on the life of the people, these codes made life in community possible" (*EJA*, no. 36).

---

[31] Daniel Groody provides an interesting, compelling "meta-narrative" framework for understanding the themes of justice and liberation in Scripture. Unfortunately, his treatment is too complicated to include here. See ch. 2 of *Globalization, Spirituality, and Justice: Navigating the Path to Peace* (Maryknoll, NY: Orbis Books, 2007).

One of the most important aspects of justice found in the Law of ancient Israel is a concern for the poor and powerless. As the US bishops observed, "The specific laws of the covenant protect human life and property, demand respect for parents and the spouses and children of one's neighbor, and manifest a special concern for the vulnerable members of the community: widows, orphans, the poor, and strangers in the land" (*EJA*, no. 36). In the Covenant Code of Exodus, Yahweh commands the new nation of Israel,

> You shall not molest or oppress an alien, for you were once aliens yourselves in the land of Egypt. You shall not wrong any widow or orphan. If ever you wrong them and they cry out to me, I will surely hear their cry. (Ex 22:20–22)

Aliens, widows, and orphans were all disenfranchised in ancient Israel's patriarchal society. They were the most vulnerable, powerless members of society. This passage on the importance of caring properly for aliens, widows, and orphans is not an aberration in the overall vision of justice in the Torah. On the contrary, one finds similar passages in Deuteronomy, where "defraud[ing] a poor and needy hired servant" or "[violating] the rights of the alien or of the orphan" are prohibited (24:14, 17).[32] Thus the books of the Law make it clear that the ancient Israelites understood maltreatment of the least advantaged members of society to be a violation of God's Law and a fundamental form of injustice.

Showing concern for the poor and treating vulnerable persons justly were not special acts of kindness; they were understood as minimal demands of justice.[33] God heard the cries of the Israelites enslaved in Egypt; likewise, those who understood themselves to be God's people were called to hear the cries of the oppressed and to respond with compassion. Christians today understand themselves to be God's people—descendents of Abraham and the people of ancient Israel. They understand themselves to be descendents of the people of the covenant at Sinai. As such, the demands of the covenant have some force for them even today when they hear these readings proclaimed at liturgy. In these biblical themes, the principle of the preferential option for the poor—one of the central principles of contemporary Catholic social teaching on economic matters—is clear (*EJA*, no. 87).

The Prophets of Ancient Israel

The Hebrew Scriptures are filled with accounts of ancient Israel's struggles to remain faithful to the demands of their covenant with Yahweh. The prophets were religious authorities in ancient Israel who took their countrymen to task over fidelity to the covenant. Today, if people think about prophecy at all, they

---

[32] Donahue, "The Bible and Catholic Social Teaching," 21.

[33] Ibid., 15.

likely associate it with predicting the future; however, this was not the primary role of the ancient prophets. The prophets did sometimes make dire predictions about the future, but their primary role was to assess whether Israel was being faithful to the covenant. They warned that if Israel failed to live up to its obligations, disaster would result—the country would suffer war, famine, or a similar calamity. So their predictions about the future were not instances of soothsaying so much as reminders that God would punish Israel if it failed to live righteously.

The prophets used two main criteria to assess whether ancient Israel was being faithful to the covenant: right worship and preferential option for the poor. Right worship checked whether the Israelites were worshipping only Yahweh or were committing idolatry. The preferential option for the poor checked how well the society was caring for its most vulnerable members. These criteria can be understood as a dual measurement of justice, gauging whether Israel was in right relationship with God and giving Yahweh his due, and whether there were just relationships among the members of the community.[34] Thus as the US bishops explained:

> The substance of prophetic faith is proclaimed by Micah: "to do justice, and to love kindness, and to walk humbly with your God" (Mi 6:8, RSV). Biblical faith in general, and prophetic faith especially, insist that fidelity to the covenant joins obedience to God with reverence and concern for the neighbor. (*EJA*, no. 37)

The ancient prophets had harsh words for the rich and powerful of their day. Their admonitions echo across the centuries and warn those similarly situated today: "Thus says the Lord: For three crimes of Israel, and for four, I will not revoke my word; Because they sell the just man for silver, and the poor man for a pair of sandals. They trample the heads of the weak into the dust of the earth, and force the lowly out of the way" (Am 2:6–7).

The New Testament

One can find substantial continuity between the themes of justice in the Old and the New Testaments. The prophetic concern for the poor and vulnerable echoes throughout Christian Scripture, perhaps loudest in the Gospel of Luke. Luke's account of the birth of Jesus (Lk 2:1–20) depicts the Son of God being born in a stable among shepherds (a group that lived on the margins of society). Luke's Gospel also offers a powerful prayer (often called the *Magnificat*), spoken by Jesus' mother, Mary:

> The Mighty One has done great things for me, and holy is his name. His mercy is from age to age to those who fear him. He has shown might with his arm, dispersed the arrogant of mind and heart. He has

---

[34] Burghardt, "Worship and Justice," 39.

thrown down the rulers from their thrones but lifted up the lowly. The hungry he has filled with good things; the rich he has sent away empty. (Lk 1:49–53)

As the US bishops observed, "Jesus, especially in Luke, lives as a poor man, like the prophets takes the side of the poor, and warns of the dangers of wealth" (*EJA*, no. 49).

Luke's Gospel is not the only one to emphasize God's special concern for the poor and marginalized. One of the most powerful passages in any of the Gospels is Matthew's account of the Last Judgment (25).[35] That story tells how Jesus will return in glory at the end of time to divide the "sheep" (those who will be saved and live eternally with God) from the "goats" (those who are to be eternally separated from God, or damned). In this story, those who are saved are told this is because they showed mercy to people in need of compassion. Jesus tells them, "I was hungry and you gave me food, I was thirsty and you gave me drink, a stranger and you welcomed me, naked and you clothed me, ill and you cared for me, in prison and you visited me" (Mt 25:35–36). Note that Jesus tells the righteous that they showed mercy to *him*. In this passage, Jesus identifies himself with those most in need of mercy. He says, "Amen, I say to you, whatever you did for one of these least brothers of mine, you did for me" (Mt 25:40).

The Scriptures do not provide detailed solutions to today's pressing economic and social problems. But for people who turn to the Scriptures for guidance on how to live and what sort of people to become, it is clear they should show a deep concern for the poor and vulnerable. As Matthew's Gospel indicates, Christians are asked to look to the poor—to "these least brothers of mine" (Mt 25:40)—when they seek out the face of Christ. The prophets and Matthew warn that a person's eternal fate hangs on how they treat the powerless. More positively, this passage from Matthew's Gospel suggests that those who would show their love for Jesus Christ should direct that compassion toward "one of these least ones" (Mt 25:45). In these ways, liturgy can foster concern about justice.

When the assembly gathers for liturgy, Scripture is not simply read, but preached. The Word is "broken open" in a homily in which a member of the clergy helps the community understand the text and reflect on its implications. While the connections between concern for widows and today's economic challenges may not always be readily apparent to the average churchgoer, a good preacher can make such links clear.[36] The bishops recognized this when they wrote, "We call upon our priests, in particular, to continue their study of these [social and economic] issues so that they can proclaim the gospel message in a way that challenges the faithful but that also sustains and encourages their vocation in and to the world. Priestly formation in our seminaries will also have to

---

[35] For the discussion of Matthew 25 in *EJA*, see no. 44.

[36] Burghardt, "Worship and Justice," 39.

prepare candidates for this role" (*EJA*, no. 361). The Catholic Church has done little to encourage and assist priests in making these connections. As a result, the potential of liturgy to illuminate the implications of the Gospel for economic life has not been fully realized. If the US bishops remain serious about the need to help the whole Catholic Church understand the social justice implications of the Gospel, developing new forms of homiletical training for priests and deacons should be a top priority.

Intercessory Prayer

The late Dr. Mark Searle, a Catholic theologian who specialized in liturgical theology, claimed the primary purpose of the Liturgy of the Word is not to console the church. Rather, the Word is addressed to the church to stir it to action for the sake of the world.[37] Searle explained that some scholars believe liturgy in the early Christian church was modeled on the *qahal* of the Old Testament—assemblies convened by prophets, priests, or kings in ancient Israel in which people were called to hear the Word of God anew and to recommit themselves to living according to the covenant.[38] The gatherings were an occasion to remember how God had called the community to live, and to recommit oneself to living according to that promise.

The Prayer of the Faithful is a key moment in the liturgy for measuring the distance between the world as it is and the world as God would have it become. Occurring just after the Liturgy of the Word, the Prayer of the Faithful consists of a series of prayers of petition to God on behalf of the needs of the world, to which the congregation often replies, "Lord, hear our prayer." These intercessory prayers provide a vital link between action in the liturgy and Christ's presence and ongoing action in the world.[39] Praying for others requires those who pray to grow in solidarity with the world because otherwise they do not really mean what they pray. A key part of the reality of intercessory prayer is encountering the needs of the world.

In the proclamation of the Word combined with the prayers of intercession, the assembly develops a deep sense of the distance between the realities of the present day and what is called in theological terms the "eschatological future," that is, the Reign of God. Let me explain. When Christians pray the "Our Father" (a prayer that the Gospels suggest originated with Jesus), they pray, "Thy Kingdom come; Thy will be done on Earth as it is in Heaven." The

---

[37] Mark Searle, "Private Religion, Individualistic Society, and Common Worship," in *Vision: The Scholarly Contributions of Mark Searle to Liturgical Renewal*, ed. Anne Y. Koester and Barbara Searle (Collegeville, MN: Liturgical Press, 2004), 199.

[38] Mark Searle, "The Pedagogical Function of the Liturgy," in *Vision: The Scholarly Contributions of Mark Searle to Liturgical Renewal*, 70.

[39] Saliers, "Liturgy and Ethics," 28.

"Kingdom of Heaven" or the "Reign of God" is a vision of the ultimate future for the human race. It is a vision of the way things should be. Christians believe that Jesus revealed the shape of that world in his words and deeds. The Reign of God or Kingdom of Heaven is marked by love, forgiveness, justice, and so on. When Christians pray "Thy Kingdom Come," they are praying for God to make that world a reality. They do so with the hope that one day God's will shall in fact be done and with a mindfulness of their own calling to begin to live their lives now according to the rules and values of that Kingdom.

Praying for justice requires a deepened awareness of the facts of present injustice and cultivates a desire for the realities of injustice to be changed. It should move us to a deeper sense of the bonds that unite us as a human family and inspire us to "search for those social and economic structures that permit everyone to share in a community that is a part of a redeemed creation" (*EJA*, no. 365).

The Mystical Body of Christ

So far the links between justice and various parts of the liturgy have been discussed. However, it is also possible to link the liturgy taken as a whole to the pursuit of justice in the world. Virgil Michel explains how this might be the case. Writing in the 1930s, Michel sees the world moving toward two unacceptable social and political models: collectivism and individualism, both of which he labeled as "un-Christian" and "pagan at heart."[40] Individualism exalts the individual—it rejects the value of community and tradition and even goes so far as to refuse to recognize any authority superior to humankind (i.e., rejecting God). Individualism (often associated with Western capitalism) leads people to the conclusion that their sole duty is to look out for their own self-interest, which in turn results in a society of each against all.[41] "Collectivism" (i.e., totalitarian communism) is no better in Michel's view. While individualism overemphasizes the importance of the individual, collectivism wrongly ignores the individual rights of human persons.[42] On this point, Michel's view resonates well Catholic social thought; for example, in *EJA*, the US bishops warn of an "exaggerated individualism" that marks our present age (no. 345).[43]

---

[40] Virgil Michel, "The Liturgy: The Basis of Social Regeneration," *Orate Fratres* 9 (1934–1935): 537.

[41] Ibid. Michel writes, "There was then no longer any master superior to man. Man was his own supreme authority, his own sole lawgiver, not only in religion but in all the fields of human conduct, especially also in economic life."

[42] Ibid., 538. "This is the true danger of Collectivism: that it destroys or absorbs the individual. For it the individual does not count for anything. Authority and obedience is everything, and the human person is nothing" (539).

[43] Catholic social teaching has often been seen as a "third way" that navigates a middle ground between capitalism and collectivism. See Stefano Solari, "The Corporative Third Way in Social Catholicism (1830–1918)," *European Journal of the History of Economic Thought* 17, no. 1 (2010): 87–113.

VIRGIL MICHEL

Virgil Michel was born into a large Catholic family in Minnesota in 1890. He entered the novitiate of the Benedictine order at St. John's Abbey in Collegeville, Minnesota, in 1909 and became a monk in 1913.[44] During his short life (he died in 1938), he constantly spoke and wrote about the privileged role of liturgy in the formation of Christians.[45] He was part of a team that prepared a series of texts for elementary schools called the "Christ-Life Series in Religion," which emphasized full participation in liturgy as fundamental for catechesis (i.e., "religious education," the process of learning about the content and implications of Christian faith). He took a similar view of the importance of liturgy for adult Catholics. A tireless advocate for full participation of the laity in the Eucharistic liturgy, he called such participation "the people's sacrifice."[46] For Michel, the central feature of living a moral life (or what he called "the Christ life") was active, regular participation in the Eucharistic liturgy. Michel saw the liturgy to be the key not only for sustaining a vital Christian life for individual Catholics but also as the "indispensable basis of Christian social regeneration."[47] He embraced the view of Pius XI, who held that social regeneration was impossible without the true Christian spirit. He made the case for this view in a series of columns published in the journal he founded, which is now known as *Worship*.[48]

Michel believed only a Christian view of the human person and society grounded in the doctrine of the Mystical Body of Christ could overcome the communitarianism versus individualism conundrum. According to the doctrine of the Mystical Body of Christ, every member of the church is united to Christ as a member of Christ's own body because she or he is a member of the church.[49] However, the body of Christ does not absorb and assimilate people in a manner that destroys their individual identity and personhood; on the contrary, this notion of the church gathered as "one body" with Christ as its head simultaneously allows

---

[44] R.W. Franklin, "Virgil Michel: An Introduction," *Worship* 62, no. 3 (1988): 194.

[45] Jeremy Hall, "The American Liturgical Movement: The Early Years," *Worship* 50, no. 6 (1976): 472–87.

[46] Virgil Michel, "The Mass as the People's Sacrifice," *Orate Fratres* 1, no. 7 (May 15, 1927): 208–14.

[47] Michel, "Liturgy," 545.

[48] Ibid. The series "Natural and Supernatural Society," which appeared in *Orate Fratres* 10, nos. 6–10 (April–Sept. 1936), is also central for understanding Michel's vision.

[49] For a lengthy, authoritative presentation of this doctrine, see Pope Pius XII, *Mystici corporis Christi* (Encyclical on the Mystical Body of Christ), June 29, 1943, *http://www.vatican.va/holy_father/pius_xii/encyclicals/documents/hf_p-xii_enc_29061943_mystici-corporis-christi_en.html.*

individual members of the church to remain truly themselves and to flourish in ways that suit their unique character.[50] Thus the mystical body of Christ points to a way for the individual and the whole (of either Christ or of society) to relate that stands apart from both collectivism and individualism.

Michel held that the church gathered at Eucharist perfectly embodied this model of human society, and he also saw liturgy to be the method of communicating the doctrine of the Mystical Body of Christ to believers and ultimately to the rest of society.[51] For Michel, the mystical body is not so much a doctrine as a vibrant reality that should come to life in each person, especially as he or she participates in liturgy.[52] A conscious awareness of how one is a member of the mystical body of Christ engenders an experience of solidarity. It helps people to understand that even though they have a unique identity, even though they are loved as individuals by God, they are simultaneously members of the body of Christ. Their good, their identity, their very being is tied up with Christ and his body, the Church. Recognition of this deep connection is the first step on the path toward social justice.

Michel often explained the concept of the mystical body in terms of the communion of saints, another traditional doctrine of the Church, which holds that there is a fundamental unity and connection among all Christians, living and dead. The current *Catechism of the Catholic Church* explains:

> Since all the faithful form one body, the good of each is communicated to the others. . . . We must therefore believe that there exists a communion of goods in the Church. . . . As this Church is governed by one and the same Spirit, all the goods she has received necessarily become a common fund.[53]

The idea here seems to date back to medieval views of grace, holding that through their good works, all good Christians contribute to a common treasury of merit from which all members of the church can draw in their need. Kenneth Himes explains that Michel believed "just as there is a responsibility on the part of all believers to promote the spiritual well-being of others by contributing to the common treasury of merit, so too there is a serious responsibility to promote the material well-being of others by serving the common good."[54] One can hear a clear echo of this sentiment in *EJA* in which we read, "*Social justice implies that persons have an obligation to be active and productive participants in the life of the society and that society has a duty to enable them to participate in this way*" (no. 71, italics in the original).

---

[50] Baxter, "Reintroducing Virgil Michel," 505.

[51] Himes, "Eucharist and Justice," 202.

[52] Ibid., 202–3.

[53] *Catechism of the Catholic Church*, no. 947, http://www.vatican.va/archive/ENG0015/_P2B.HTM.

[54] Himes, "Eucharist and Justice," 206.

■ NOT BY LITURGY ALONE: LITURGY AND CATECHESIS

By turning to the revitalization of liturgy, the US bishops could do much to advance their cause of promoting a Christian vision of economic life in the United States. Liturgy has much to offer in terms of content and leading every-day Catholics toward an emotional and intellectual commitment to social change. At the same time, it would be unwise to rely upon liturgy alone for such formation. Liturgy alone would not serve a formational function, especially with regard to the promotion of a faith-based commitment to the regeneration of society. As the US bishops recognize in *EJA*, catechesis and other forms of edu-cation are crucial for advancing the social mission of the Church:

> Through her educational mission the Church seeks: to integrate knowl-edge about this world with revelation about God; to understand God's relationship to the human race and its ultimate destiny in the Kingdom of God; to build up human communities of justice and peace; and to teach the value of all creation. By inculcating these values the educational system of the Church contributes to society and to social justice. (no. 341)

Thus, as the Church pursues a renewal of liturgy, it must also seek to weave liturgy into a fabric of catechesis (i.e., religious education) and other aspects of the life of the parish and the broader church (e.g., Catholic schools and uni-versities). In other words, liturgical ministry must be linked to catechesis and social ministry.[55]

How to do this effectively is the crucial question. The US bishops devoted considerable attention and resources to writing *EJA*. They conducted numerous listening sessions at which they consulted with experts in the fields of economics, politics, ethics, and other relevant disciplines. A similar sense of urgency and of the need to listen and consult experts and the laity should mark a new undertaking by the bishops to understand how better to form members of their own Church.

It is not possible to give a complete answer as to how the connections among liturgy, catechesis, and social ministry should be fostered, but let me sketch briefly two possible models that might be piloted independently or ide-ally in combination with each other.

The first model develops a parish-based program of liturgy-based catече-sis that includes strong connections among liturgy, catechesis, and social action. John Roberto has described one promising program in which a theme for each month of the year is chosen from the lectionary readings that has a direct con-nection to an issue of social concern (e.g., "Feed the hungry!"). The parish pas-toral team then designs programs around that theme for a variety of catechetical

---

[55] Gilbert Ostdiek, "Liturgy and Justice: The Legacy That Awaits Us," in *Liturgy and Justice*, ed. Anne Y. Koester (Collegeville, MN: Liturgical Press, 2002): 1–17, at 14–5.

ministries (children, teens, adults). These programs are supplemented by at-home kits, articles, ideas for individual action, opportunities to participate in political action or direct service, or group prayer outside the context of the Eucharistic liturgy.[56] This approach might also be centered on a series of vir-tues (e.g., "Becoming a Compassionate People" or "Embodying Hospitality").[57] The key to this model would be to make participation in liturgy an occasion for intentional moral formation as well as to connect the formation that takes place liturgically with opportunities for conversational reflection, service, and prayer outside the Eucharistic liturgy.

The second model focuses on members of the Church community who are already engaged in outreach or social ministries. This approach has been piloted by Catholic Charities in the Diocese of Brooklyn, New York. Catholic Charities has partnered with a number of parishes in the diocese that provide direct services (such as the provision of food, clothing, or shelter) to the poor. Catholic Charities employs a community programming and organizing direc-tor in four geographical regions of the diocese. One of the primary tasks of these organizers is to connect with people who work in parish outreach min-istries and to develop programs that help those people link what they do with the overall mission of the parish. The program includes small group discus-sions, prayer, and workshops on Catholic social teaching. The program is still in development, but the next planned phase entails discussing links among various issues of social justice and linking outreach work to political action. For example, a program in a northern Queens neighborhood (a section of New York City in the Diocese of Brooklyn) has begun to discuss sources of food and issues of food production in connection with the parish's efforts to run a food pantry and soup kitchen. Men and women, whose involvement in social outreach had previously been limited to providing direct service to the poor, now see their role and their faith in a new light. Prayer, reflection, service, and catechesis are being woven into a mutually reinforcing web.

∎∎ THE CHALLENGE OF "LIFELESS LITURGIES"

An objection can be raised against the line of argument presented so far; namely, that although liturgy *theoretically* may be a rich resource for linking social jus-tice and Christian faith, it is less certain that this can be so in practice. Writing nearly three decades ago, Margaret Farley made the bracing observation that "many Christians experience the liturgy today, the public forms of worship in

---

[56] John Roberto, "Weaving Together Liturgy, Justice, and Catechesis," in *Liturgy and Justice: To Worship God in Spirit and Truth*, ed. Anne Y. Koester (Collegeville, MN: Liturgical Press, 2002), 139–46.

[57] Christopher P. Vogt, "Fostering a Catholic Commitment to the Common Good: An Approach Rooted in Virtue Ethics," *Theological Studies* 68, no. 2 (2007): 394–417.

the church, as deadening not enlivening, impoverishing not enriching."[58] Mark Searle agreed, writing that dead liturgies in many ways simply reflect the cultural values of the times (rather than challenging them); as such, they tend to be private, functional, and individualistic.[59] Similarly, British sociologist Bryan Wilson claims the view that American churches have a communal orientation that can work against the rampant individualism of our age is false and self-delusional.[60]

These criticisms are quite damning. They point to the sorry state of the vitality of the local church in some places. However, these criticisms are not really arguments against the importance of liturgy per se or of its potential so much as they are warnings that liturgy is not a magical or "automatic" antidote to the challenges Christian communities face. Indeed these criticisms point to the necessity of a concerted effort to revitalize the liturgical life of the Church. It is a reminder that the proposals suggested here would require not only thinking about liturgy in new ways but also dramatically improving the quality of parish liturgies in many places. On the other hand, it is not necessarily true that the Church would have to revitalize liturgy and then make connections between liturgy and justice. Instead, helping everyday Christians to see the connections between their lives in the world and their lives at prayer in church might serve as the catalyst for improving the quality and vitality of parish liturgies.

■■ CONCLUSION

Three features should characterize programs and efforts to integrate liturgy and social justice ministries. First, they should attempt to develop new forms of liturgy that can further the spiritual and moral formation of those who participate in them. The Eucharistic liturgy holds great promise for formation, but liturgy is a much wider reality than the Eucharist. This fact has been lost on many Catholics since the liturgical reforms of Vatican II, which had the unintended consequence of destroying many lay devotions.[61] That trend must be reversed. Communities might turn to the liturgical year as a school of prayer or seek to model themselves after the lay confraternities of centuries ago.[62] Other local

---

[58] Margaret A. Farley, "Beyond the Formal Principle: A Reply to Ramsay and Saliers," *Journal of Religious Ethics* 7, no. 2 (Fall 1979): 192.

[59] Searle, "Private Religion," 193.

[60] Bryan Wilson, *Religion in Secular Society* (London: Watts, 1966), 91, cited in Searle, "Private Religion," 186-87.

[61] Vincent Miller, *Consuming Religion: Christian Faith and Practice in a Consumer Culture* (Washington, DC: Georgetown, 2004), 218.

[62] For more on a model of formation grounded in the liturgical year, see James M. Schellman, "Initiation: Forming Disciples for Christ's Mission in the World," in *Liturgy and Justice: To Worship God in Spirit and Truth*, ed. Anne Y. Koester (Collegeville, MN: Liturgical Press, 2002), 129–37, at 134. For more on the lay confraternities, see Keith Pecklers, *Worship: A Primer in Christian Ritual* (Collegeville, MN: Liturgical Press, 2003), 144.

churches might draw from the more recent example of the gatherings of the Sant' Egidio community in Rome on Wednesday evenings for prayer and lay preaching, one of many models that might be explored and nurtured.[63]

Second, efforts to integrate liturgy and social justice should include the creation of a mediating space in which people can gather to work out the social and political implications of the understanding of justice that emerges from their renewed life. This is already explicitly a part of the program in the Diocese of Brooklyn described above, but it would be an important feature of any effort to promote social justice via liturgy. The formation of a loving community would be a major accomplishment, but even that should be but the beginning of a much larger process of the transformation of all creation.[64] Furthermore, it seems the need to explore the social and political implications of what people are learning and experiencing would almost inevitably arise. The fact is contemporary Christian communities do not function as complete cultures or societies that exist on their own.[65] Contemporary Christians belong to multiple communities.[66] For example, a person might be a Catholic, a Californian, a member of the Democratic Party, and so on. Negotiating the sometimes competing claims of such various identities is not an easy task; it is one that should be explicitly addressed as a dimension of moral formation and the pursuit of social justice.

Finally, an essential quality of any program of formation is that it must strengthen and foster popular lay agency in the church. The laity should be regarded as subjects in the process of their formation; they must be empowered to act. This would require the bishops to embrace a new model of what it means to be a teacher and leader in the church. Just as university professors have been asked to expand their view of pedagogy from a model in which the teacher simply dispenses knowledge to a model in which the teacher designs learning activities that students experience inside and outside the classroom, so there is a need to rethink the pedagogy of catechesis and the role of bishops as teachers. What is required is not merely the articulation of ideas about social, political, and economic justice, but a building of an infrastructure of formation for the church. The task of building that infrastructure is one that bishops, pastors, and lay parish leaders must engage together.

---

[63] For more on the Community of Sant' Egidio, see *http://www.santegidio.org/*.

[64] John P. Hogan, "People of Faith and Global Citizens: Eucharist and Globalization," in *Liturgy and Justice: To Worship God in Spirit and Truth*, ed. Anne Y. Koester (Collegeville, MN: Liturgical Press, 2002), 47–61, at 48.

[65] Miller, *Consuming Religion*, 24–5.

[66] Searle, "Private Religion," 53.

FOCUS QUESTIONS

1. What are some of the reasons given in this chapter for why a Christian movement for social justice must be linked to the liturgy? What is your assessment of the validity of those claims about the importance of liturgy?

2. Is it right to think of the liturgy as a means of promoting social justice? Explain.

3. How does the Eucharist sanctify those who celebrate it? In what ways does it help Christians to become more holy or better disciples of Jesus Christ?

4. How does the liturgy encourage those who participate in it to understand themselves and their place in the world? How does this self-understanding lead people toward personal conversion and toward acting to promote justice?

5. What specifically are some of the things a person must do to live in fidelity to the demands of a relationship with God and with his or her neighbors? As you look at the world today, what violations of right relationship do you see?

6. *EJA* calls for Americans to have a special concern for the poor and powerless. What are the biblical bases for this "preferential option for the poor"?

7. Which model of combining liturgy and catechesis proposed here is most promising? What else should churches do to help Christians integrate worship, faith formation, and a commitment to justice?

CONTRIBUTORS

Mark J. Allman is professor of religious and theological studies and faculty associate in the Center for the Study of Jewish-Christian-Muslim Relations at Merrimack College. His first book, *Who Would Jesus Kill? War, Peace, and the Christian Tradition* (Anselm Academic, 2008), won the College Theology Society Book of the Year Award. He serves as coeditor for the *Journal of the Society of Christian Ethics* and on the board of directors for the College Theology Society.

María Teresa Dávila, a Roman Catholic laywoman, is assistant professor of Christian ethics at Andover Newton Theological School. Her main area of interest is understanding the intersection between Christian values and principles, such as the option for the poor, and US civil society. Through this lens she examines issues such as immigration, consumerism, and class identity.

Daniel K. Finn is the William E. and Virginia Clemens Professor of Economics and the Liberal Arts and professor of theology at Saint John's University in Collegeville, Minnesota. He is a past president of the Catholic Theological Society of America, the Society of Christian Ethics, and the Association for Social Economics. His recent books include *The True Wealth of Nations: Catholic Social Thought and Economic Life* (Oxford University Press, 2010) and *The Moral Ecology of Markets: Assessing Claims about Markets and Justice* (Cambridge University Press, 2006).

David Hollenbach, SJ, holds the University Chair in Human Rights and International Justice and is director of the Center for Human Rights and International Justice at Boston College, where he teaches Christian social ethics. His most recent books include *Driven from Home: Protecting the Rights of Forced Migrants* (2010) and *The Global Face of Public Faith: Politics, Human Rights, and Christian Ethics* (2003), both published by Georgetown University Press. He has frequently been visiting professor of social ethics at Hekima College of The Catholic University of Eastern Africa, Nairobi, Kenya. He was president of the Society of Christian Ethics and received the John Courtney Murray Award for outstanding contributions to theology from the Catholic Theological Society of America. He also served as a consultant to the original drafting committee of *Economic Justice for All*.

Thomas Massaro, SJ, is dean of the Jesuit School of Theology of Santa Clara University at Berkeley. Previously he taught social ethics for fifteen years at Weston Jesuit School of Theology in Cambridge and its successor, the Boston College School of Theology and Ministry. He holds a doctorate in Christian social ethics from Emory University. He has written several books and many articles on topics related to Catholic social teaching and public policy, including *Living Justice: Catholic Social Teaching in Action* (Rowman and Littlefield Publishers, 2008) and *United States Welfare Policy: A Catholic Response* (Georgetown University Press, 2007).

Alex Mikulich is research fellow on race and poverty at the Jesuit Social Research Institute, Loyola University, New Orleans. He is coauthor of *The Scandal of White Complicity in U.S. Hyper-incarceration: A Nonviolent Spirituality of White Resistance* (Palgrave MacMillan, 2012). Mikulich is a founder and coleader of Louisiana for Fair Lending and Louisiana Catholics Committed to Repeal of the Death Penalty.

Rebecca Todd Peters is associate professor and chair of the Religious Studies Department at Elon University. Her book *In Search of the Good Life: The Ethics of Globalization* (Continuum, 2004) won the 2003 Trinity Book Prize. She is coeditor of *Teaching Undergraduate Research in Religious Studies* (Oxford University Press, 2011); and *Justice in the Making* (2004), *Justice in a Global Economy: Strategies for Home, Community, and World* (2006), and *To Do Justice: A Guide for Progressive Christians* (2008), all published by Westminster John Knox Press. Peters is currently working on a book on solidarity ethics.

Margaret R. Pfeil is assistant professor of moral theology at the University of Notre Dame and a faculty fellow of the Joan B. Kroc Institute for International Peace Studies. She is a cofounder and resident of the St. Peter Claver Catholic Worker community in South Bend, Indiana.

Christopher P. Vogt is associate professor of moral theology at St. John's University in New York City. He is the author of *Patience, Compassion, Hope, and the Christian Art of Dying Well* (Rowman and Littlefield, 2004). His most recent published work is "Catholic Social Thought and Creation," in *Green Discipleship*, edited by Tobias Winright (Anselm Academic, 2011). Vogt's current research examines connections among virtue ethics, social ethics, and moral formation.

INDEX

Illustrations, sidebars are indicated with i, s following the page number. Footnotes and endnotes are indicated with n followed by the footnote or endnote number. The abbreviation *EJA* denotes references to *Economic Justice for All*.